Sponsored

Agrolimen

49. GENERAL VIEW OF THE PALATINE HILL WITH THE ARCH OF CONSTANTINE, c.1806

Watercolour, heightened with gouache, the figures in pen and black ink, D & C Blauw papers laid down on canvas, 76.6 x 126.6 cm
Lausanne, Musée cantonal des Beaux-Arts
Inv. 851

Literature: Agassiz 1927, p. 40; Haskell, Chessex 1985, n. 1; exh. cat. London 1985, n. 6; exh. cat. Lausanne 1986, n. 10; exh. cat. Rome 1987, n. 9; exh. cat. Lausanne 1998b, p. 54

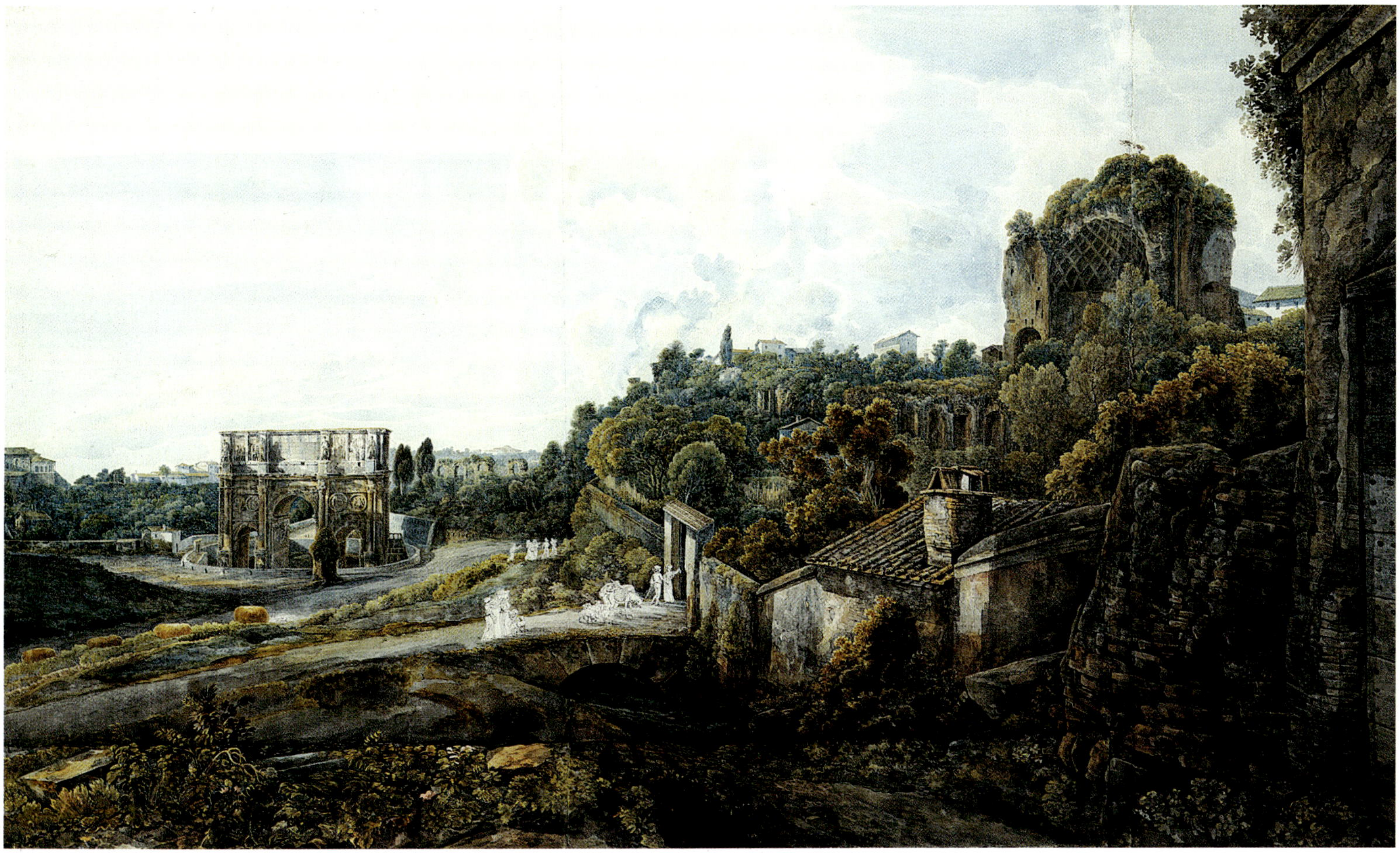

48. THE GROTTA DEI PAGGI, MALTA, 1800–1806

Watercolour and oil, papers laid down on canvas, 86.5 x 121.5 cm
Lausanne, Musée cantonal des Beaux-Arts
Inv. 825

Literature: G. A. Guattani, *Memorie enciclopediche romane sulle Belle Arti*, Rome, t. II, 1807, pp. 72–73; K. L. Fernow, 'Bericht aus Rom November 1808' in *Journal des Luxus und der Moden*, janvier 1809, pp. 37–38; Agassiz 1927, p. 38; B. Hartwig, *Bayerische Staatsgemäldesammlungen, Neue Pinacothek, München*, Bd. 3, Munich 1978, pp. 65–68; Chessex 1982, p. 67; exh. cat. London 1985, n. 50; exh. cat. Lausanne 1986, n. 98; exh. cat. Valletta 1989, n. 11; exh. cat. La Chaux-de-Fonds 1997, p. 29; exh. cat. Lausanne 1998b, p. 112

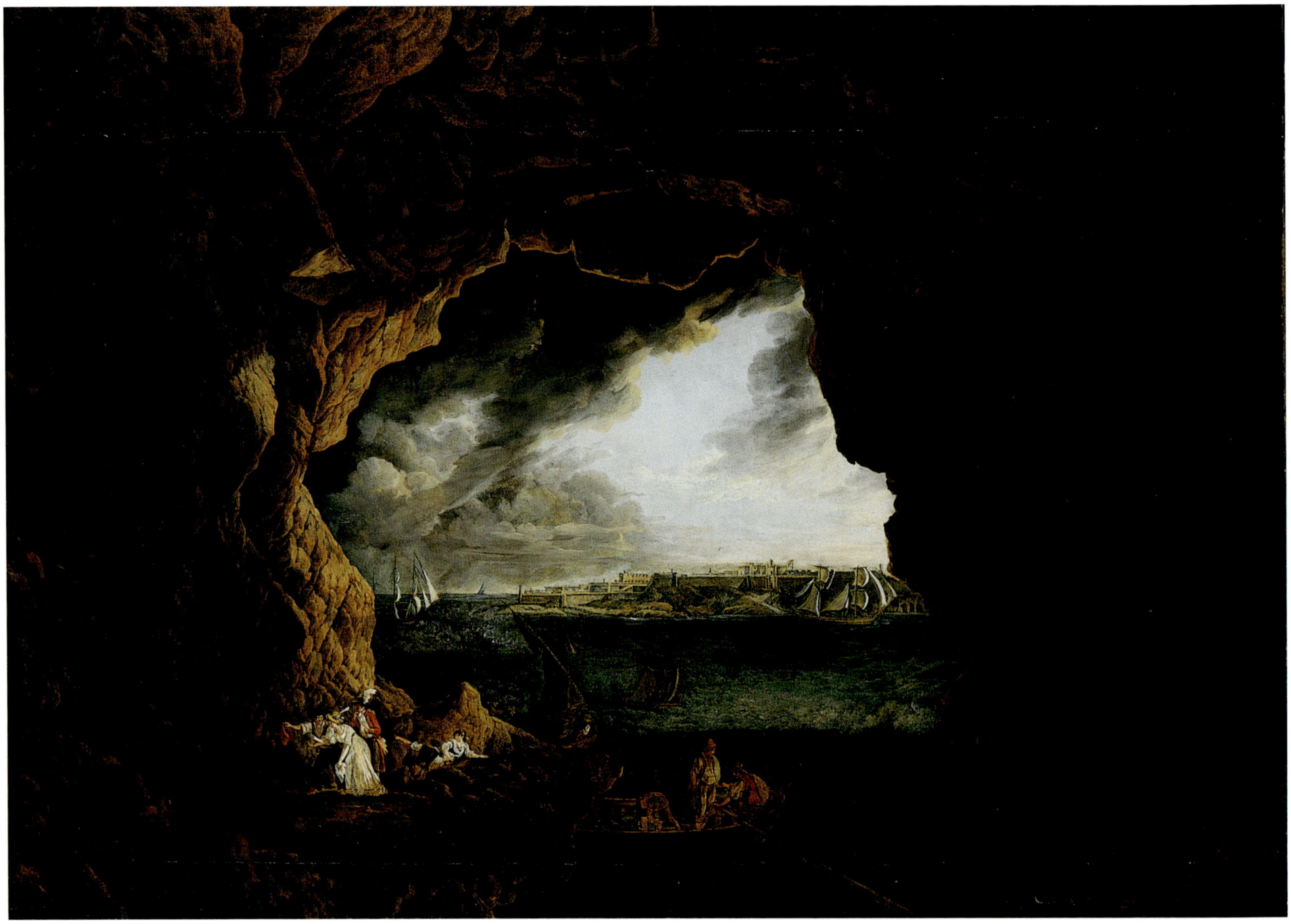

WHAT HUMA-NITY?

The human figure after the war (1940—1966)

Exhibition Curator

Àlex Mitrani

MUSEU NACIONAL D'ART DE CATALUNYA

TABLE OF CONTENTS

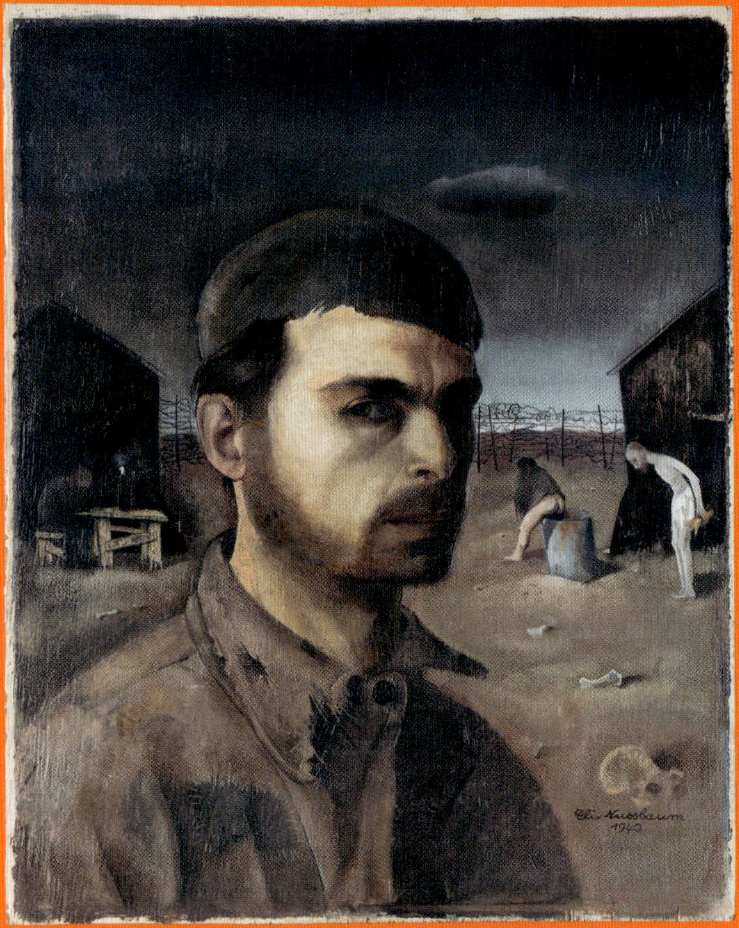

WHAT HUMANITY? FIGURES BETWEEN DESTRUCTION AND RECONSTRUCTION

Àlex Mitrani

The extent of the disaster

Today, as at other key moments in history, the question of humanity is urgent and unavoidable. Who do we want to be, as a community? How do we want to define ourselves and project ourselves into the future? How can we break the atavistic vice of violence and domination that is destroying us? How can we attain a human condition that is imbued with meaning, beauty and justice? What image, what dream, should we build of ourselves?

On the eve of the Second World War, when fascism and violence loomed threateningly and had already triumphed in Spain, the Martinican writer Aimé Césaire wrote a long poem vindicating the dignity of the African people in the context of colonialism. Although he spoke from a position of marginality, his meditation nevertheless acquired a universal, humanist dimension:

> "Partir
> Comme il y a des hommes-hyènes et des hommes-panthères je serais un homme-juif
> un homme-cafre
> un homme-hindou-de-Calcutta
> un homme-de-Harlem-qui-ne-vote-pas
>
> l'homme-famine, l'homme-insulte, l'homme-torture on ne pouvait à n'importe quel moment le saisir le rouer de coups, le tuer –parfaitement le tuer– sans avoir de compte à rendre à personne sans avoir d'excuses à présenter à personne
> un homme juif
> un homme-progrom
> un chiot un mendigot
>
> mais est-ce qu'on tue les remords, beau comme la face de stupeur d'une dame anglaise qui trouverait dans sa soupière un crâne de Hottentot ?"[1]

Describing pain and humiliation, daring to look them in the eye, leaves those of us who discover these things from the outside looking bewildered, stunned. The identification of the victims, the excluded, those stripped of their condition of full humanity, may move us, but above all it questions us and forces us into moral reaction. At the time when Césaire was writing, the holocaust and insane violence were still only at the gates, but it was already possible to see that the fundamental problem, in the new twentieth-century world of hyperbolic globalisation, was the human condition. In expressing the outrage and pain he felt before the subjection and degradation of suppressed races and groups, Césaire defended *négritude* not only as a form of recovered identity, but also as the source of a new humanism: "the work of man is only just beginning".[2]

Felix Nussbaum
Self-portrait in the Camp, 1940
Neue Galerie New York

In more formal manner and from a position of cultural privilege, Albert Camus would express similar feelings in his Nobel Prize acceptance speech in 1957. It was twelve years since the end of the Second World War, but Camus still warned about the need to prevent global destruction. Art should take a step forward in response to this situation ("the time of irresponsible artists has passed"), becoming engaged (and here one could mention all the nuanced political positions opposed to Jean-Paul Sartre's militancy). For two decades, art, having struggled under the weight of a time that had stood still during the war and projecting towards a future as urgent as it was uncertain, particularly in the European context, was defined by the attempt to digest the apocalyptic episode of the conflict and by movements towards the reconstruction of human, moral and emotional coherence. This crisis is reflected in representations of humanity, in images of implacable mirrors placed before us by artists, in which deformations are not capricious alterations, but elements emerging from a veritable interiority.

Jean Cayrol, who was deported to Mauthausen and later wrote the commentary for Alain Resnais' renowned film *Nuit et Brouillard* (Night and Fog), explained the link between the human question, the experience of the camps, the image and the heroic role of the survivor which ushered in a type of art he called *lazaréen* (Lazarean) in an allusion to the miracle of the resurrection of Lazarus. After the catastrophe, "the world no longer has a human face. After the return, thinks the deportee, who has found his face again, who has been able to enter into their features again, who has not suffered facial operations. Do we ever know who is beside one? [...] It is always a mass that the Lazarean personage has before their eyes, even in the simplest face."[3] Recognising the face, reconstructing the figure, restoring humanity, all seem like parts of the same process. How could one not think here of the repetition, simplified to the extreme and repetitive to the point of stereotype, of Jean Fautrier, with his hostages, as we can see in the illustrations he made for the collection *Dignes de vivre* (1944), by the iconic poet of the resistance, Paul Éluard, who sang of the possibility of a humanity cleansed of its perversion:

> "Nous jetons le fagot des ténèbres au feu
> Nous brisos les serrures rouillées de l'injustice
> Des hommes vont venir qui n'ont plus peur d'eux-mêmes
> Car ils sont sûrs de tous les hommes
> Car l'ennemi à figure d'homme disparaît."[4]

The response to annihilating aggression went beyond political and military action to become a human and personal challenge that can still interest us today. The studies of the neuropsychiatrist[5] Boris Cyrulnik provided vital inspiration for this exhibition. Cyrulnik's theory of resilience as a survival response to trauma has an individual but also a collective psychological aspect in that it is embedded in specific historical phenomena and, in his case, is linked to the personal experience of escape from the Shoah as a child. Cyrulnik also explains that resilience is constructed from two distinct moments, that of the shock or initial impact, when the emotions are overflowing and paralysed, and that of the subsequent elaboration in the form of a representation that establishes distance and enables us to master the event. The event is thereby converted, in a way, into a story or an image that we can assimilate. Cyrulnik's description of these two stages is identical to Immanuel Kant's typically modern definition of the experience of the sublime, in which he explains how, through aesthetic distancing, we can achieve an intellectual and moral elaboration of terrible events or ideas that completely overwhelm us. Postwar art, it seems to me, is greatly concerned with this process.

Postwar art has been the subject of many studies. We can highlight particularly the in-depth work of Lionel Richard,[6] Laurence Bertrand Dorléac, Sarah Wilson and others on its links with existentialism.[7] Exhibitions have provided excellent terrain for research and review, with extensive projects exploring the impact of the Second World War on culture and mindsets, as reflected through the artistic production of the time.[8] We note an evolution from more formalist readings, governed by the narratives and hierarchies established by the protagonists themselves, concerned for the centrality of Paris and New York and for a certain avant-garde logic suggesting the predominance of artistic options related to abstraction, towards interpretations that are in a more cultural key, open to the artistic diversity of the moment, multiplying visions and foci of interest in the peripheries. In this sense, ambitious projects like *Postwar: Art between the Pacific and the Atlantic 1940-1965* seem to us to be exemplary. We now hope to contribute our own grain of sand, focusing on a particular, though central, aspect: that of the human condition as depicted by artists in their representations of the human figure. Accordingly, we shall consider essentially figurative art here.

Figuration is a vague and controversial historical term. The dispute between abstraction and figuration was as noisy as it was short-lived, and was resolved in favour of the former in the 1950s. The debate about conscript art and the dilemma of whether to return to tradition or, after the period marked by the great wars, to plunge into the revolutionary and experimental, generated a certain primordial association between the human figure and humanism. An example is the exhibition *Manifeste de l'homme témoin* (Paris, Galerie du Bac, 1948). In his introduction, the critic Jean Bouret championed figurative art as opposed to the supposedly snobbish esotericism of the abstract artists, quoting the philosopher Alain: "The human body is the tomb of the gods". This was an argument that often fell into the simplistic and opportunistic, and tended to hinder the advance of figurative art. On Bernard Buffet and his followers, the critic Julián Gállego spoke of a "rococo in reverse".[9] While taking into account these oppositions and how the quality and importance of ideas and works was judged, these pieces interest us for their historic power, before banalization set in.

A contemporary gaze can help to distinguish archetypes and symbols of great historical significance, as Keith Lowe has brilliantly demonstrated. Moreover, in his foreword to the catalogue of the important assembly-based exhibition *Art et résistance* (Paris, Musée des Arts Modernes), André Chamson affirmed that: "Generous despite its present harshness, life will enable us to see this heroic history become transformed into myth before our very eyes". A historical consciousness was clearly felt, and the need for human reflection was manifested in a way that was as diverse as it was constant. This is why, in contemporary historiography, it is useful to go beyond a strictly stylistic and artistic archaeology, eschewing hierarchies, as this enables us to link and compare works that, although from different contexts, which raise common dilemmas. We cannot and will not produce an exhaustive exhibition here, but rather will reveal and link works that can help us to recognise the ideas, intuitions and images generated by reflections on the idea of humanity at a historic moment that continues to be projected up to the present day.

If we may focus on one specific motif, the representation of the figure (while being aware of all the nuances that one might establish, taking the view, for instance, that the performances of Murakami Saburo of the Gutai group, bursting through a row of paintings, are also manifestations of the figure in action), then the cultural and chronological framework can be expanded in the same way. There are many postwars, and each different country underwent its own processes at its own rhythm. We have taken the year 1940, at the start of the Second World War and just after the end of the Spanish Civil War – the latter understood as the direct prelude to the former – as the starting point for our exhibition. One particular writer can help us to understand this connection, and in the most striking fashion. Felix Nussbaum, who died at Auschwitz, left testament to the anguish and senselessness of the persecution of the Jews, an episode that laid bare the inhumane dimension, the horror and madness of a war the likes of which had never been seen before. Nussbaum painted the physical and moral despair and misery of the camps, but he did so in images constructed from the visits he made to prison camps for Germans in France, in Sant Cebrià de Rosselló (Saint-Cyprien). These were the same camps where, almost immediately before this, Republican fugitives from the Spanish Civil War had been confined, inmates drawn with pathetic *costrumbrismo* by the Catalan artist Josep Bartolí.

The silence of bodies

In 1940, Salvador Dalí painted *The Face of War*, a cranium with skulls in its eye sockets and putrid mouth, an image both allegorical and premonitory of the horrifying, insane destruction that was to come. This despairing image, a kind of sinister *ouroboros*, presaged absolute terror, ruthless and inexorable. The headline to the report on the death camps featuring photographs by Lee Miller published in *Vogue* read: "Believe It". To believe it, documentary images and witness accounts are essential. The horror caused by these signs of the unimaginable have been widely dealt with (but never resolved). Giorgio Agamben reflected on the ambiguity between the figure of the witness and that of the martyr, observing that "the thing, in art, is not the legitimacy of the testament but the need for the record and the creation of the collective memory".[10] Accordingly, art should respond, on the one hand, to the need for the communal, that is to say, final political elaboration of what happened. But, on the other hand, the intimate nature of the event and the depth of the wounds explain why, despite the breach between the experience and its representation, pain had to emerge and had to be expressed. In Écorces, Georges Didi-Huberman observes that: "It is unimaginable, then, to have to imagine despite everything."[11] Didi-Huberman also highlights the importance of the skin, in its fragility, both as emblem and as tenuous but indelible record of scars. On the subject of the origins of perversion, he concludes, however, that "the reified language of the Third Reich mechanises all humanity – and that is why humanity will have to mechanise itself. Its poverty will be relentless harshness, absence of fluidity and plasticity".[12] It is as if life, organic and turgid, were faced by its inhuman extinction, its desiccation. The horrific rigidity of the executioners imposed rigidity on the body of the victim, which became cadaver.

One could not look at the camps (Goya had already warned about violence: "One can't look"), but they could be imagined, as Lasar Segall, a Lithuanian-born Jew resident in Brazil, did. Segall had already captured the horror of the pogrom and the sufferings of emigration. From his Brazilian home, in touch with the émigré community (he corresponded by letter with Stefan Zweig shortly before that latter's suicide in Petrópolis), he now produced a series of drawings before the world discovered the camps, before photographs of their horrors became known, surprising us with his sharp lucidity. He draws a woman with her hand held to her mouth, in a gesture of desperation, with huge, rolling eyes whose interior reveals rigid, cadaverous bodies. His groups maintain their solidarity and tragic unity as they pass through doors that open into a terrible darkness into which they will be dissolved.[13]

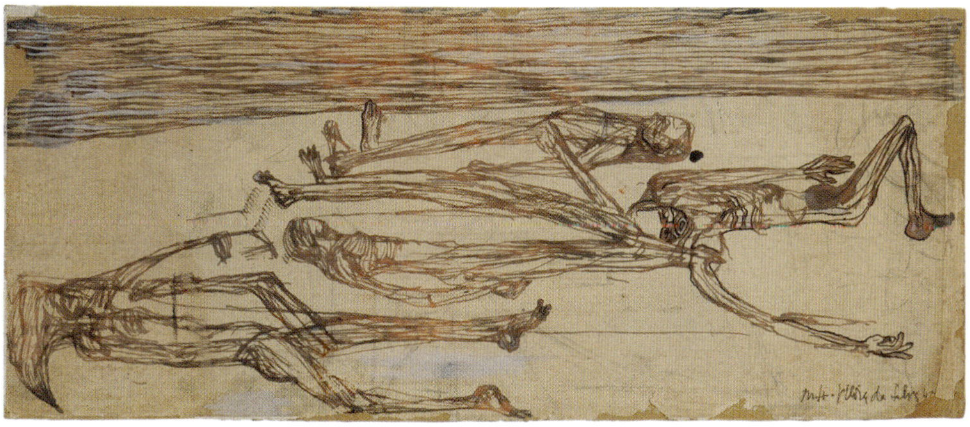

Maria Helena Vieira da Silva. *The field of the dead,* 1940
Col. Fundaçao Arpad Szenes-Vieira da Silva. FASVS (D0129)

The most harrowing of the direct testaments is that of the Slovenian Zoran Mušič, who was imprisoned at Dachau. Mušič made a series of drawings *in situ*, in the weeks leading up to the liberation of the camps, as if he wished to retain the images and memory of what he saw. However, immediately afterwards he buried these memories and began to create poetic paintings evoking nostalgic Dalmatian landscapes. He then went on to produce informalist textures, focusing on stone and earth that became – in appearance only – abstract. In the 1970s, from the detritus would rise once more, as if disinterred, the bodies of the cadavers in the series *Nous ne serons pas les derniers* ('We Are Not the Last'). As occurred with so many others (see, for example, the striking case of the Austrian Roma Ceija Stojka or that of Shelomo Selinger), images of the camps, the "landscapes of corpses", as he called them, re-emerged in his work many years later.[14]

However, the most iconic image of the victims was that created by Pablo Picasso, who, obviously, did not have first-hand experience of the camps or the war. Picasso worked with photographs in grey tones to create a new work, the latter-day equivalent of his *Guernica*, which at first he entitled *The Massacre* but which he

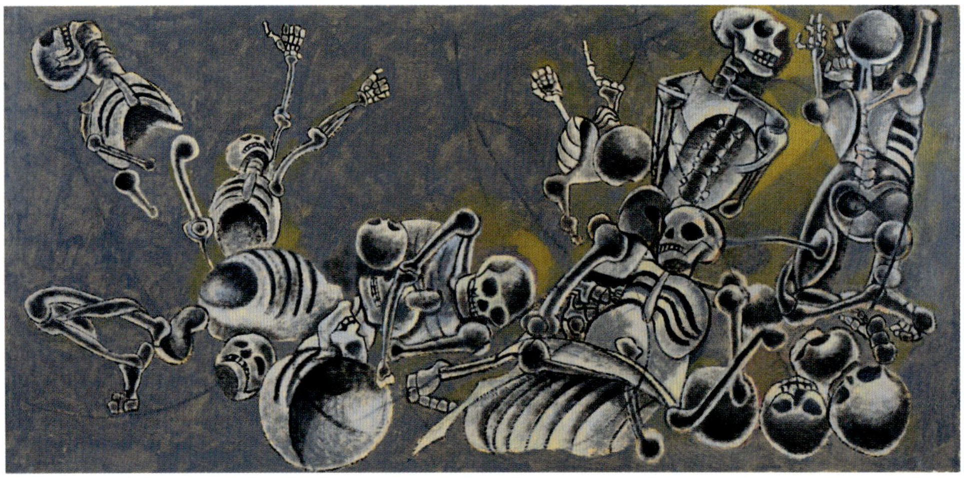

Erró. *La Danse macabre*, 1955
Collection of Reykjavík Art Museum

later renamed as *The Charnel House.*[15] The collective imagination projected onto this painting the impact of the camps, in total incoherence with the still life seen in the upper section. A few years later, in 1952-53, the Spanish artist José Vela Zanetti, in exile in Santo Domingo, followed in the footsteps of the great Mexican muralists and painted a huge mural on the UN building in New York with the title *The Route to Freedom*, which later became better known as the *Mural of Humans Rights*. The great frieze began on the left with an evocation of the prisoners of the camps, but translated to a heroic, powerful dimension, glorified in their tragedy. In the legendary 1946 exhibition *Art in Republican Spain. Spanish Artists of the Paris School*, the sculptor García Condoy presented a piece, *The Fall of Man at Auschwitz* that must be understood in generic key: the whole of humanity has fallen into decay. Also in 1946, the Portuguese artist Maria Elena Vieira da Silva, in exile in Rio de Janeiro, showed, alongside her work *Disaster*, which depicted the terrible maelstrom in which all humanity was drowning, a small drawing of bodies made from almost transparent, evanescent threads. The Islandic artist Erró, who later became known for his powerful pop iconography, became obsessed with images of skeletons engaged in a macabre, mechanical dance, reflecting the collective imagination's persistent but amalgamate fantasy of the spectacle of death and the destruction of bodies. The stunning horror of the atomic bomb would be more suited to abstract expressions,[16] but some artists, like Josep Maria Subirachs, also drew it as a symbol of the apocalypse.

Recognition and expiation

In *La douleur*, Marguerite Duras describes with uninhibited and loving precision the fragility of the body of the survivor Robert Antelme: "En haut, le cou pénétrait à l'interieur du squelette, il collait en haut des mâchoires, s'enroulait autour des ligaments comme un lierre."[17] Primo Levi wrote that, in the camps, "There is nowhere to look in a mirror, but our appearance stands in front of us, reflected in a hundred livid faces, in a hundred miserable and sordid puppets".[18] When the famous Spanish comedian Miguel Gila found himself in prison with the great popular poet Miguel Hernández, he says that he did not recognise him, destroyed as he was by humiliation and suffering, as he would not have recognised himself .[19] Gila later survived a firing squad, by pure chance, buried under a pile of dead bodies. So, how can we recognise the victim in their dignity and individual personality? In his controversial monument to the martyrs of Oradour, Apel·les Fenosa chose an emblematic maternity. In his reaction to the bombing of Rotterdam in *La Ville détruite* (1947), Ossip Zadkine also explored the gesture of raised arms.

Despite his early death, Francis Gruber was the most influential painter of so-called existentialist or miserabilist figuration. After the war he worked always with the same male model to produce a series of works, oils and drawings, ranging from the allegorical *Job* to *Hostages,*[20] which was shown alongside his study in the 1946 exhibition *Art et résistance* de 1946 and Picasso's *The Charnel House*. At the time of *Guernica* and the death camps, Gruber vindicated the progressist and revolutionary value of the painting of history.[21] Crudely, but not cruelly, he clinically studies the angles of a sordid corpse, the folds and the exhaustion. He finds a physiognomy that seems to him, in its precarious dignity, to be a personage that can become a unifying element through the fragility and the sensitive truth of the body. In contrast, Jean Fautrier, in his famous *Hostages* series, creates an image of complete simplicity, a rustic profile with a prehistoric, mineral air, as if out of time. One fascinating aspect of Fautrier's investigations was the invention of what he called "multiple originals". This is an attempt to overcome the elitist nature of painting and the sacralisation of the unique work by adopting a hybrid procedure that combines the manual with the mechanical to obtain different versions of the same painting, thus anticipating the stance taken by certain later proponents of conceptual art. But there is also a philosophical aspect in the renunciation of the individuality, not only of the person represented, but also, in a certain way, of the author. Warhol used repetition and serialisation to allude to media desire, and Fautrier seems to seek a formulation of primordial and democratic humanity, at once both popular and mythical.[22]

Fautrier's *Hostages* are said to have been inspired by the noises of torture and execution that he heard from his house during the war. The Polish artist Wladyslaw Wróblewski also evokes these horrors in a realist style that eschews western genealogies (if his work cannot be connected with that of Jean Hélion), his art imbued with a sinister serenity. Although Wróblewski evokes the figure of the child, he keeps pathos under restraint. Rather, a dismembered body, like that of an infant, causes a strange feeling reminiscent of surrealism. Perhaps artists could no longer imitate the emotional observation of a Goya, nor replicate the clinical coldness of a Manet. The subject is not a simple one, as the controversy that surrounded Picasso's *Massacre in Korea* (1951) shows. However, at times a more discreet testament in a minor key can take on considerable emotive power. Such is the case of Gonçal Sobrer, who created what can be considered one of the first performances in Spain in 1966, overlooked by the censor on its publication in a catalogue that same year, perhaps due to a misinterpretation suggested by the artist's burlesque tone. *Execution Dance* was inspired by Sobrer's childhood memories, when trucks passed through the Poblenou district of Barcelona where he lived, heading for Somorrostro beach, the scene of brutal executions.

A fairground shooting range featuring Hitlerian faces can be considered a representation of the figure of the monster that forms part of this universe of violence for, as Sartre wrote: "Once it is manifested, the inhuman becomes part of the human."[23] Tooth-filled mouths, aggressive disfiguration, horror and the grotesque all emerge regularly as a possible exorcism of the demonic nature of humanity. What is shocking, though, is the proximity between the heads of the monsters and the expiatory figure of Christ or the saints, in the case of Bacon, who surrounds his cross with an ordinary urban landscape, cars and all. We find ourselves somewhere between horror and pity. As Sarah Wilson points out, the theme of the Crucifixion is frequent among postwar artists, as it takes on a new significance, one both historical and universal.[24] As early as 1945, writing about Fautrier, Francis Ponge notes the emergence of a new religion, that of humanity versus executioners, in which: "The firing squad replaces the crucifixion. Anonymous man replaces the Christ of the paintings."[25]

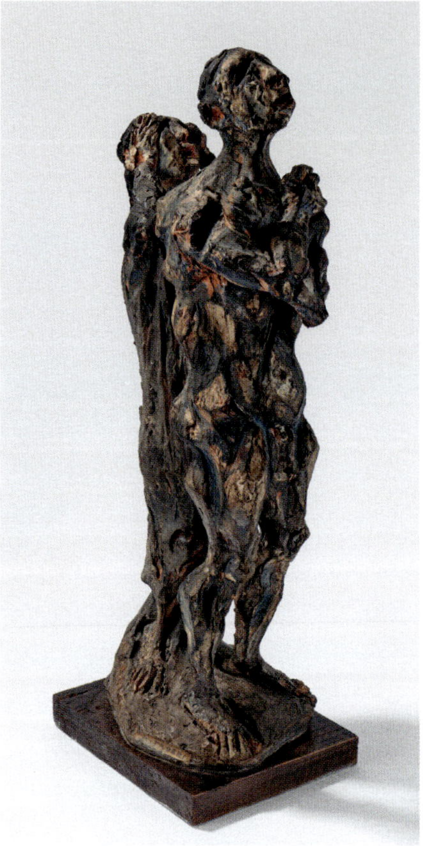

Agenore Fabbri. Sketch for the *Monument to the Unknown political prisoner*, 1952
Finarte: Modern and Contemporary Art

In his educational book *Introduction aux existentialismes* (1944), reprinted several times in its day, Emmanuel Mounier attempted to present and define existentialism as a complex movement in which an atheist existentialism dialectically confronts a Christian existentialism (as proposed by Gabriel Marcel). In art, this proximity between religion and existentialism is confirmed and made visible in works generated by commissions for artistic and liturgical revival linked to the magazine *L'Art Sacré* in the 1950s and confirmed by the Second Vatican Council. In Spain, this renewal produced interesting results, despite the conflictive and ambiguous situation imposed by Francoist National Catholicism. We can highlight two works in particular. Firstly, the statuary that Jorge Oteiza was commissioned to make for the Sanctuary of Arantzazu, of national and spiritual importance to the Basque people, evokes a humanity at once titanic and hollow. One perceives a profound interrogation of the human, represented by the dichotomy between the full and the empty, in the paradoxical relation between the density of the body and its negative emptiness. When the Vatican prohibited the works, his 1950 sculptures were left abandoned on the roadside. Secondly, Josep Maria Subirachs produced an ensemble of the twelve apostles and Our Lady for the Sanctuary of La Mare de Déu del Camí, with elongated forms, volumes converted into strata and scarifications and severe, drawn faces, described by the critic and poet Joan Eduard Cirlot as follows: "on a scheme comparable with the roughest work of a rural Romanesque, the sculptor obtains a cracked contraction, a fossil sadness".[26]

The solemnity of religious art finds a place in the slow, ambivalent reification of humanity that is evident, particularly, in postwar sculpture. In Germaine Richier's *L'Ogre*, the subject seems to be in a process of metamorphosis, halfway between erect human being and a monstrosity that continues to pursue it. Richier's friend, Agnès Varda, who photographed the artist in her studio, also seems to seek the rehabilitation of the human being in her microhistories of individuals. Despite its horror of its own actions and its own misery, humanity seems able to rise once more. Sartre sees Alberto Giacometti's characters, firstly, as "martyrs of Buchenwald", but then as "Ascensions". Despite its modest size, Giacometti's 1947 sculpture *Bust d'home* (Bust of a Man), is supported by a proportionally large base which lifts and elevates the work. Notwithstanding the differences between them, in both Richier and Giacometti flesh and the body seem to become tangible once more in the skin and the texture. Sculpture, which eschewed the heavy weight of classical idealism, did not renounce the human. Other sculptors might also have been included in this exhibition. For instance, the French artist César with his apocalyptic humour; the British practitioners Lynn Chadwick with her robotic figures, and Eduardo Paolozzi with his burnt-out creatures. A place could also have been found for the Catalans Francesc Torres-Monsó and José Subirà-Puig. Francesc Saumells interpreted their work in religious key. We should also remember the more abstract work of the Aragon artist Pablo Serrano and his "vaults for man". Agenore Fabbri, impressed by Picasso, adopted a line of expressionism as regards materials and surfaces, creating dramatic faces. Marino Marini, a leading figure in postwar Italian sculpture, used a less prickly language and evoked happiness and freedom more than pain. He also made a *Prisoner*, a work that represents an exception in his entire career, as the piece lies on the ground, renouncing all verticality. And another gaze emerges, also exceptional and completely on the margins: that of Louise Bourgeois, who, with a small, totemic statue, prepares an exploration of the female identity that will become revolutionary in the future.

The possibility of hope

When does a war end? One thing is armistices and the ceasing of military actions and another is the situation of pain, violence and injustice that is perpetuated or lives on in inertia or sequelae. Saul Steinberg composes an image, in collaboration with the photographer Inge Morath, in which we can perceive the irony but also the melancholy of errant humanity that has accepted and conquered a diaspora that will accompany it always with their masks. In 1949, Pierre Tal-Coat, who had already made a series of *Massacres* in allusion to the Spanish Civil War, painted profiles under water, human figures that disappear beneath the ripples. The case of Spain is outrageous, as the victory of fascism and its long duration left large sectors of the population in a situation of despair and defeat. At the time when the Second World War was just beginning, Spain was materially and spiritually devastated after the atrocities of its civil war. In his poem *Insomnia* (1940), Dámaso Alonso exclaimed: "Madrid is a city of more than a million corpses."[27] From exile, the Catalan writer Mercè Rodoreda narrated the private lives of the vanquished. In *Nada*, Carmen Laforet offers an bitter description of grey postwar Barcelona. The painting *Silence*, by Juana Francés, illustrates that state of consternation and censure that only artists can transgress, often clandestinely or through enforced discretion and modesty.

Marino Marini. *Prisoner*, 1943
Museo Marino Marini

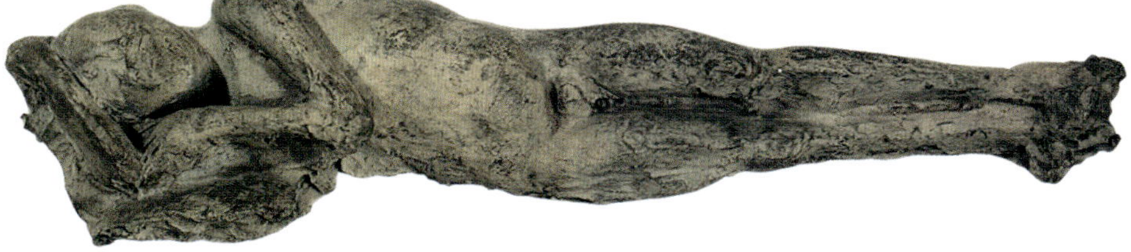

In the context of Francoist censorship, when politics could not be manifested in complete freedom, opting for an expressive, modern but deliberately constrained avant-garde figuration was a valid strategic solution and ethical position. Peasants, veiled women, faces hardened by misery, urban solitudes and rural isolation, apparently atavistic tragedy that nevertheless contained what was a perforce elliptical denouncement of the excluded, repressed social classes, gave way to a realism that cannot be compared to the avant-garde experiments in more open and propitious countries. From the Lorcan primitivism of Josep Guinovart to the implacable naturalism of solitude as portrayed by Antonio López, the use of popular themes and descriptions of poverty and vulnerability among groups apparently excluded from modern times can be seen as a vindication of human dignity and a protest against structural injustices. Despite their apparently local subject-matter, such works achieve a certain degree of universality. It is interesting to note the possible analogies between different and distant contexts, such as the dramatic but profoundly empathetic denunciation of the Brazilian artist Candido Portinari. The deep melancholy of a traumatised, repressed survivor of the *Leva del biberón* (the "baby bottle" levy of boys aged 14-18 sent to the Republican front at the end of the Civil War) like Joan Brotat, an artist of the humblest origins, fluctuated between nostalgia for lost innocence and latent anguish. The weird demons and night visions of the Catalan group Dau al Set, whose members included Joan Ponç, Modest Cuixart and Antoni Tàpies, express a deeply-felt distress that contains and explores anger.

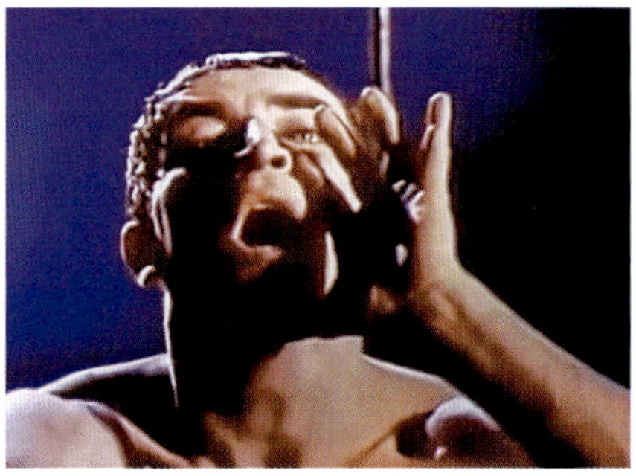

Still from *Symphonie pour un homme seul* (1957)
Music: Pierre Schaeffer and Pierre Henry (1949-1950)
Choreography: Maurice Béjart (1955)
Director: Louis Cuny
14 min.

There is a fight against uncertainty. The Polish artist Franciszka Themerson draws an individual deep in reflection before an enigmatic labyrinth. The *Symphonie pour un homme seul* by Pierre Schaeffer and Pierre Henry (1950), converted into a ballet by Maurice Béjart (1955), evokes the situation of crisis and rehabilitation in which humanity finds itself. However, optimism, if not frivolity, was possible. In his role as emblem of *La Libération*, Pablo Picasso was the main representative of this more positive mood, with his figures of the shepherd with the lamb in his arms, revisiting a Christological iconography, and other allegorical drawings featuring a revived Mediterranean serenity that manages to tame the beast. The leading architect of the modern movement, Le Corbusier, devised a scale of proportions known as *Le Modulor*, the starting-point for once more championing the utopian project of modern architecture in time of reconstruction. However, it is without doubt the search for a radical, regenerating primitivism that best suggested the possibility of rebirth, based, not on the ideal of maturity and plenitude of classical humanism, but on an innocence conquered by renouncing the perversions of civilisation to find renewing energy and honesty once more. We note the emergence of the dream of paradise, the return to nature, the reappearance of the myth of Adam and Eve, now stripped of the threat

Candido Portinari. *Dead child from the series: Emigrants*, 1944-1945
Museu de Arte de São Paulo Assis Chateaubriand.
Doação Assis Chateaubriand, 1948. MASP.00326

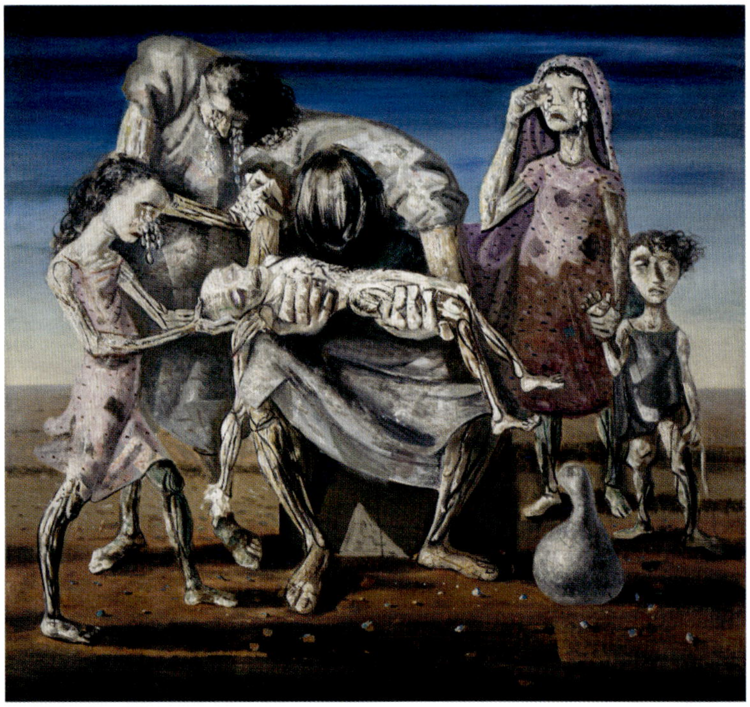

of sin. Although there was still the danger of a certain over-simplification, and his dramatic series *Barcelona* on the theme of the fascist bombings was overlooked, Miró was interpreted in this key. According to the critic Joan Perucho, writing in the Catalan magazine *Ariel*: "We need to return to the primary emotion of man towards things, towards the world: the babbling of a child and of primitive man. Emotion without prejudices, purity of soul".[28] In this way, Perucho prefigured the role that Miró, a key figure in the Catalan avant-garde, would play. His supposed naïveté was not such – on the contrary – but we can appreciate that the archaic simplicity of an early humanity could represent a dream, a model to oppose the mirages of progress and the hypocrisies of common sense and the conformities that had been violated by totalitarian fanaticism, if they had not actually collaborated with it. At the same time, less programmed, and discreet, but strangely recurrent, we can see the development of the theme of pregnancy and motherhood, the iconography of hope *par excellence* which also permits great nuance, of the totemic women of the Catalan-Chilean artist Roser Bru and the enigmatic mothers of Parvine Curie (which she made while living in Barcelona and signing her works as Arlette Martí). Baltasar Lobo, an artist from Zamora with close ties to Picasso, goes from the motif of the woman with skull to a sensual celebration of a joy that become physical, bodily.[29]

At times, artists achieve promising moments of serenity and nobility. Among his obsessive series of skulls, Luis Fernández creates the dignified effigy of the resistant whose sacrifice has not been in vain. Take, for instance, *The Philosopher*, by Norman

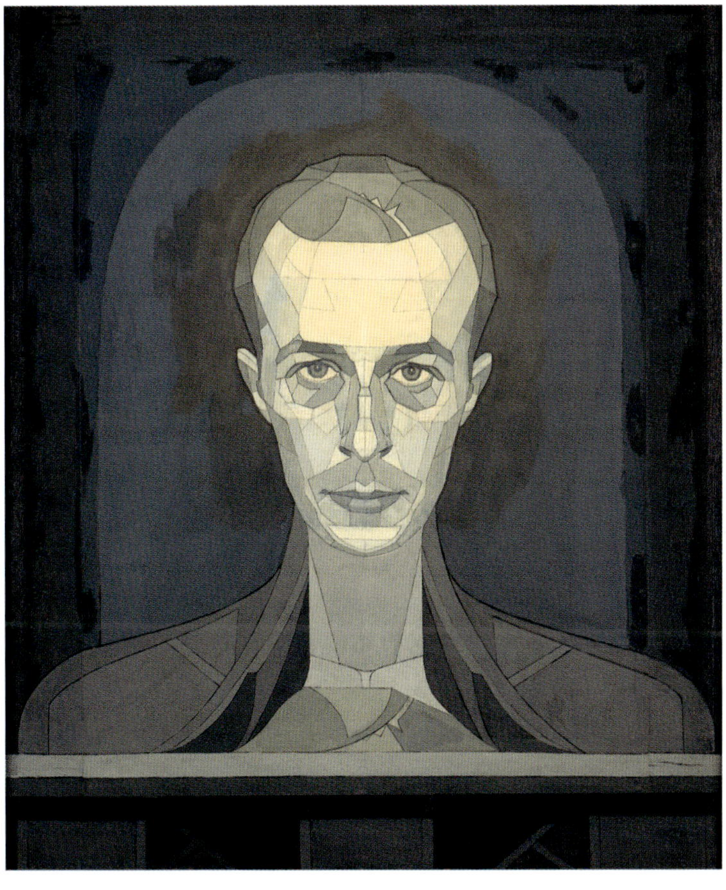

Luis Fernández. *Portrait of a young man (Le Résitant)*, 1944-1945
The Menil Collection, Houston (USA). Access. # 1978-105 E

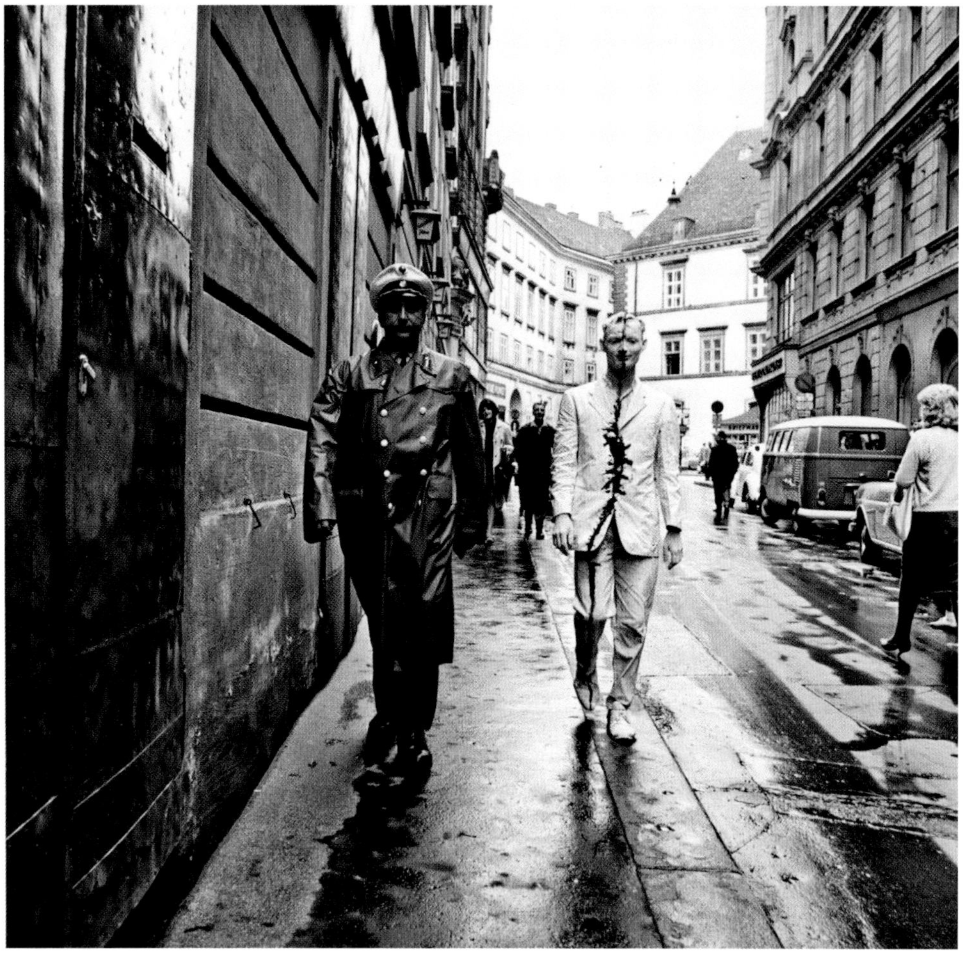

Günter Brus. *Viennese walk*, 1965 (1989)
S/W Photograph acquired in 1989, G 725/1

Narotzky, a New York-born artist who lived in Barcelona, with his works of spectral gentleness and Buddhist tranquillity, or the huge, serene but vibrant heads of his compatriot Leon Golub. As we know, Golub would evolve towards themes directly linked to the denunciation of structural violence in civilisation in the second half of the twentieth century. These are possible images of a humanity that attempts, despite all, to make itself known, to achieve the resilient placidity of rehabilitation from the wound while accepting the trauma. The vital anxiety and intimate suppurations that led to the existentialist trend would give way, in time, to the resurgence of new generations, new concerns, new conflicts. The feminism of Niki de Saint Phalle or Mari Chordà, the performance art that vomits out repressed violence, and the serenity of the false order recovered by Günter Brus, race issues in the United States of America, decolonisation, which becomes unstoppable, and the rejection of war; all this sweeps us into dynamics that are not so much introspective as active, both as individuals and as groups. As the Valencian artist Juan Genovés seemed to foresee, new struggles, communal now, are looming into view.

What humanity, tomorrow?

The Russian writer Romain Gary, nationalised French, who served in the air force and became a war hero, denounced the absurdity of war and its cruel and incomprehensible world in his novel Éducation européenne (1945). However, immersed in this pain and valiantly accepting his duty to engage in the struggle against aggression and injustice, Gary discovered that there existed a special "refuge" for resistance and hope: "La vérité c'est qu'il ya des moments dans l'histoire, de moments comme celui que nous vivons, où tout ce qui empêche l'homme de désespérer, tout ce qui lui permet de croire et de continuer à vivre, à besoin d'une cachette, d'un refuge. Ce refuge, parfois, c'est seulement une chanson, un poème, une musique, un livre."[30]

There are moments in history... but perhaps they are not as transitory as we would like to think. In her essay *Persona y democracia* (Person and Democracy, 1958), the philosopher María Zambrano, after evoking the concentration camps and deliberating on the contradictions inherent in the definition of the human within the necessary temporal and historical condition in which we live, which, in the end, is always the present, reminds us that: "Pues solamente se es de verdad libre cuando no se pesa sobre nadie; cuando no se humilla a nadie, incluido a sí mismo. La condición humana es tal que basta humillar, desconocer o hacer padecer al hombre –uno mismo o el prójimo– para que todo el hombre sufra. En cada hombre estan todos los hombres."[31]

1 Césaire, A., *Cahier d'un retour au pays natal*, Paris, 1983, p. 20.
2 *Cit. supra*, no. 1, p. 57; translation by the author of the article.
3 Cayrol, J., *Nuit et brouillard*, Paris, 1997; translation by the author of the article.
4 Éluard, P., "La dernière nuit", *Dignes de vivre*, Paris, 1944, p. 53.
5 Cyrulnik, B., *Je me souviens...*, Paris, 2010.
6 Richard, L., *L'art et la guerre. Les artistes confrontés à la Seconde Guerre Mondiale*, Paris, 1995.
7 See, among others: Wilson, S., "New Images of Man: Postwar Humanism and its Challenges in the West", Enwezor, O., *Postwar: Art between the Pacific and the Atlantic, 1945-1965*, Munich, 2016, pp. 344-355.
8 We may mention, among others: Morris, F., *Paris Postwar. Art and Existentialism 1945-1955*, Londres, 1993; A.D., *L'art en Europe. Les années décisives 1945-1953*, Zurich, 1987: A.D., *L'écriture grifée*, Saint-Etienne, 1993; A.D., *Eu ropa de postguerra. Art després del diluvi 1945-1965*, Barcelona, 1995; A.D., *Sota la bomba. El jazz de la guerra d'imatges transatlàntica*, 1946-1956, Barcelona/Madrid, 2007; A.D., *Arts a Catalunya, 1950-1977*, Barcelona, 2015; A.D., *Campo cerrado. Arte y poder en la posguerra española, 1939-1953*, Madrid, 2016; Enwezor, O., *Postwar: Art Between the Pacific and the Atlantic, 1945-1965*, Munich, 2016; Bertrand Dorléac, L.; Munck, J., *L'art en guerre. France 1938-1947*, Paris, 2012.
9 Gallego, J., "La pintura de Bernard Buffet", *Goya*, Madrid, 1954, 1.
10 Agamben, G., *Lo que queda de Auschwitz*, Valencia, 2014 [1999], p. 26.
11 Didi-Huberman, G., *Écorces*, Paris, 2018, p. 30; translation by the author of the article.
12 Didi-Huberman, G., *Le temoin jusqu'au bout*, Paris, 2012, p. 44; translation by the author of the article.
13 Waldman, B. *et al.*, *Visões da guerra. Lasar Segall*, São Paulo, 2012.
14 Clair, J., *Zoran Music à Dachau*, Paris, 2018 [2001].
15 Daix, P., *Les après-guerres de Picasso (1945-1955) et sa rupture avec Aragon*, Paris, 2006, pp. 22-24.
16 A.D., *Lo nunca visto. De la pintura informalista al fotolibro de postguerra (1945-1965)*, Madrid, Fundación Juan March, 2016.
17 Duras, M., *La douleur*, Paris, 2001, p. 73.
18 Levi, P., *Si esto es un hombre*, Madrid, 2019, p. 26; translation by the author of the article.
19 Cascante, J. (ed.), *El libro de Gila*, Barcelona, 2019.
20 On this work and the question of the title, see: Wilson, S., "Francis Gruber: espace politique, espace eschatologique", *Francis Gruber, L'oeil à vif*, Lyon, 2009, pp. 65-76.
21 Bernard-Gruber, C.; Vanazzi, A., *Francis Gruber*, Paris, 2002, p. 117.
22 Schwarz, D., *Jean Fautrier: Matière et lumière*, Paris, 2018, p. 21.
23 Besnier, J.-M., "Les années Sartre", *Obliques. Sartre et les arts*, Paris, 1981, p. 432; translation by the author of the article.
24 Keith Lowe also observes how the holocaust has become Christianised in imagery and has become linked to the Crucifixion. Lowe, K., *Prisioneros de la historia*, Madrid, 2022, pp. 90-91.
25 Ponge, F., "Note sur les otages, peintures de Fautrier", *L'atelier contemporain*, Paris, 1977, p. 29; translation by the author of the article.
26 Cirlot, J. E., *Subirachs*, Barcelona, 1960.
27 Alonso, D., *Hijos de la ira. Diario íntimo*, Madrid, 1944.
28 Perucho, J., "Miró", *Ariel*, 9/1946, 5, pp.68-69; translation by the author of the article.
29 Bolaños, M., *Baltasar Lobo*, Lleó, 2002.
30 Gary, R., *Éducation européenne*, Paris, 2020, p. 76.
31 Zambrano, M., *Persona y democracia*, Madrid, 2019 [1958], p. 108.

HUMANITY IN RUINS

Paula Barreiro

In 1957, an internal communication distributed among the members of Equipo 57 ('Team 57') read, with its idiosyncratic spelling, something like: 'Everyonez afraid = therza strong intellectual and political reprezive direktion. Anyone a bit suspekt of being a bit rebelliuz or intelligent is publikly denounzed as a kommunist or dangerouz… everything is on the blak market if at all = no alkohol or turpentine or tobako or food – this is the worst part of the woar and the post-woar (*sic*)'. This message perfectly sums up the state of panic and paranoia caused by the repression and shortages that spread anguish among the Spanish people in the late-1950s. To the disaster of a three-year fratricidal struggle was added the post-war desire for revenge in a period of violence and economic hardship that was pushing many in Spain to physical and mental limits. With the prisons overflowing with political prisoners, the letter circulated around young artists merely reflects the mood in a fearful society. And although the alliance established between the United States and Spain in 1953 had garnered international legitimacy and considerable sums of foreign currency for the regime, most ordinary Spanish people, scarred by the war and subsequent repression, formed no part of the propaganda narrative that, a few years later, would begin to be rolled out under the slogan 'Spain is different'.

Anguish

In the 1950s, Spanish artistic culture was undergoing very much the same epistemological, cultural and social transformations that the massacre of World War Two had engendered elsewhere. The existential anguish epitomised by the thinking of Jean Paul Sartre and Albert Camus, despite the differences between the two philosophers, had filtered into both literary and artistic culture from the earliest. In 1942, Josep Maria de Sucre painted the deformed head of a man/skull, clearly reminiscent of Munch, titling his work *Twentieth-Century Anguish*. The distressed gaze of a half-sketched, hallucinatory creature illustrated the fall of a continent into the clutches of fascism. The work took on particular significance in the context of Spain, a supposedly neutral country that unashamedly supported the Axis powers and committed the most atrocious outrages against its own citizens. The traumatic experience of the Spanish Civil War was followed by a long period when any opposition was completely eradicated from the social scene under a strategy already methodically implemented during the conflict and known as 'cleansing and punishment operations'.

It is no surprise that, in response to the well-oiled machine of repression, self-censorship and fear were rampant. These circumstances were masterfully captured by several artists. In *Silence* (1953), Juana Francés alludes to the sequestering of freedoms from the perspective of a gender bias that was considerable in such a deeply patriarchal society, where women (and the artist herself) were at a clear disadvantage. The painting shows a girl with narrowed eyes, her mouth covered by a hand (hers, or that of another). The ambiguity of the figure – we do not know whether she is silent or is being silenced – reinforces the melancholy air of the image, which features dull tones, a hieratic figuration and rounded volumes. The gaze off towards a plane that we cannot see and whose nature we can only guess

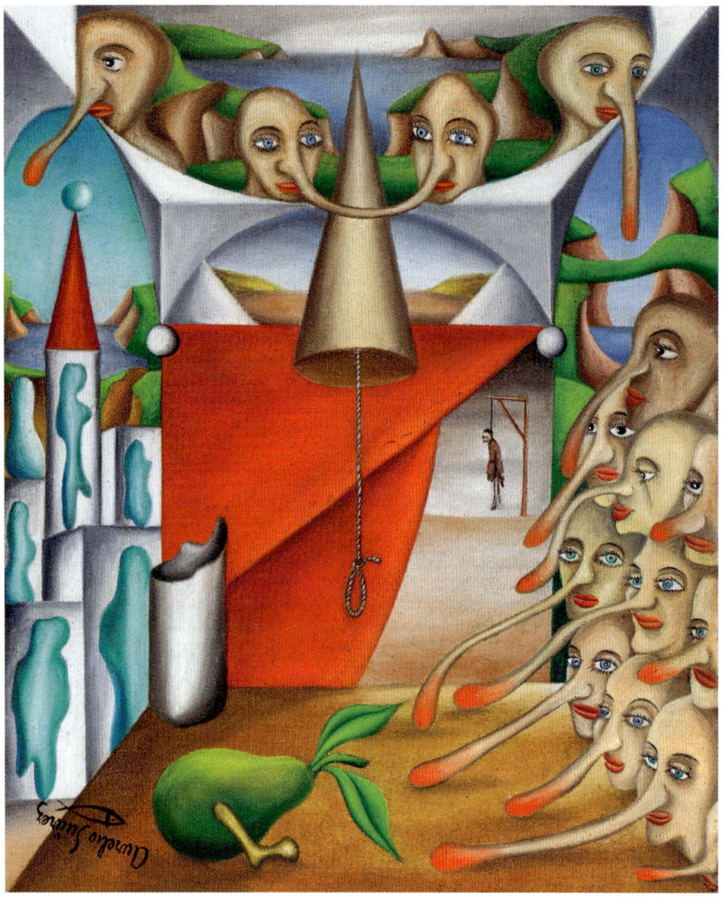

Aurelio Sánchez. *Rope smell*, 1947
Courtesy of Galería Guillermo de Osma, Madrid

at due to the woman's sorrowful attitude, seems to indicate a scene of pain and violence, one that, in the Spain of the 1940s, could only be alluded to (and with little by the way of safety guarantees) in satirical or surreal fashion.

In 1947, from the isolation of his studio, the Asturian artist Aurelio Suárez dared to paint the contours of different types of violence (political, economic, sexual, etc.) that were assailing the country. In *The Smell of the Rope* (1947), Suárez paints a carnivalesque universe in which the fear of being next on the scaffold is made explicit. In the centre of the composition is the noose ready for a new victim, eyed by a chorus of giggling characters with elongated, phallic, playful, deceitful noses. Under the veil of farce, they share the burden of handing down an implacable, imminent sentence. The work illustrates in its images the politics of fear that the regime imposed on Spanish society. It not only alludes to the caprices of sequestered justice, but also underlines the compulsory participation of citizens in a violent, criminal system.

Resistance

If the dictatorship had turned the Spanish people into witnesses of and participants in violence, then, following the tenets established on the Republican side during the war, thought, art and writing became instruments of resistance. After the withdrawal, the role of art as a weapon of denunciation became clearly evident even in the internment camps where Republican artists were sent. Josep Bartolí was among those who made drawings depicting the disintegration of his comrades in the sordid surroundings of their enforced confinement in Le Barcarès. Adhering to his own adage that 'the idea is more important than the painting', he sketched on paper what Jaume Grau, also a prisoner, described as the daily reality of the camps: 'mutilated men, broken men, defeated men', in short, 'men in ruins'. In his nervous pencil strokes, Bartolí constructed a visual manifesto that bears witness to the violence and physical and moral destruction of his compatriots, a document denouncing the atrocities of internment from its earliest days.

In postwar Spain, such images were dangerous and condemned to clandestinity, but they nevertheless existed. This was the case of the series of more than two hundred drawings by José Manaut Viglietti. Produced in 1943 and 1944 while he was serving his sentence as a political prisoner at Porlier and Carabanchel, sketches, drawings and even small oil paintings testify to the harsh conditions at the overcrowded prisons of Franco's regime during what the dictatorship called the 'victory years'. And, although the subject never ceased to be taboo, it eventually seeped into the practices of the young avant-garde. In 1950, Joan Ponç represented in *The Prison*, a dramatically expressive of work of great poetic depth, the vulnerable naked body of a prisoner abandoned to his fate in a dreary moonlit cell.

The revenge-obsessed policies pursued by the dictatorship in Spain tinged the existential absurdity of the postwar period with a different kind of desperation and a peculiar impetus. The awakening of a critical consciousness gathered force during

José Manaut. *Prisoners lying on mats*, n.d.
Universitat de València

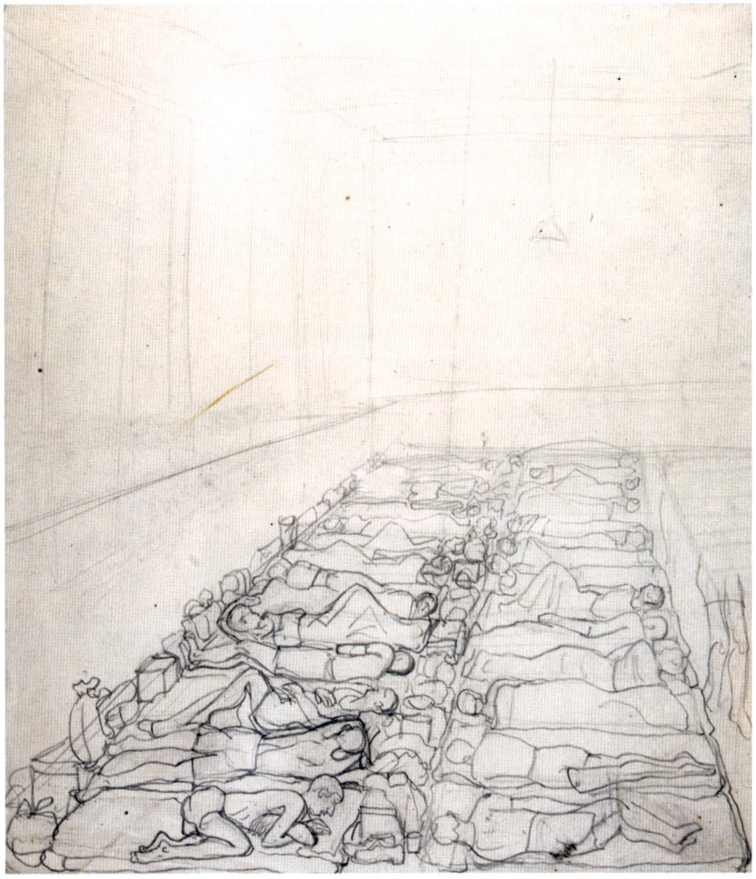

the university demonstrations of 1956, when a vision of art as protest began to take shape. Sartre, opportunely introduced as part of an avant-garde engaged in socio-political concerns, was a vital element in this process. The French intellectual had been a figure of reference for the resistance movement against fascism in World War Two, and his reputation among Spanish clandestine left-wing circles remained intact. Writers, art critics and artists found in his ethics of engagement the keys to constructing an existential – and highly moral – discourse on the artist's responsibility in the social sphere and, therefore, the incitement to take part in the *praxis*.

Testament

Accentuating the avant-garde's mission to denounce social realities, the artistic culture of the 1950s made extensive use of the Sartrean concept of *testament*. Within the context of the dictatorships and in line with the pathos found in the figurative practices of the European postwar period, the choice of figuration enabled artists to depict and protest against suffering. In his monumental, Picasso-influenced painting *The Defeated* (1956), Marc Aleu denounced, with great expressive force, the fate (and class) of the losers (represented by a desperate humble family). Death, hunger and powerlessness were the daily bread of the working classes, chief among the victims of Francoist ruthless vengeance.

Nevertheless, Spanish art also began to explore the territories of abstraction, finding in this style an excellent medium for expressing anguish. The spread of informalism enabled artists to find a language that, while still very much their own, was also adapted to the international context. Manolo Millares and Antonio Saura masterfully described the contours of man in ruins by progressively reducing colour, gesture and the expressive value of material. With its use of painstakingly worked sackcloth, Millares' work *Homunculus* (1960) seems to allude to Guanche mummies (which the painter had been familiar with from childhood), suggesting the shroud of a tortured anthropomorphic creature.

Delving deeply into the dark sorrows of a humanity in physical and moral ruin, these works, while participating under the aegis (and great rejoicing) of the dictatorship in the internationalisation of the Spanish avant-garde, also formed part of the forces of culture against Francoism that began to take shape in the late-1950s. Both Millares' tortured sackcloth and Antonio Saura's monstrous crucified creature (*Crucifixion*, 1962) articulated an existential unease that was shared with the rest of Europe, their canvases subtly embodying the normalised violence that dwelt within the social body of the dictatorship.

1 Letter CINN 0001, Equipo 57 Collection, Centro Andaluz de Arte Contemporáneo, Seville.

2 Preston, P., *El holocausto español: Odio y exterminio en la Guerra Civil y después*, Barcelona, 2013, p. 23 (translated from the English by Catalina Martínez and Eugenia Vázquez).

3 Haro, N., 'Mujeres artistas e imágenes de la opresión femenina en el realismo crítico. Revisando la historia oficial del antifranquismo', Aliaga, V.; Mayayo, P. (ed.), *Genealogías feministas en el arte español (1960-010)*, León, 2013, p. 165.

4 Jiménez-Blano, M.D., *Campo Cerrado. Arte y poder en la posguerra Española 1939-1953*, Madrid, 2016 (exhibition catalogue, Museo Nacional Centro de Arte Reina Sofía).

5 Grau, J., *Ulysse dans la boue. Journal des camps français, 1939-1944*, Perpiñán, 2014, p. 549 (author's own translation). Thanks to Eva Raynal for the reference.

6 Bartolí, J.; Molinw i Fábrega, N., *Campos de concentración*, México D.F., 1944.

7 See Barreiro López, P., *Vanguardia y crítica de arte en la España de Franco*, Madrid, 2021.

8 On collaboration, see Marzo, J.L.; Mayayo, P., *Arte en España (1939-2015) Ideas, prácticas, políticas*, Madrid, 2015. On their role in combating Francoism, see Núñez Laiseca, M., *Arte y política en la España del desarrollismo (1962-1968)*, Madrid, 2006.

FROM POSTWAR TO OUR WAR: THE WRETCHED OF THE EARTH

Sarah Wilson

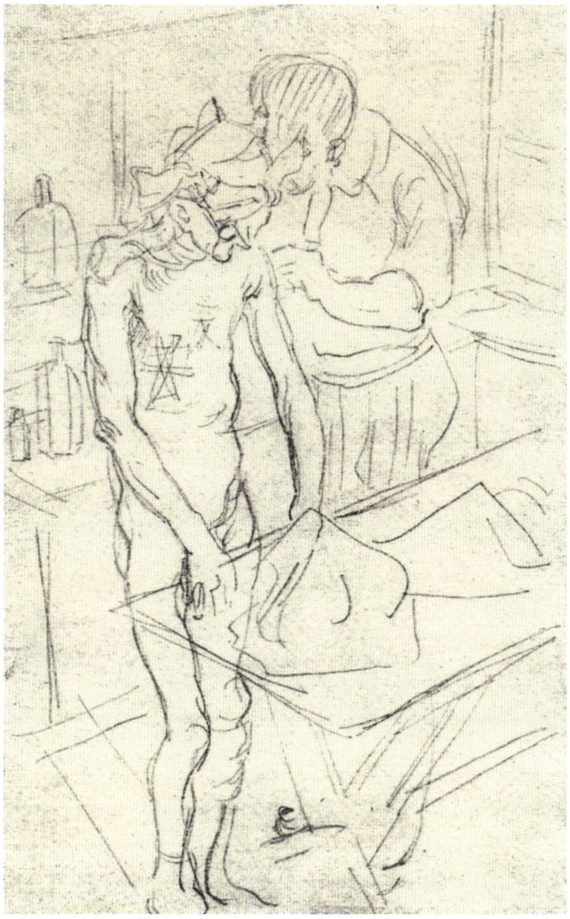

Boris Taslitzky. *Professor Halbwachs a few days before his death at Buchenwald,* 1945

Which Humanity? Francis Gruber's painting *Les cadavres* was shown in *Art and Resistance* at Paris's national museum in 1946. Almost monochrome, it is rich with pallid modulations of ground colour and of skin tones. A model, elongated, slightly foreshortened, lies face downwards, one arm invisible under the weight of his body, knees bent. A protruding sternum shelters the concave, empty stomach in shadow; a fist is still clenched. The darker hand, face and foot suggest forced labour out-of-doors; the body stripped naked after death. The second male form to the right is cut off, knees in the air. Beyond compassion, the viewpoint interrogates the spectator. Are we the Nazi, looking down, so close we could give the corpse a last kick? Or are we — like Gruber's friend, Boris Taslitzky — a starved, inmate-survivor, who must lift the dead weight onto a makeshift cart with other corpses, en route for the *charnier*? A kerb runs across the top of the painting, where a red rose, stem crushed, adds a strange note of romanticism. What contrast with the artist's clothed portraits in interiors or exteriors where ruined doors open onto blank skies.

Which Humanity? asks questions about perpetrators when it shows victims. Depictions of crowds interrogate the behaviour of collectivities. Ethics and decision-making were at the heart of Jean-Paul Sartre's existential philosophy. This exhibition traverses the period of Sartre's *Being and Nothingness* (1943), *Existentialism is a Humanism* (1946) and *Portrait of the Anti-Semite* (1947). Responses included the Nuremberg trials, the Geneva Convention, the setting up of structures under the aegis of the United Nations such as UNESCO; the "banality of evil" was discussed in Hannah Arendt's *Eichmann in Jerusalem* (1963) following her *Origins of Totalitarianism* (1951): debates continued in the 1960s.

Art was compelled to respond to the Second World War's plural endpoints: victory, the revelation of the concentration camps, the final atrocity of the atomic bomb. The brutal divisions of territories at Yalta in 1945 meant families separated, the displacement of peoples and proxy wars in rival spheres of influence. Colonial and imperial competition for raw materials — food, petrol, uranium — conceived "man" as expendable labour or cannon fodder. French forces bombed Sétif on victory celebration day, May 8, 1945: thousands of casualties anticipated later bloodshed in Algeria, the "war with no name" for a territory conceived as part of "greater France": echoes of a "special military operation" today.[1]

"Cold War" is a misnomer for a period rife with more wars, more victims. Picasso's *Massacre in Korea,* 1951, anticipated the war in Indochina, playing out in Vietnam, where the Communist/anti-Communist territorial divisions and direct American involvement used peoples as pawns in the ideological struggle between the USA and USSR. *Which Humanity?* concentrates on atrocity and victimhood in Europe

—even imagined from faraway Brazil. 1966 as an endpoint includes the invasion of Hungary by the USSR in 1956: totalitarian rule from afar tolerated no dissent.

To return to the *Art and Resistance* exhibition in 1946: it also showed Picasso's *Le Charnier*, its complex monochrome composition a pendant to his *Guernica*. A domestic scene with tangled bodies under a table, it triggered a debate about style within the French Communist party. Taslitzky's on-the-spot camp drawings inspired his vast, expressionist panorama, *The Small Camp, Buchenwald,* shown in June 1946.[2] Both works contrast with Gruber's simplicity.

These years were marked not by celebration but mourning, the return of the *déportés* (citizens deported by collaborators), purge period murders and revenge killings.[3] The shaving and branding with swastikas of women accused of sex crimes inspired transgender artist Prinner's illustrated poem *La femme tondue*: "Catcalls —Whore!— Tart!— Carcass!— Piece of shit!" are complemented by frenzied hands, trapped in this so-called "ugly carnival".[4]

The entire postwar humanist discourse was gender-specific, including the conference on Humanism in Geneva 1949.[5] The discourse of "man" ignored victims such as the "forgotten women of Buchenwald";[6] see Julio Gonzales' screaming peasant-woman, and Apel·les Fenosa's flaming female martyr, commemorating Oradour-sur-Glane (an entire village population were set on fire in a church). The forgotten female sculptor Françoise Salmon commemorated Auschwitz victims in Paris's Père Lachaise cemetery in 1949 and the deportation from Hamburg on the site of the Neuengamme camp in 1965. From the inevitable rape in Renato Guttuso's Picassoid *Trionfo della morte,* 1943, to Josep Maria Subirachs' sculpture *Europa,* 1953, the female body, with its long history in art, signified both abjection and classical tradition. Europe's back, arched off the ground, invokes *Rape of Europa* tropes long past; her Cold War complement is Henry Moore's *Falling Warrior, 1957-60*, recalling the dying Trojan hero with shield from the Doric Temple of Aphaia.

Which Humanity? also asks religious questions: *Eli, eli, lama sabachthani?* Surely God has forsaken man? Throughout Catholic Europe, the tortured and humiliated body was retransposed to the Crucifixion: witness Bernard Buffet's *Lapidation*. A spate of church reconstructions demanded a modern sacred art: see the apostolic figures by Subirachs for the Sanctuary of La Virgen del Camino, León (Spain). In Protestant countries, Christ also became a symbol. Graham Sutherland's *Crucifixion*, with its black brush-strokes and streaming blood, is based on Matthias Grünewald's Isenheim altarpiece. His Byzantine *Christ in Glory in the Tetramorph*, a grandiose tapestry, dominated the nave of the new Coventry Cathedral in 1962. This moment coincided with the much-delayed embrace of modernism by the Vatican: Sutherland's *Crucifixion* is housed in the Vatican museum. While Francis Bacon depicted a mere scaffolding for the beast-like figures in his *Fragment of a Crucifixion*, the cross's very presence attests to the impossibility of its symbolic destruction.

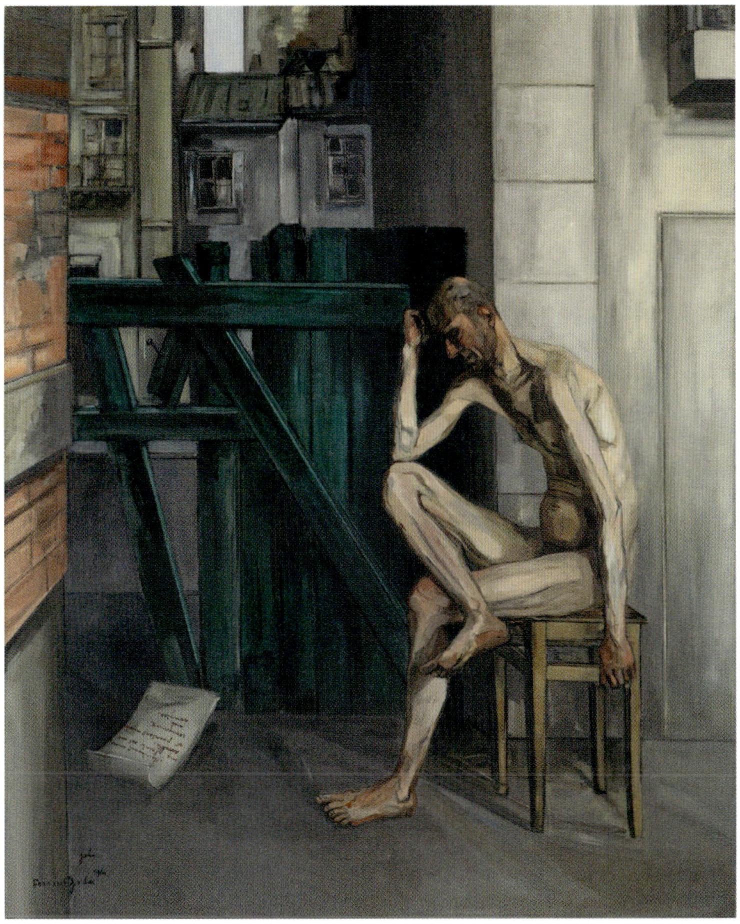

Francis Gruber. *Job*, 1944
Tate Gallery

Communist atheism and existentialism offered alternative frameworks for response to Nazi atrocity in a period of growing secularisation. Neutral figures — the undifferentiated masses of Lasar Segall's *Visions of War,* 1940-1943 — responded to a predicament in which the outcast meant first the Jew, then other persecuted groups (homosexuals, Roma, or Communist resistants). Existentialism was able to confront deeper epistemological challenges with its dialectic of being and nothingness.[7] "Witness drawings" of the dying made in camps must be fundamentally differentiated from later recollections or sympathetic imaginings (Segall in Brazil). Moreover, the distance between Taslitzky's drawings of Maurice Halbwachs, Professor of the Collège de France, humiliated and naked in the Buchenwald infirmary and Halbwach's posthumous publication *On Collective Memory* is deeply uncanny.[8]

The existentialist impact on postwar painting and on sculpture had a *locus classicus*: Sartre's relationship with Alberto Giacometti's bronze, emaciated figures. Germaine Richier "queered" postwar existentialist sculpture with her nature-eroded humans, insects and Christs. Her London retrospective of 1947 inspired the "geometry of fear" generation of English sculptors, including Reg Butler, whose quasi-erotic female *Figure in Space* (adapting the armatures of both Richier and Giacometti) followed his major success in Britain's group show at the 1952 Venice Biennale: rugged surfaces signalled scarred bodies, while tradition (figurative sculpture in bronze) was maintained with pride.

Sartre's powerful discussion of the gaze and its relationship to the Other, embodied in Giacometti's sculptures, is transposed to the looks of many portrait heads in *Which Humanity?*: the late cubist mode of Jordi Mercadé, the intense and questioning self-portrait by Antoni Guans, the anguished doubt of Norman Narotzky's *The Philosopher,* or the piercing gaze of the figure by American painter Leon Golub. Female portraits by male or by female artists seem more composed. Even if in mourning (Edouard Pignon's *Catalane)*, a link is implied to motifs of maternity and rebirth. Maternities in sculpture are joyous and smooth; see the work of Baltasar Lobo, as early as 1946. Postwar dwellings to house new families were constructed all over Europe (including the East) in styles derived from Le Corbusier, whose Unité d'Habitation de Marseille (1947-52) preceded his great Ronchamps chapel, completed in 1954; the first postmodern building.

The Cold War had its agendas in the arts: London's Unknown Political Prisoner competition of 1953 was funded, unbeknownst to organisers and competitors, by the CIA.[9] Now, anguished figures (Angelo Fabbri's terracotta figure) pointed silently to the Soviet gulag. Motifs of mourning, melancholy and reflection upon the Holocaust persisted. The International competition for an Auschwitz monument was launched in 1958. *New Images of Man* was the last international humanist exhibition at the Museum of Modern Art in New York in 1959.

In the 1960s, international Pop, absorbed or parodied in Europe, introduced bright colours (Mari Chordà); abstractions, where Op joined Pop, offered design ideas to the fashion world. Female artists were emboldened: Niki de Saint Phalle, "seized the gun" for her shooting paintings. Women claimed full emancipation in the privileged West, whose "economic miracles" extended to Spain and Catalonia.

This was no climate for "the work of memory". Yet, as Sartre prefaced Frantz Fanon's *Wretched of the Earth* in 1961, the colonial question became more acute: the Algerian claim for freedom anticipated Black civil rights demonstrations in America and anti-Vietnam protest.[10]

While Fautrier's hostage paintings of 1956 were provoked by the Soviet invasion of Budapest — an anguished repeat of his 1945 series — memory retrieval took longer for Slovenian artist, Zoran Mušič. After his Dachau drawings came the *informel* landscapes: only in the 1970s did stones turn to skulls. Finally, in the 1980s, Maurice Blanchot composed *Writing the Disaster*, Jean-François Lyotard was able to write *The Differend, Heidegger and "the Jews"* and preface the art of Ruth Francken, a Jewish émigré from Prague, deeply affected by Ludwig Wittgenstein's "sear of silence".[11]

It is Giorgio Agamben's *Bare Life, Homo Sacer*, 1995, which takes us back to Francis Gruber's painting *Job*, 1944 and his male cadavers of 1946 — the year David Rousset, concentration camp survivor and future gulag specialist analysed "the concentrationary universe".[12] Crucial for Agamben were Robert Antelme's camp memoirs, Carl Schmitt's thoughts on politics and sovereignty, Michel Foucault's biopolitics and René Girard's unacknowledged study of violence, the sacred and the scapegoat: "Because the victim is sacrificed it is criminal to kill him — but the victim is sacrificed only because he is to be killed."[13] What might this ambivalence signify as regards the spectacle of victims in *Which Humanity?* "The Camp as the 'Nomos' of the Modern" has been crucial to theorising the *Homo sacer* as one with "an outcast, a banned man, tabooed, dangerous [...] accursed".[14] Guber's contemporary portrait of Job, abandoned, crying out to God, is that of the citizen-subject reduced, as was Antelme, to a state of "bare life".[15]

We live though a loop in time. Accusations of "Nazi", old tanks, shattered buildings, mud, pain and the obscenity of propaganda have revived, with crowds in flight, broken families, shattered and wounded bodies. News bulletins give this exhibition a new urgency: yesterday seems all too close to today.[16]

1 The postcolonial positioning of Okwui Enwezor was to the fore in his great exhibition *Postwar. Between the Pacific and the Atlantic*, Munich (with my essay "New images of man. Postwar humanism and its challenges in the West", pp. 344-349).

2 Wilson, S., "*Le Charnier* or *Buchenwald*", *Picasso / Marx and socialist realism in France,* Liverpool, 2013, 4, pp. 99-101.

3 Boudrel, Ph., *L'épuration sauvage*, 1944-1945 (2002), Paris, 2008.

4 Brossat, A., *Les Tondues. Un carneval moche*, Paris, 1992 (Paris, 2015).

5 Barth, K. *et al.*, *Pour un nouvel humanisme*, *Rencontres Internationales de Genève* (Neuchâtel, Éditions de la Baconnière, 1949).

6 *Les femmes oubliées de Buchenwald,* Paris, 2005.

7 Sartre, J.-P., *L'Être et le Néant, essai d'ontologie phenoménologique,* Paris, 1943 (*Being and Nothingness,* London, 1958).

8 Halbwachs, M., *La m*émoire collective, Paris, 1950 (Coser, L. A. (ed.), *On Collective Memory*, Chicago, 1992).

9 Lapp, A., "The Freedom of Sculpture, the Sculpture of Freedom: the International Sculpture Competition for a Monument to the Unknown Political Prisoner", *Sculpture Journal,* 1998, 2, pp. 113-122.

10 See Gervereau, L. *et al.* (eds.), *La France en guerre d'Algérie, novembre 1954-juillet 1962,* Nanterre, 1992 (catalogue of the exhibition in Musée d'histoire contemporaine-BDIC, including Niki de Saint Phalle etc.)

11 Blanchot, M., *The Writing of the Disaster*, Nebraska, 1986 (French edition 1980); Lyotard, J.-F., *L'Histoire de Ruth*, 1984; Lyotard, J.-F., *Heidegger and "the Jews"*, Minneapolis, 1990 (French edition 1988); Lyotard, J.-F., "Sear of Silence/La brûlure du silence", *Ruth Francken*, 1991.

12 Rousset, D., *Univers concentrationnaire,* Paris, 1946; Rousset, D., *Le Livre blanc sur les camps de concentration soviétiques*, Paris, 1951.

13 Girard, R., *Violence and the Sacred*, Baltimore/London, 1977 (French edition 1972). Introduction quoted in English in Pierpaolo Anonello, "Sacrificing Homo Sacer: René Girard reads Giorgio Agamben", *Forum Philosophicum*, 2019, online.

14 Agamben, G., *Homo Sacer, Sovereign Power and Bare Life* (1995), Stanford, 1998, 166-171 ff.

15 Antelme, R., *L'Epsèce humaine*, Paris, 1947 (Paris, 1957).

16 Wilson, S., "Writing the disaster: Trauma and reconstruction in postwar France", Gillen, E.; Weibel, P. (ed.), *Facing the Future, Art in Europe, 1945-1968*, Brussels, pp. 88-101. This exhibition moved to the Pushkin Museum, Moscow, with a catalogue in Russian: how tragic in retrospect.

ART AND VIOLENCE

Nausikaä el Mecky

Art and violence have a fascinating, confusing relationship. After the occurrence of real-world violence, art can be essential for a society to heal. On the one hand, by exposing brutality and injustices and making them known to the world. On the other hand, by providing images of comfort and beauty, that can remind us—even in the harshest of times—that humans are not simply cruel and destructive. And yet, art does not simply respond to real-world atrocities, a canvas is not just a projection screen on which events are projected and processed, it can also be the site of new, artistically created violence. Images can be inherently destructive and repressive, sometimes in ways we would not even notice. Therefore, at times it's hard to determine what kind of relationship a work of art even has with violence: it may *look* gorgeous and peaceful, but it is inherently oppressive. Or quite the opposite: it can look destructive, yet its intention is to uplift us. Art is sometimes idealised as the place where we rise above both the mundanity and the horrors of the world, where our noblest tendencies are passed on to current audiences and future generations. Perhaps this is the reason museums can seem like temples or churches, where we interact with images respectfully, meditatively, as we briefly enter a higher ground. But artists are not holy beings: art is not immune from either our noblest or our ugliest tendencies, and as such, it will also reflect our most violent impulses. Still, violence is not always a bad thing in art. In this essay, I would like to go a bit deeper into this confusing, contradictory topic, by exploring four ways in which art and violence are related, and show how art can assuage, show, hide, and commit violence.

Showing the violence

War, repression and genocide are instruments of erasure: of beauty, of dignity, of entire peoples and their culture. Images can counteract—and shed light on—that black hole of war and obliteration. Works such as Josep Bartolí's *View of the Camp,* in *Concentration Camps*, or Zoran Mušič's *Dachau. Four Hanged Men* expose and immortalise the horrors that were meant to be happening out of sight. Art is not just a document that brings atrocities out into the open, it can also deepen empathy and activate us to prevent such violence in the future. Figurative works which show brutality most shatteringly may be very different, and in some ways opposed to press photos of atrocities. First of all, they can be a lot more intimate, as we look through the filter of the artist's gaze at people behind barbed wire, or at the arms lifting up a baby as in Lasar Segall's *Visions of War.*

The distortion of photorealistic reality can make images of violence all the more poignant. After all, the visual surface of things can at times be a screen that hides the true nature of things. Immediately after the war, the landscape was filled with scars: burnt fields, ruined houses—yet many survivors' bodies told a false story, as though nothing had happened. Meanwhile, the broken bodies of the victims had been buried or burnt. So how do you show that interior landscape of pain? By going beyond what can be seen, by showing the anguish caused by weapons of war not as literal bombs or soldiers falling from the sky with parachutes, but as a black, synaptic blob with eyes, as in Helios Gómez' *Air-born Pain (Parachute with an Eye).* And by simplifying, twisting and pushing the depiction of the human body far beyond the literal, to wring out the violence as it was felt, to push those collective wounds into the open and start healing. The twisted, impossible bodies of Anton Prinner's *La femme tondue* speak of suffering and grief in bodily and metaphorical terms. Similarly, Honorio García Condoy's sculpture *Buchenwald or the Fall of Man*, through its wrenched column of bodies, shows pain, cruelty and mass murder in a way that rejects anatomical reality in favour of bringing out a deeper truth of suffering. Sometimes, the only way to understand the inconceivable is through images that blend the familiar and unfamiliar, since that is often how people describe war or other traumatic events: as something impossible, even as they are living it.

Assuaging the violence

As anyone who has experienced grief will know, it is impossible to only focus on the horrible. Art can also provide a portal of hope, without pretending that the cruelty never happened, showing how grief and beauty can, despite everything, co-exist and even nourish each other. A segment from the 1964 song *Nim Wstanie Dzien* (Before the Day Rises), by Polish poet Agnieszka Osiecka, encompasses the cycle of violence and joy in detail that is gruesome yet comforting:

The sun will embrace us
From earth heavy with blood
Once more wheat will be born
A golden dust

[...]

Breads will emerge from ovens
And look, where there was only smoke
Flowers will scar over the war trail
Rose-coloured[1]

This sense of re-birth, of rising above or beyond, may be gleaned in e.g. Laurent Jiménez-Balaguer's *Untitled* or in Antoni Tàpies' *Man*, but loss is not forgotten in these images, as death and something otherworldly appear to be present: hurt and hope are interwoven in images that look tranquil, but may have been wefted together by violence.

Hiding the violence

And yet, other kinds of peaceful, soothing images can actually be criminal and repressive, acting like a smokescreen to distract from inhumanity. It may not be a coincidence that Hitler, Stalin and Mao all tried to control art and used it as a tool to airbrush the murderousness of their regimes. Artists were prosecuted and murdered, or forced to work in a way that was in service to the authorities. Such works were meant to be understood as clearly as a message on a Post-it—no room for ambivalence or personal interpretation. Here were happy people,

1 Translated from the Polish by N. el Mecky.

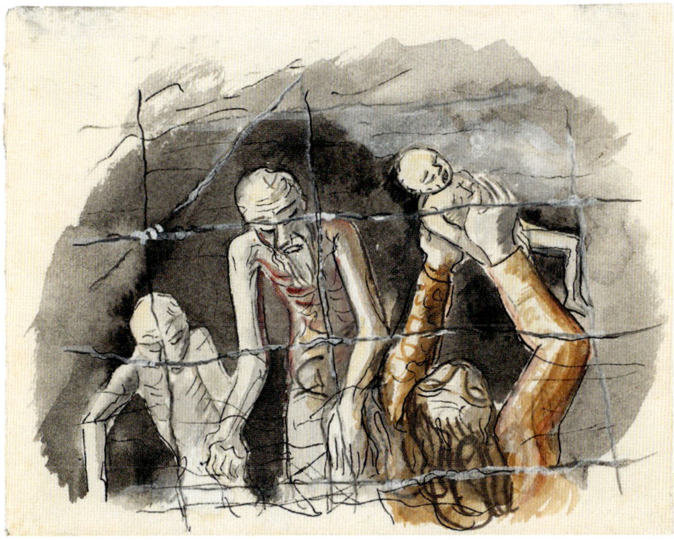

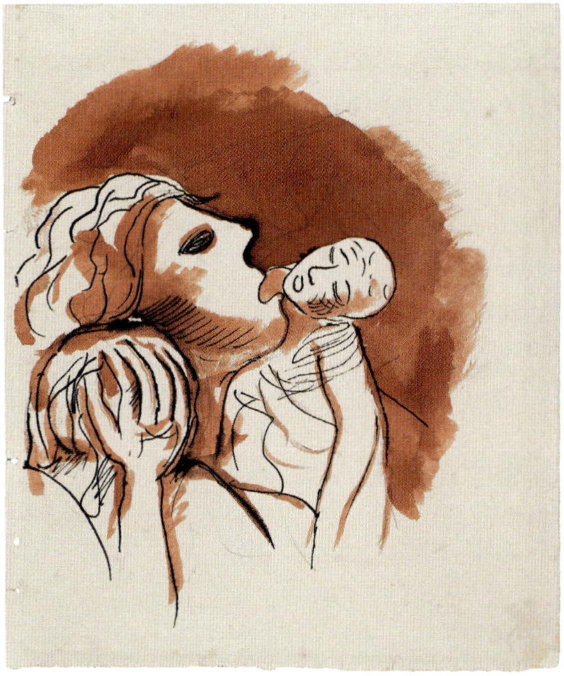

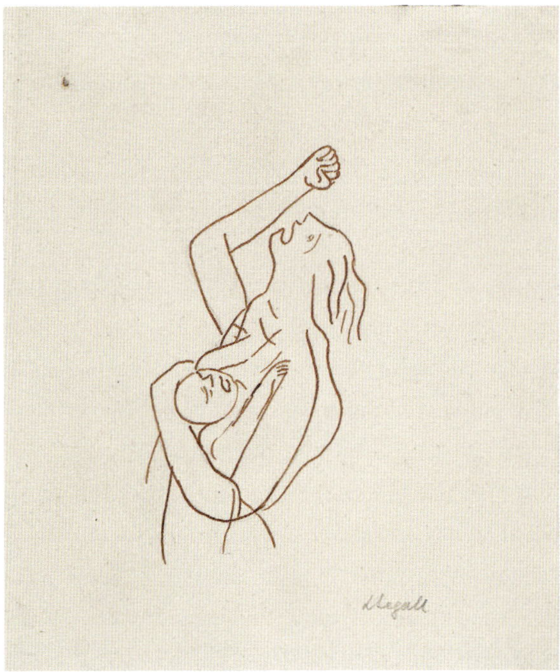

Lasar Segall
Vilnius, Lithuania, 1891 –
São Paulo, Brasil, 1957)
Drawings from the sketchbook
Visões de guerra
1940-1943
Mixed technique on paper,
15.5 × 19.5 cm approx. /
19.5 × 15.5 cm approx.

heroic people, cast in the eternal sunlight of their glorious regime. If there was any reference to violence, that was glorious, too: brave soldiers, winning, or, if absolutely necessary, dying bravely and gratefully for their fatherland. Such art embodies suppression by concealing violence twice over: the violence of artists forced to work in a specific way according to a checklist; and it hides the immeasurable violence perpetrated by repressive regimes. A cruelty that is supposedly justified, as it is in pursuit of the utopia shown in propagandistic art. Its images of meadows, flowers and happy people can be more brutal than the most visceral depiction of pain.

Committing the violence

It is no surprise that many artists wanted not only to expose the violence that had happened, but to attack the traditional notion of art itself. It could also be used as a creative tool: destruction and artistic creation need not be opposites. Thus, Robert Rauschenberg erased a drawing by Willem de Kooning in the name of art, Gustav Metzger used acid as paint, which left his canvas in shreds. Niki de Saint Phalle in her *Shooting Paintings*, such as *Tir Gambrinus*, used a rifle to blow up balloons filled with paint, which were covered with white plaster, the bullets creating such spectacular splatters of paint that they would have made Jackson Pollock jealous. In these acts, destruction creates its own beauty.

CoBrA: showing, assuaging, committing and repressing violence all at once

The short-lived CoBrA (1948-51) movement appears to bring together all the aforementioned aspects of art and violence. An international movement, its name is an acronym of Copenhagen-Brussels-Amsterdam. Its intents were both idealistic and disruptive: seeking a kind of rebirth in their embracing of the childlike, there was also an aggression in their approach. Constant, one of its members, believed art to be 'spiritual weapon', whereas another, Christian Dotremont, wanted an art that was 'as natural as the shattering of a windowpane or the growth of a city'. Its founders believed in vitality, in harmony, as well as in exposing the bourgeoisie for its role in the horrors of Nazism.

Though it references children's art, CoBrA is far from cutesy, and miles away from the happy, well-behaved children so often employed in propaganda art. Just like many children are fascinated by the grisly and macabre, so CoBrA works can have a violent, at times nightmarish quality. Employing the schematic shapes typical of the drawings of young children, the movement's artists splattered on the paint. 'My paint is like a rocket which describes its own space,' stated Karel Appel, one of its most well-known members (*Young Boy with a Ball*). CoBrA used the 'inability' of small children to render bodies, animals and perspective 'correctly' and embraced these supposed failures as beautiful. Their paintings are populated with strangely flattened beasts, terrifying-yet-adorable stick figures, globby paints or the unevenness of an undisciplined, passionate child: lots of paint in one part of the work, the canvas left raw in the other. It is both a return to innocence after the world wars and a cathartic release of raw, red-hot energy, an art that is disruptive as much as it is life-affirming. That explosiveness proved contagious: fistfights broke out at a poetry reading held at the 1949 CoBrA show at Amsterdam's municipal museum, whilst newspapers severely condemned the works as 'Madness elevated to the status of art', as 'Botch, Blotch and Splotch'. Now, as with many movements that started off as a rebellion against the status quo, CoBrA has become accepted, decorative even: it can now be found on coffee mugs and placemats in many Dutch households. That in itself could be considered a kind of demise. But perhaps worse is that even this movement had a repressive side: Ernest Mancoba, an early member from South Africa, was marginalised both by the movement's artists and, until recently, by art historians. A similar fate befell its various female artists, such as Anneliese Hager, who, bogged down with housekeeping, could only make her innovative work at night, and was subsequently ignored by art history. CoBrA thus is art that is uplifting in its vitality, it engages with raucous wildness as well as totalitation darkness, and yet contains this element of repression of women and artists of colour underneath its exalted surface.

This last part may be the worst and most slippery element of the relationship between art and violence. When depictions of events which are not part of the main historical narrative are deemed irrelevant—or when artists who fall outside of the art canon quietly disappear, the suppression of such images happens softly, in the margins. It is a violence that is invisible, yet it is a fundamental aspect of art.

RE-LEARNING TO LOOK AT THE HUMAN IMAGE

Jordi Ibáñez

It is well worth mentioning at the outset certain historical novelties that are inextricably linked to our idea of the representation of horror and the image of the human. Clearly, these historical novelties are not, in reality, so new, but they continue to charge forwards amid overwhelming technological progress. There is photography, there is film and video, there is the extraordinary spread of the Internet, and there are images created by Artificial Intelligence. We may well say that these technological powers have produced, and continue to produce, an image of the human – a "human-image" – that should be distinguished from other ideas and visual experiences of a historically and culturally defined human image. It is impossible not to think about humanity before and after photography, or about the differences between seeing with the power of conviction of the cinema and seeing the real thing at the time – *in vivo*, as they say. The forging of fact into image is decisive, and if the image seems very real, or even replaces what is real, then we enter a completely new dimension in cognitive, moral and political terms. Of course, we already had Goya's etchings of the *Disasters of War*. It is a well-known commonplace. But what was there before that, as far as we know? Callot's etchings of the Thirty Years' War? Is, for example, Poussin's *The Massacre of the Innocents* valid as a representation of horror? And to what can we compare Titian's *The Flaying of Marsyas*, at the Prado, in which we see the satyr skinned alive? Perhaps with the terrible photographs of the death by a thousand cuts in China that so fascinated and obsessed Georges Bataille? We can look at Fautrier's heads of tortured people. But will we be able to hold our gaze at photographs of *gueules cassées*, faces disfigured by shrapnel and bombs in the First World War? Would we say that photography shows to be intolerable images that painting transforms into something else? However, at times the two media become interwoven and create a conflict that is not so much between painting and photography as between art and documentation and testimony. The Vietnam War, for example, was filmed and photographed to an extraordinary degree. Perhaps more than any of the wars of the twentieth century and those we have seen in the twenty-first so far. The conflict did not produce great painting, it is true, but it did generate collages, primitivist drawings, posters and silk-screen print series. One particular case, the massacre perpetrated in the village of My Lai, well documented by photographs published in magazines such as *Life* (cruel irony of the title!), scandalised public opinion, which was already opposed to the war, and even generated considerable discussion – and a shocking poster – as regards the right of the United States to continue to show a painting like *Guernica* at MoMA. Francis Frascina devoted an important article to this case and the debate it generated. And although the Gulf War was, according to Baudrillard's *boutade*, a war that "did not take place" due to the planned, calculated lack of images – United States military leaders had learned the lesson of Vietnam – the invasion of Iraq once more brought disturbing images, such as the tortured prisoners at Abu Ghraib, to our eyes.

Seeing or not seeing is key. One thing is for them to tell you about it. And quite another thing is the image. Before photography, before film, there was the account and there was the graphic representation – painting, drawing, engraving – or the *immediate* vision of the horror. In his memoirs, Giacomo Casanova describes the horrific, meticulously planned, slow torture to death suffered by a manservant, Damiens, who had dared to stab Louis XV with a penknife. Readers of Foucault are familiar with the litany of horrors that Damiens suffered, because the French philosopher opens his book *Discipline and Punish* with a discussion of the case. Indeed, Foucault uses sources that describe the torture in much greater detail than the Venetian libertine's account. But Casanova, who was several times obliged to turn away his face from the "dreadful sight", which lasted four hours, interests us because he records the complacency with which his noble friends and the general public of Paris followed Damiens's slow agony. Peter Weiss has Sade recall the execution in his play *Marat/Sade* (I use its short title here). In Weiss's text, the infamous marquis affirms that the guillotine, used so productively to cut off heads during the Reign of Terror, was certainly a technological advance, but not a moral one, as the public continued to be as inhuman as they were fifty years previously. Moreover, on the subject of sensitivity to certain spectacles, we may remember that public executions did not cease in France, for example, until as late as 17 June 1939. In Spain – though this, given our country's history, affords little by way of distinction – the so-called Pulido Law ended public executions in 1900. So, why so *late* in France? Or perhaps we should ask, why *then*? Well, for one thing, because the spectacle of women dipping their handkerchiefs in the blood of the beheaded criminal disgusted and scandalised the authorities. It was believed that the blood of condemned men had magical power, bringing fertility. And for a similar story, one that speaks of humanity as recently as 1939, we can turn to Baudelaire's prose poem *The Rope*. However, there was another, perhaps even weightier, reason for ending public executions in France as late as 1939. Due to a technical problem with the guillotine, that last execution took nearly an hour to complete, with the sun shining down on the scene, so that it was photographed many times and even filmed. These images can still be seen on Internet where, of course, photos and films are instantly available to all. The truth is, the visibility of the event alters its nature completely. The solution? Make it invisible. Conflicts after the Vietnam War have become relatively invisible, less so when the purpose is to reveal the enemy's inhumanity. But our eyes have now lost their innocence. Have we not seen films of firing squads and other executions? Have we not seen the bulldozers piling up mountains of limp corpses for burial in mass graves at liberated Nazi camps? Images of horror should shock us, and they did. But they also hardened our gaze. After all that – to say nothing of the vast amounts of senseless violence purveyed by films and video games – we may well say that our eyes have become blinded by all the things we have seen. This is not a wise blindness, it is an inhuman blindness. But part of this blindness is due to the fact that we see what we have learned to see. Seeing is a habit, it forms part of a *scopic* regime that is, in turn, culture, and even the visual morality of a specific historic moment with its technological possibilities perfectly defined.

Having said this, it seems to me that it is easy to understand in what sense we can say that the image of the human being – the human-image – always acts as a screen, a filter or frame for the human image. We see the image of the human being that a particular historic period generates, but we do not see the human

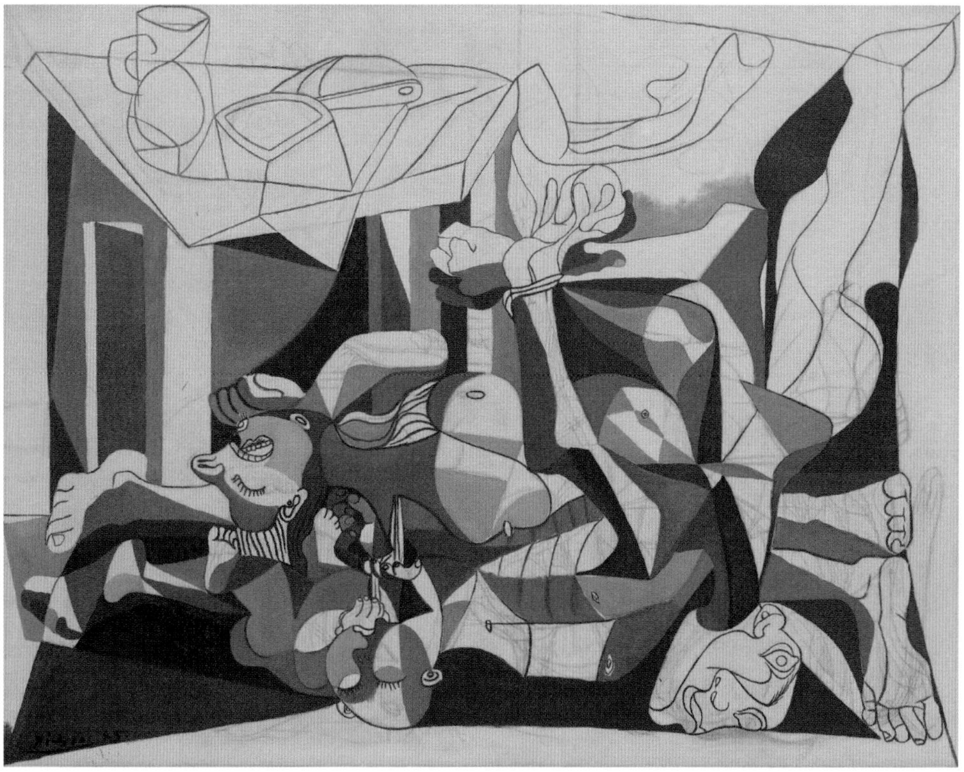

Pablo Picasso
Le charnier (The Charnel House). París, 1944-1945
Mrs. Sam A. Lewisohn Bequest (by exchange) and Mrs. Marya Bernard Fund in memory of her husband Dr. Bernard Bernard and anonymous funds. Acq. no.: 93.1971. Museum of Modern Art (MoMA), New York, USA

being *without the image*. But is it possible that, perhaps, the unimaginable human image is nothing more than an ahistorical entelechy? Here, the Vitruvian Man drawn by Leonardo da Vinci is of not more worth to us than the *Acéphale*, or beheaded human, drawn by André Masson for the magazine of the same name created by Bataille, Caillois and company. Now, the fact that it is invisible and at the same time demands to be thought about is all-important. Everything is at stake here.

In his essay *A Short History of Photography*, Walter Benjamin describes the moment when the human being was photographed for the first time. Benjamin says that it was still possible to capture a shining, a spectral aura. The technical conditions of the first photographs – the long exposure time – allowed him to play with an idea: that the human being photographed had become a spectre of the human. Giacometti broke with the surrealists precisely because he had become obsessed with the idea of portraying the human face, with capturing in painting the presence which, in the photograph, according to Benjamin's conceptual game, had become spectral. During the Second World War, which he spent hiding out in a Geneva hotel, Giacometti devoted himself to putting the limits of smallness to the test by making miniscule sculptures of people, figures the size of matchsticks which, of course, ended up slipping through his fingers. "What humanity" is a question, or an exclamation, that has attained timeless value while also demanding historical consciousness. For Giacometti, for the "optical unconscious" unleashed by photography according to Benjamin's famous theory (now degenerated into "optical unconsciousness", if I may make such a sad play on words), for the efforts of the surrealists to find the eye in the wild state – a way, paradoxical perhaps, of regaining their innocence – and for the entire denouncement of the divisive, alienating visuality that Debord posits in *The Society of the Spectacle*, the question or exclamation "what humanity" has a precise historic sense. The "scopic regime" that becomes installed with photography and the moving pictures of film and video, plus its hyperaccessibility on Internet, has brought us face-to-face with an image of the human – with an *imagery* of the human – which conditions the human image in a very different way from how this *imagery* might have functioned in times when only painting and, even, at times, only certain forms of very primitive painting, let us say, or certain prints, were accessible to the eyes of the parishioners or the inhabitants of such and such a village or hamlet, people who, in their entire lives, would only see *that*, those frescoes in the church and perhaps their own blurry image in a small mirror or reflected in the still waters of a pond. If we were to ask those primitive eyes the question "what humanity?" then, having had explained to them what on earth "humanity" was, they would probably point in answer to the Christ crucified in the village church. And if they were more bookish people – Jews, or Muslims who read the Qur'an – they might say that humanity is invisible, but that, nevertheless, it can be said, heard, recited, memorised.

In 1945, when the Second World War had ended and all the Nazi concentration and death camps had been liberated, a professor of psychology from the University of Chicago travelled to Europe to collect the oral testimony of those returning from the camps. The recordings made by David P. Boder can now be consulted in an archive of the Paul V. Galvin Library, freely accessible by Internet, catalogued under the title *Voices of the Holocaust*. This is a different kind of memory from what we can find, for example, in the testimonies recorded by Claude Lanzmann for the 1985 documentary *Shoah*, by which time the debate about the Bilderverbot and the aniconism surrounding the Nazi genocide had begun to gather force. The more elaborate – and justifiably harsh – memory became, the more demanding the imagery. The testimonies gathered by Boder do not have the narrative elaboration of memory. They are more perplexed than manifestly traumatised, more indignant even than ashamed, as if the horror were still impregnated with the quotidian. These are people anxious to tell, to explain.

We know that it took years for us to become fully and clearly aware of what the Nazi genocide industry really was. Writers like Semprún and Primo Levi describe the indifference, almost hostility, with which the accounts of those who returned from the camps were received. The horror was quickly swept away by the laws of life. But, in art, a process of re-elaboration began that was not always conscious, did not always explicitly refer to that horror. And that is the paradox, and the wonder: art transgresses the conventions, limits and habits that a historical period forges in the form of an image of the human being. Art, which also defines the regime of visuality of an age, can act at the limits of visual conventions, breaking, expanding or dissolving the rules of the day. This enables us to focus, with the same immediacy as the surprised voices still immersed in their stunned perplexity, on the human image over and above the human-image, to focus on imaginable, precarious, conflictive, complicatedly visible humanity. With painting, we almost remove the veil from over our eyes that so much photography and so much film have created. But do we see better? Perhaps we merely force ourselves to take a better look, to rub our eyes as if we were waking up from a dream. The horror might then emerge mixed with the always revolutionary, always utopian element of painterly imagery, of sculptural gesture, of the mental and manual effort that sweeps away expression and representation.

1 Frascina, F., "Meyer Schapiro's Choice: My Lai, *Guernica*, MoMA and the Art Left 1969-1970", *Journal of Contemporary History*, 07-09/1995, 30, nos. 30 and 31.

2 On this point, see the catalogue coordinated by Jean Clair for the exhibition *Crime & châtiment* at the Musée d'Orsay, Paris, 2010, pp. 206 and 299. The references are to texts by Dominique Lobstein and Philippe Nieto.

"We will all be crucified, but, silence! Don't let the children hear. Rather, let's talk about future humanity, which will be wonderful. And why should it be wonderful, future humanity? Poor humanity, how can it ever be future? It will always be present, atrociously present, divided between two calls: that of happiness, that of crucifixion. The call of crucifixion... are wars anything else?"

Joan Sales. Incerta glòria, ('Uncertain Glory'), 1956

“We were not expected to survive”

Germaine Tillion (ethnologist, hero of the Resistance)

After each war, we must mourn, take stock of the human losses and material damage. Countries are ruined, souls are wounded, and yet we must start living again.

For some people, the war never ends, even when the fighting has stopped. Prisoners of the past, these survivors only think about the horror and never regain the pleasure of living. Most of them, thanks to their dreams of the future, give meaning to their endeavours and sacrifices. The post-war period is a peculiar time when grief for what has happened is mixed with the hope of creating a new society: dancing in the ruins, crying in the cemeteries and, once again, building homes and projects for life. This is the moment when wonderful and dangerous utopias come into being.

The twentieth century was wonderful. Technology made magic progress, machines replaced men at the pit of the mines, medicine cured efficiently and social progress made us dream of equality. The shame of the twentieth century was two world wars, 50 million casualties, three genocides – Armenian, Jewish and Rwandan – and countless mass crimes, the Spanish Civil War, the Cambodian autogenocide and 60 long-running "armed conflicts" that destroy societies and pass on the trauma across several generations.

Most of the survivors remain silent in order to get on with their lives and stop thinking about the unhappiness. Those who speak pass on the horror and those who remain silent pass on the anguish. To speak is to bring back fear and suffering. Words that tell the horror make the memory bleed. Silence is more appropriate, but by remaining silent, the wounded soul conveys the anguish of emptiness, of non-representation.

In order to avoid this painful choice, a compulsion to art arises. A theatrical performance, an anthropological reflection, a novel, a film or a drawing can express what the testimonial could not express. When reality is unbearable, the work of art can make a representation of it that can be shared. Reality is not modified, of course, the dead are dead, the cities are destroyed, but an artistic production allows

WAR AND WONDER

Boris Cyrulnik

one to give a kind of images and words to what could not be said. When we can rework the representation of horror, when we do something with our wound, we modify the memory of the horror, we add the memory of what we said to the memory of what we underwent. We suffer less from the wound when, supported by our loved ones and culture, we are able to reflect on what happened to us, to make a novel, a theatrical play, a poem, a painting or a philosophical essay out of it. Horror, metamorphosed into a work of art or into an insight, changes the way we feel about the events of life. The artist, the painter or the actor become our spokespersons: they can say on stage what the wounded person could not say face to face. The diversion through the work of art gives the wounded person a link of words where they can share their story. They can write what they cannot say because spoken words are acts, heard words provoke emotions and read words are an invitation to reflection. The painter, the writer and the actor address the perfect friend, the invisible reader or the listener who will understand them perfectly. The wounded person is no longer alone!

In this sense, the first work of art that allows us to bear death, the despair of loss and the anguish of emptiness, is the staging of burial. We cannot leave to rot on the ground the body of a loved one who is dead only in reality, since in our soul they still live. We love someone who is no longer on earth and yet lives on in our memories: we talk to them, we evoke them constantly, we experience vivid feelings in our bodies even though we know consciously that death has taken them away. And so we act out their departure, our grief and our hope that they will rest in peace or that they have not died in vain. We put their body in the ground with their best clothes, flowers, jewellery, songs and words that turn their corpse into an immortal memory.

Most works of art are tragedies that have been transformed into beauty. The pyramids of Egypt, 6,000 years ago, tell with paintings, sculptures and jewels of the greatness of the deceased and their passage to the afterlife. Horses and muscular men achieving the victory by slitting the throats of the defeated were sculpted in Assyrian bas-reliefs. Napoleonic battles are magnificent with their thousands of dead lying in the snow with their speared horses. Géricault's painting of the dying on *The Raft of the Medusa* poses the moral problem of the captain who leaves the ship before protecting his passengers; Picasso's *Guernica* depicts the war crime of an air force bombing a city where unarmed inhabitants are dying; Charlotte Delbo in Auschwitz risks her life by writing poetry; and Germaine Tillion in Ravensbrück makes the deported women laugh by singing an opera inspired by Offenbach that ridicules the female SS torturers.

Human history is made up of a series of climatic, epidemic and war disasters, but each time life has reappeared, beautiful, healthy, but different because it had to overcome a trauma, which defines resilience.

There is no human life without suffering, there are no societies without wars, but at every ordeal, culture has allowed us to live again.

Marc ALEU
Karel APPEL
Francis BACON
Josep BARTOLÍ
Maurice BÉJART
Roger BISSIÈRE
Louise BOURGEOIS
Joan BROTAT
Roser BRU
Bernard BUFFET
Reg BUTLER
Armand CARDONA TORRANDELL
Mari CHORDÀ
Antoni CLAVÉ
Claude COLLET
Joan COLOM
Modest CUIXART
Parvine CURIE
Jean FAUTRIER
Apel·les FENOSA
Juana FRANCÉS
Honorio GARCÍA CONDOY
Josep Maria GARCIA-LLORT
Pere GASTÓ
Juan GENOVÉS
Alberto GIACOMETTI
Manuel GIL
Maria GIRONA
Leon GOLUB
Helios GÓMEZ
Paco GÓMEZ
Juli GONZÁLEZ
Roberta GONZÁLEZ
Eduardo GREGORIO
Francis GRUBER
Antoni GUANSÉ
Oswaldo GUAYASAMÍN
Lluís GÜELL
Josep GUINOVART
Renato GUTTUSO

ARTISTS

Lucien HERVÉ
Laurent JIMÉNEZ-BALAGUER
Ramon LLOVET
Baltasar LOBO
Antonio LÓPEZ
Marcel MARTÍ
Carlos MENSA
Manolo MILLARES
Joan MIRÓ
Henry MOORE
Inge MORATH
Zoran MUŠIČ
Norman NAROTZKY
Francis NEWTON SOUZA
Jorge OTEIZA
Pablo PICASSO
Edouard PIGNON
Joan PONÇ
Anton PRINNER
Friedrich RAUCH

Germaine RICHIER
Mercè RODOREDA
Ramon ROGENT
Niki DE SAINT PHALLE
Lluís Maria SAUMELLS
Antonio SAURA
Pierre SCHAEFFER & Pierre HENRY
Lasar SEGALL
Gonçal SOBRER
Saul STEINBERG
Josep Maria SUBIRACHS
Josep Maria DE SUCRE
Graham SUTHERLAND
Pierre TAL-COAT
Antoni TÀPIES
Franciszka THEMERSON
Josefa TOLRÀ
Agnès VARDA
Maria Helena VIEIRA DA SILVA
Andrzej WRÓBLEWSKI

The horror and the suffering caused the infamous acts of destruction and devastating violence of the Second World War drove many people into silence. Some artists, however, bore witness to all this, at times directly and viscerally (Zoran Mušič), at others through intuition and transmission (Lasar Segall). Moral perversion and the destruction of bodies at concentration camps could be intuited, explained and fixed, but often through a quasi-secret intimacy, with a horror that overwhelmed the capacity for it to be looked in the face.

THE DISASTER

MARIA HELENA VIEIRA DA SILVA
(Lisbon, 1908 – Paris, 1992)
The Disaster
1942
Oil on canvas
81.2 × 100.2 cm
Centre Pompidou, Paris. Musée national d'art moderne-Centre de création industrielle

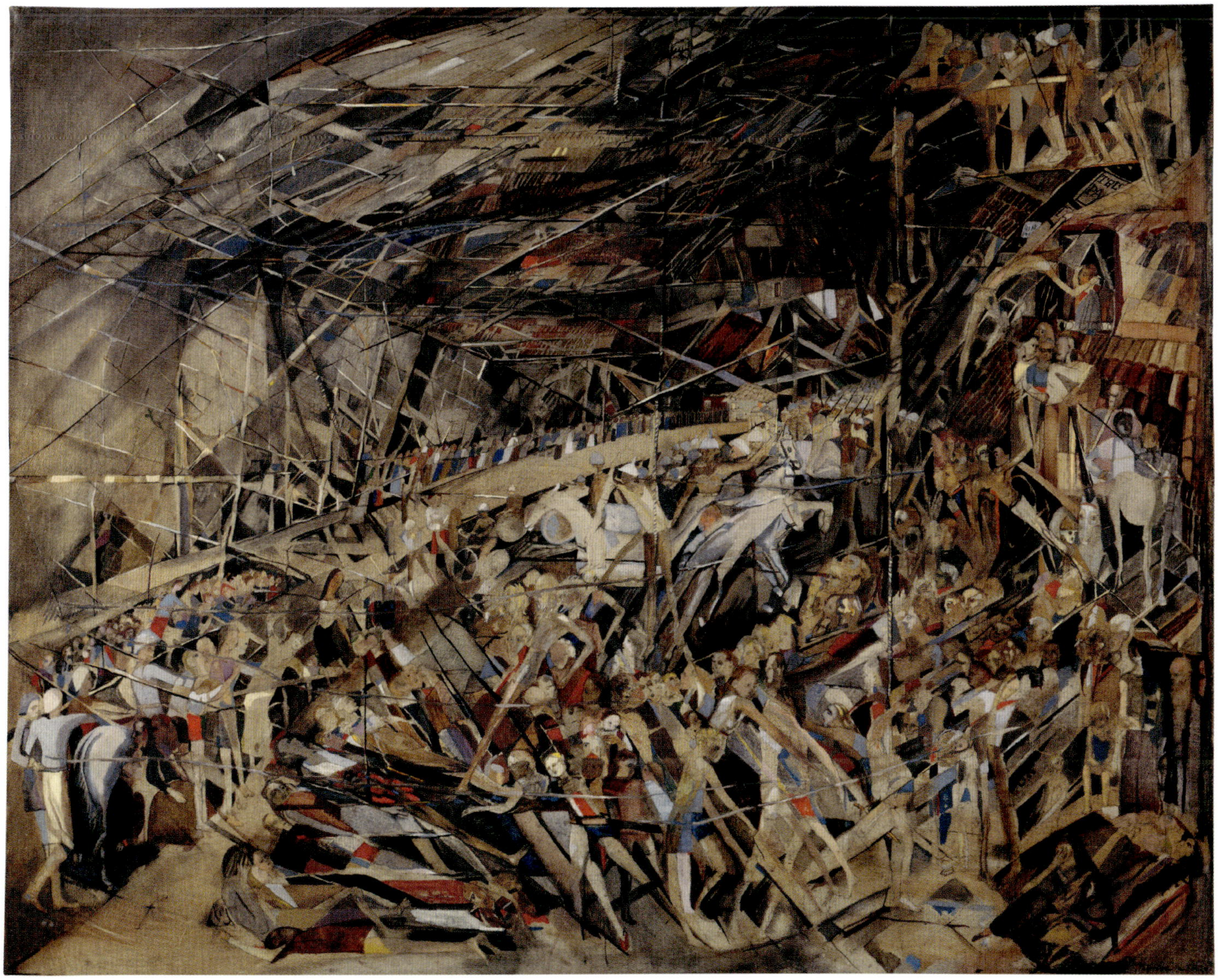

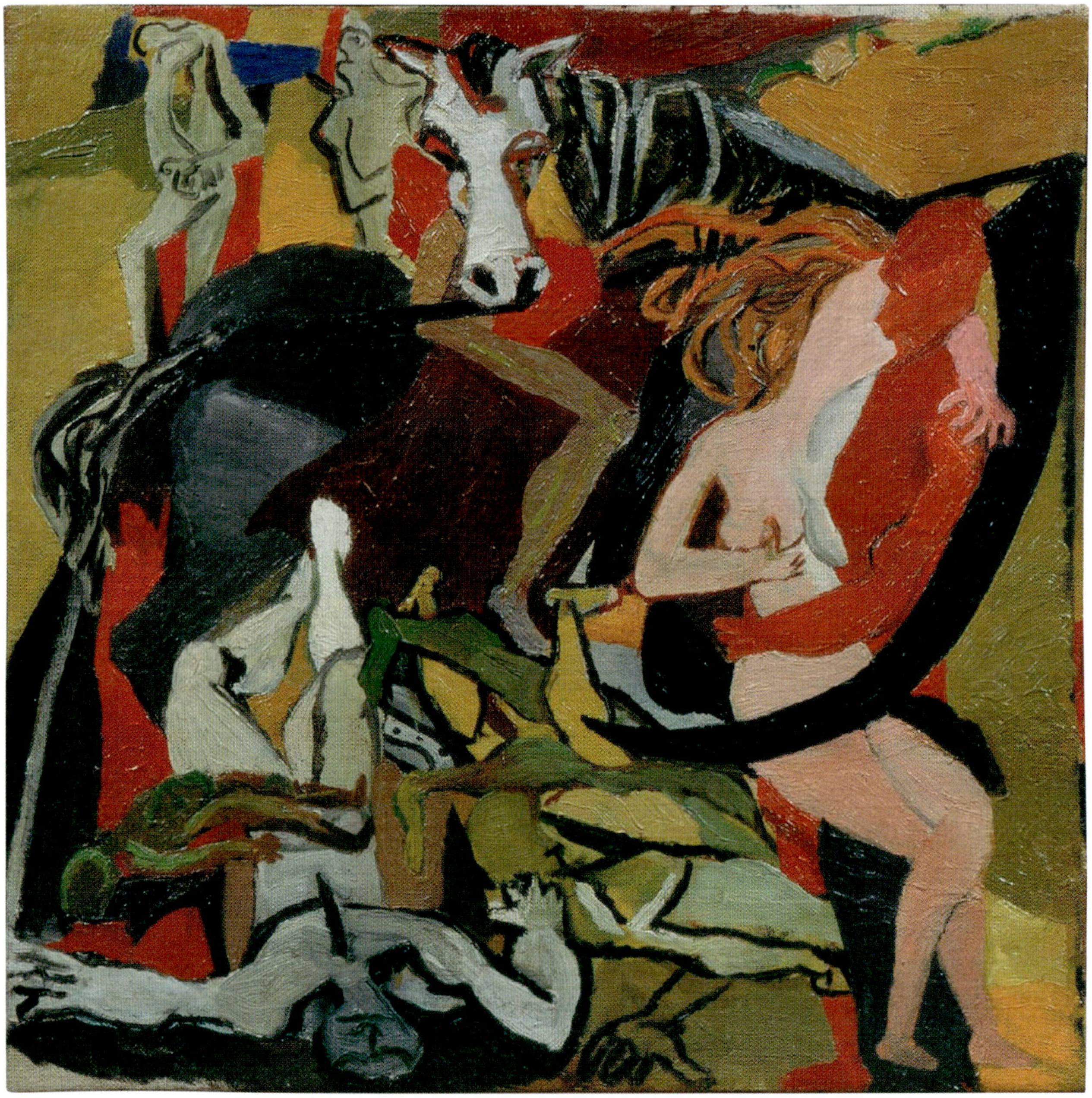

RENATO GUTTUSO
(Bagheria, Italy, 1911 – Rome, 1987)
Triumph of Death
1943
Oil on canvas
55 × 55 cm
Galleria Nazionale d'Arte Moderna e Contemporanea, Rome

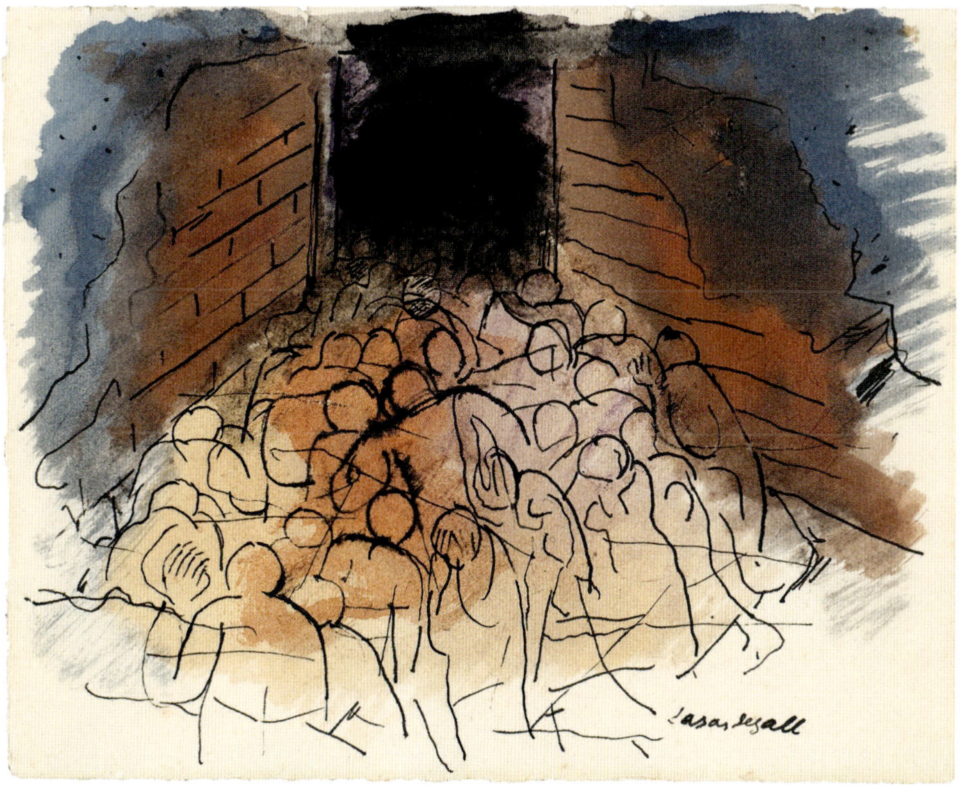

LASAR SEGALL
(Vilnius, Lithuania, 1891 – São Paulo, Brazil, 1957)
Drawing from the sketchbook *"Visões de guerra"*
1940-1943
Mixed technique on paper
15.6 × 19.5 cm
Acervo Museu Lasar Segall-Instituto Brasileiro
de Museus/Ministério da Cultura

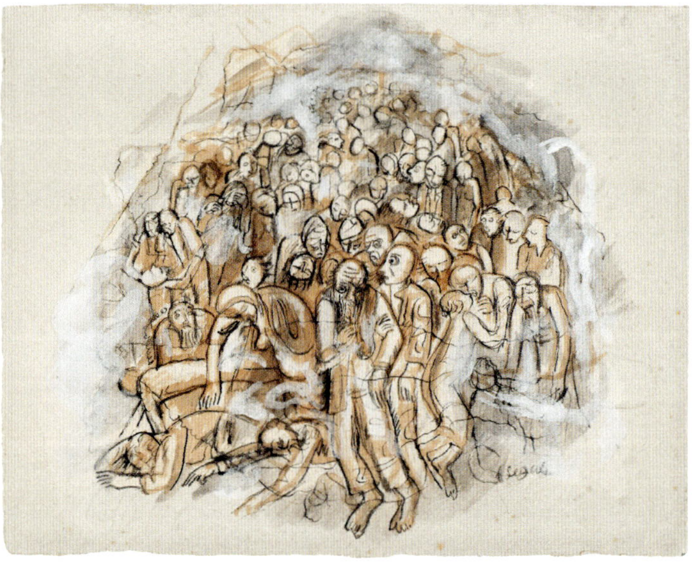
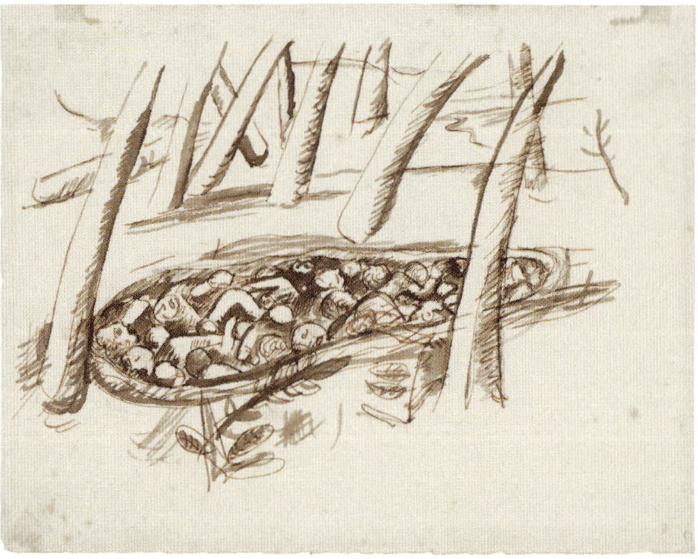
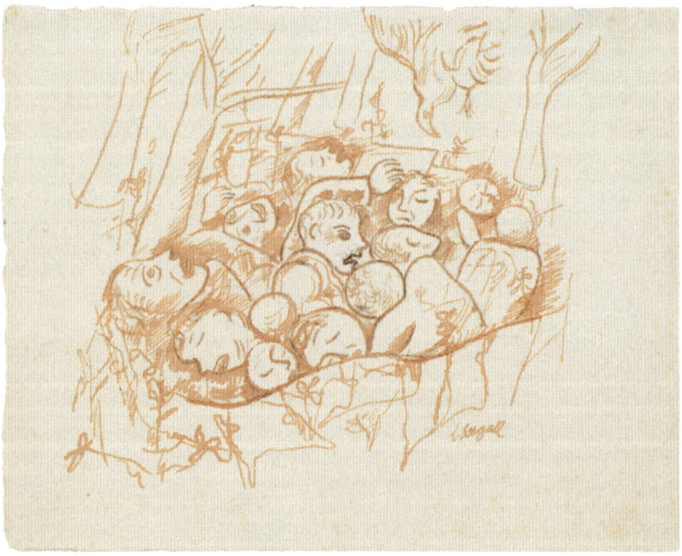
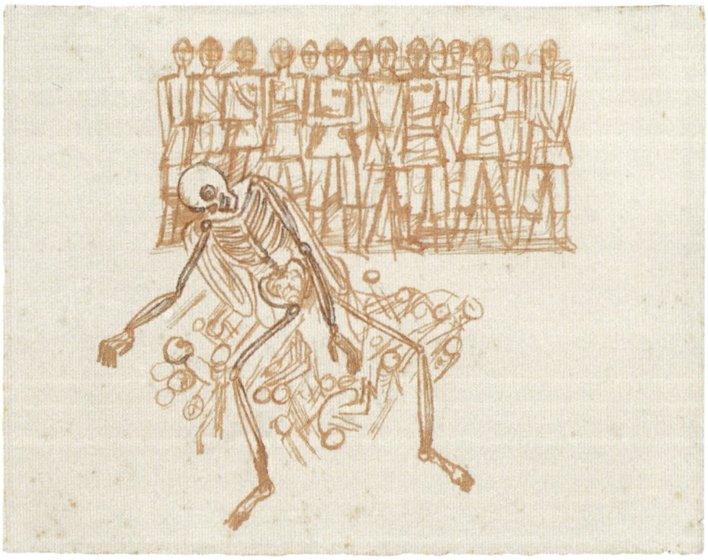

LASAR SEGALL
(Vilnius, Lithuania, 1891 – São Paulo, Brazil, 1957)
Drawings from the sketchbook *“Visões de guerra”*
1940-1943
Mixed technique on paper
15.5 × 19.5 cm approx.
Acervo Museu Lasar Segall-Instituto Brasileiro
de Museus/Ministério da Cultura

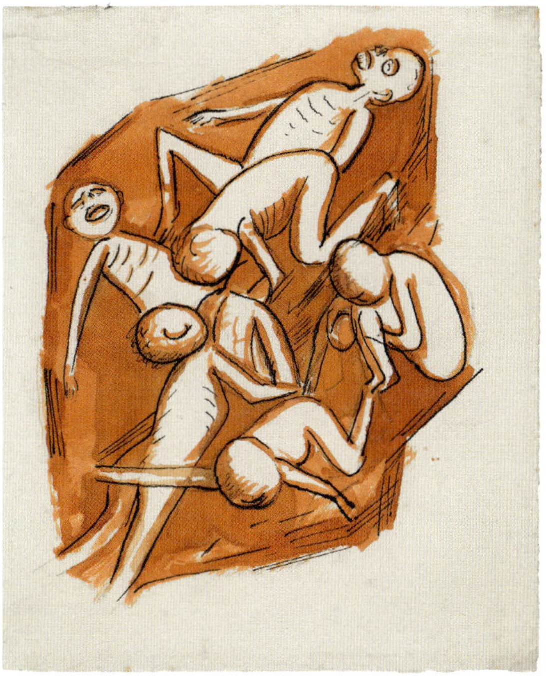

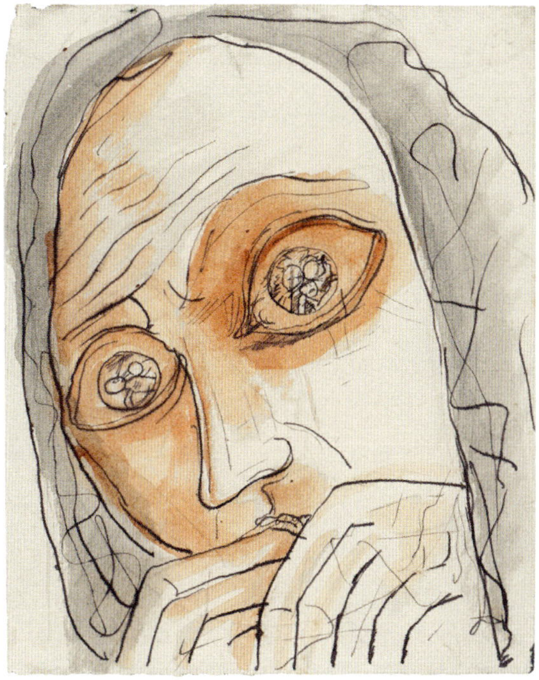

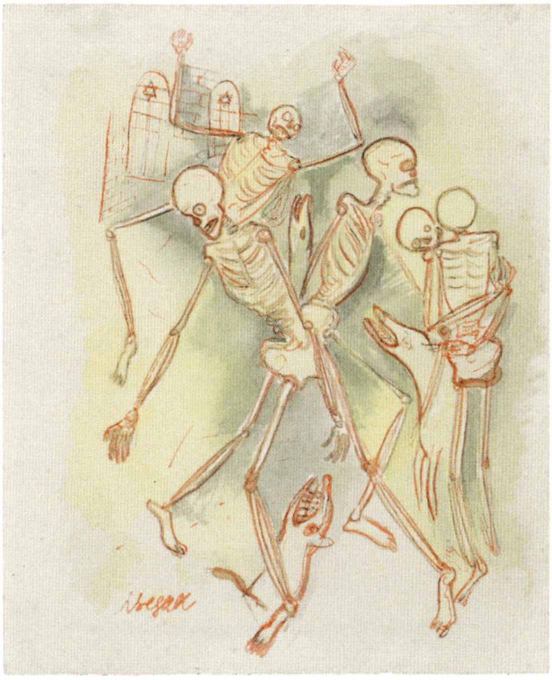

LASAR SEGALL
(Vilnius, Lithuania, 1891 – São Paulo, Brazil, 1957)
Drawings from the sketchbook *"Visões de guerra"*
1940-1943
Mixed technique on paper
19.5 × 15.5 cm approx.
Acervo Museu Lasar Segall-Instituto Brasileiro
de Museus/Ministério da Cultura

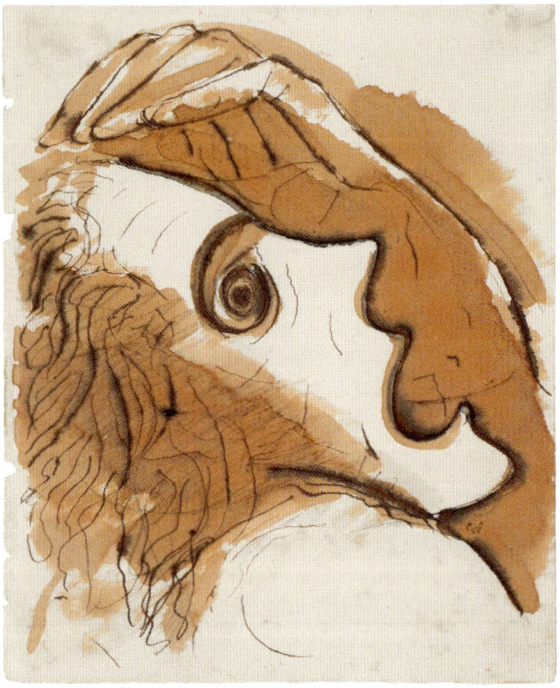

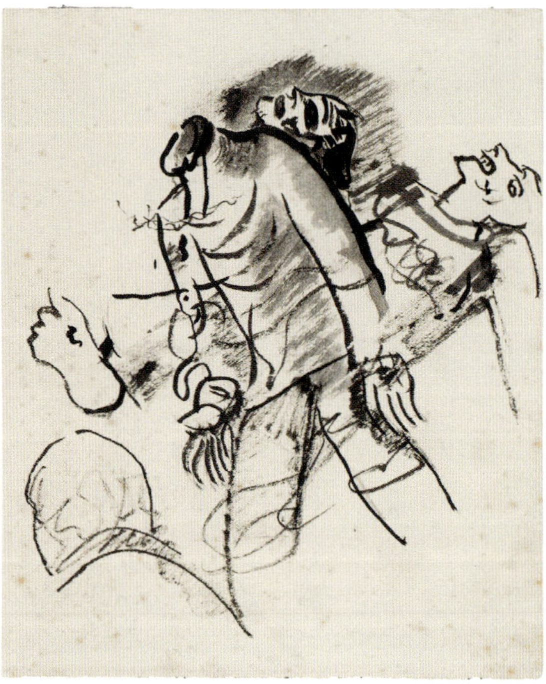

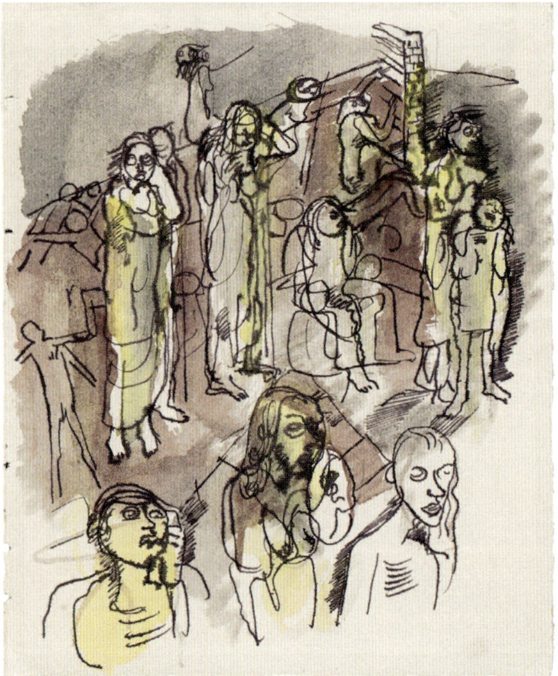

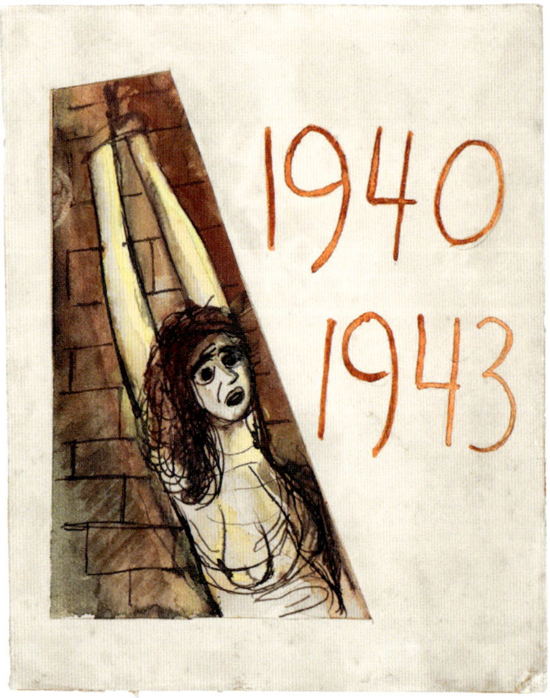

LASAR SEGALL
(Vilnius, Lithuania, 1891 – São Paulo, Brazil, 1957)
Drawings from the sketchbook *"Visões de guerra"*
1940-1943
Mixed technique on paper
19.5 × 15.5 cm approx.
Acervo Museu Lasar Segall-Instituto Brasileiro de Museus/Ministério da Cultura

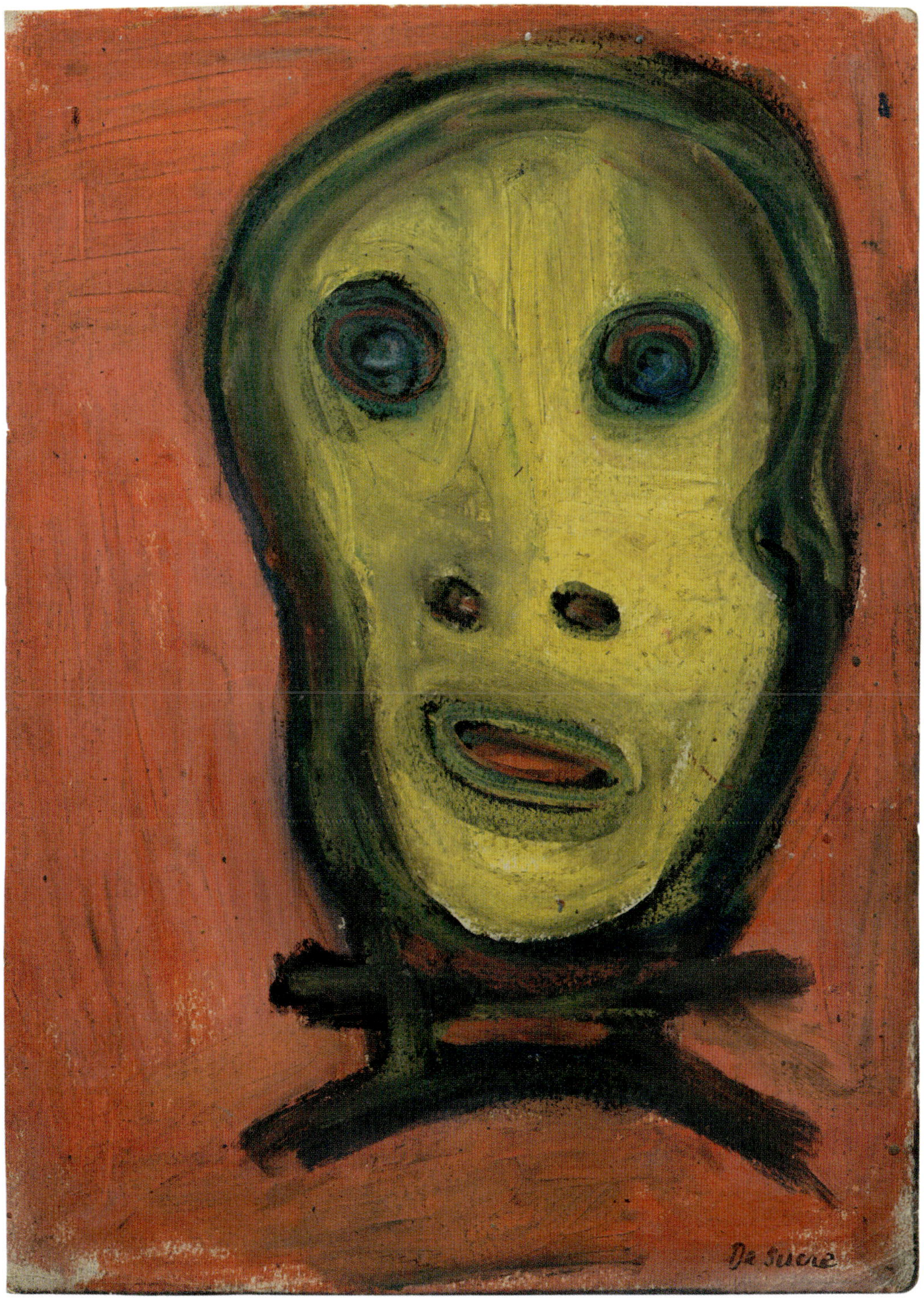

JOSEP MARIA DE SUCRE
(Barcelona, 1886-1969)
Anguish in the 20th Century
1942
Wax and ink on cardboard
33 × 23.5 cm
MACBA Collection. Deposit of the Generalitat de Catalunya. Former Salvador Riera Collection

ZORAN MUŠIČ
(Bukovica, Slovenia, 1909 – Venice, 2005)
Dachau. Four Hanged Men
1945
Brown ink on paper
33.6 × 23.1 cm
Kunstmuseum Basel, Kupferstichkabinett, Inv. 1966.112
Karl August Burckhardt-Koechlin-Fonds, 1966

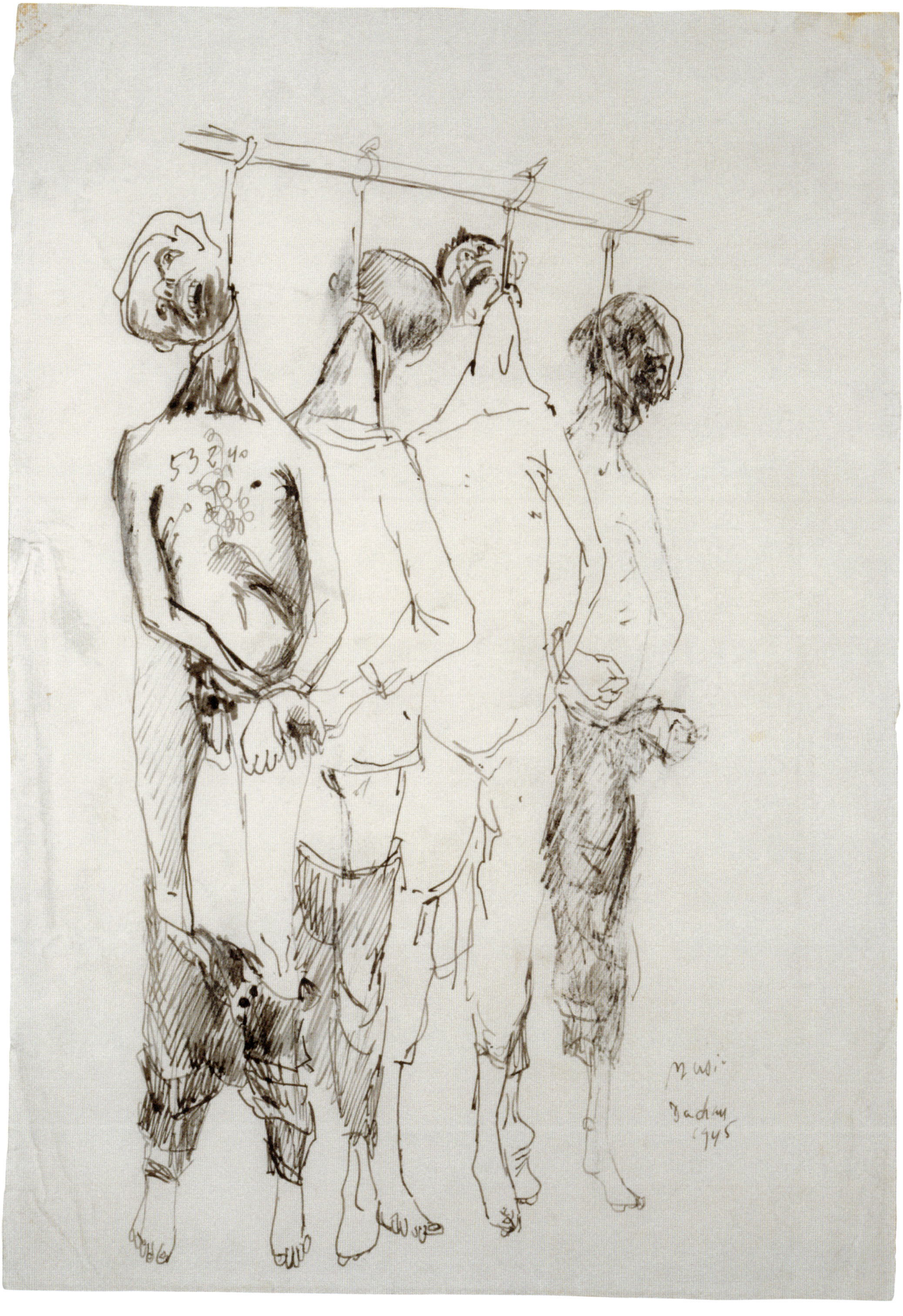

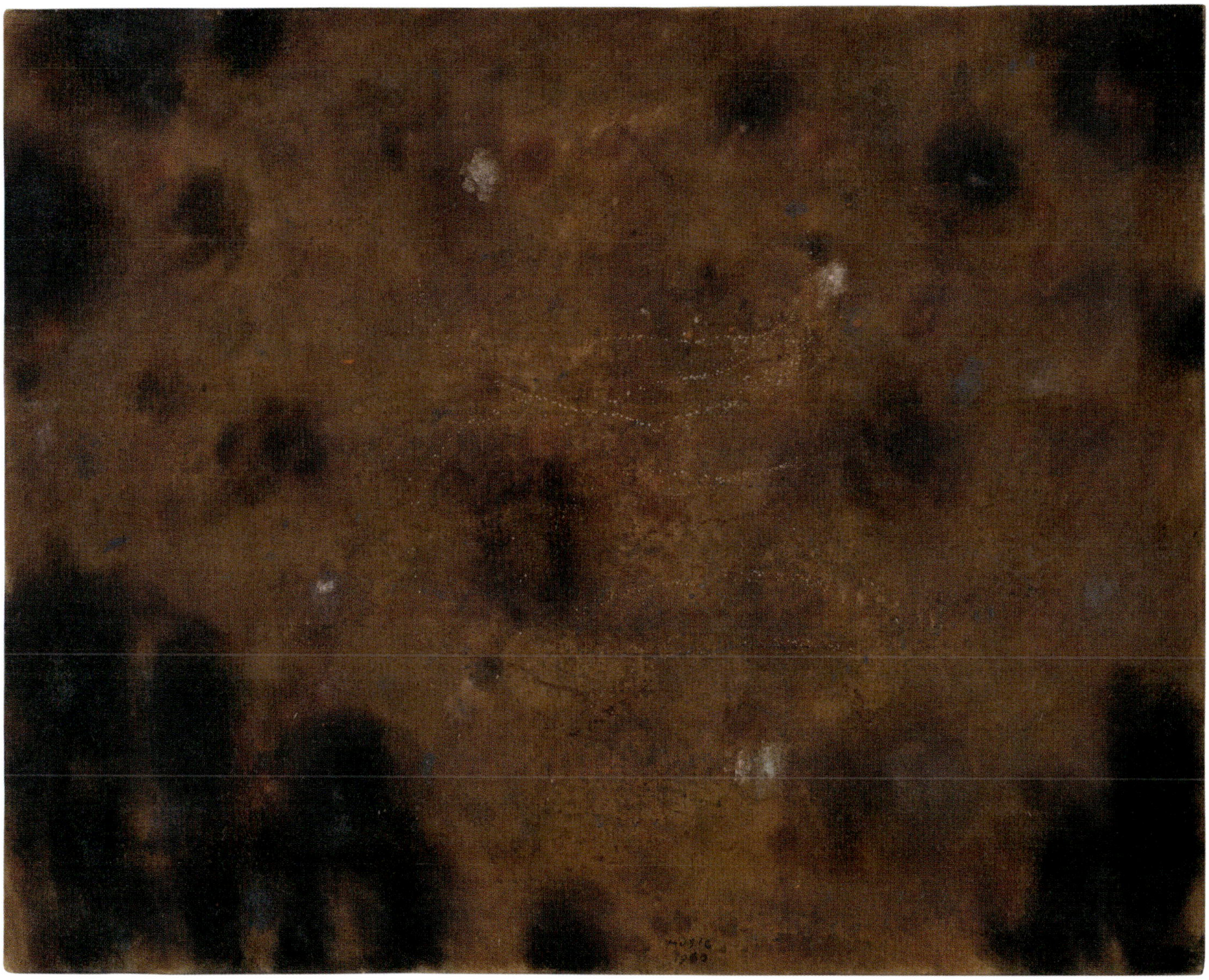

ZORAN MUŠIČ
(Bukovica, Slovenia, 1909 – Venice, 2005)
Empty Landscape
1960
Oil on canvas
130 × 160 cm
Carmen Thyssen Bornemisza Collection

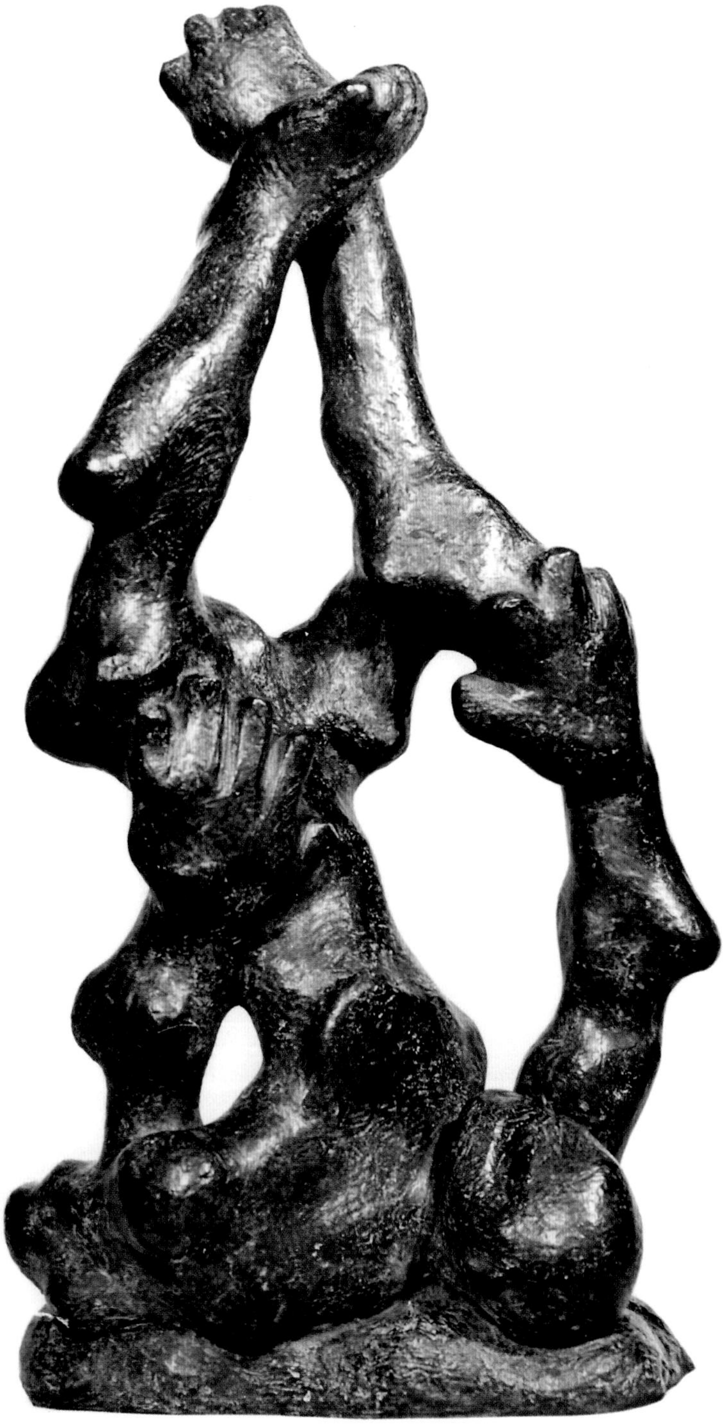

HONORIO GARCÍA CONDOY
(Saragossa, 1900 – Madrid, 1953)
Buchenwald, or The Fall of Man
1944
Bronze
78 × 41 cm
Delphine Creuze Collection

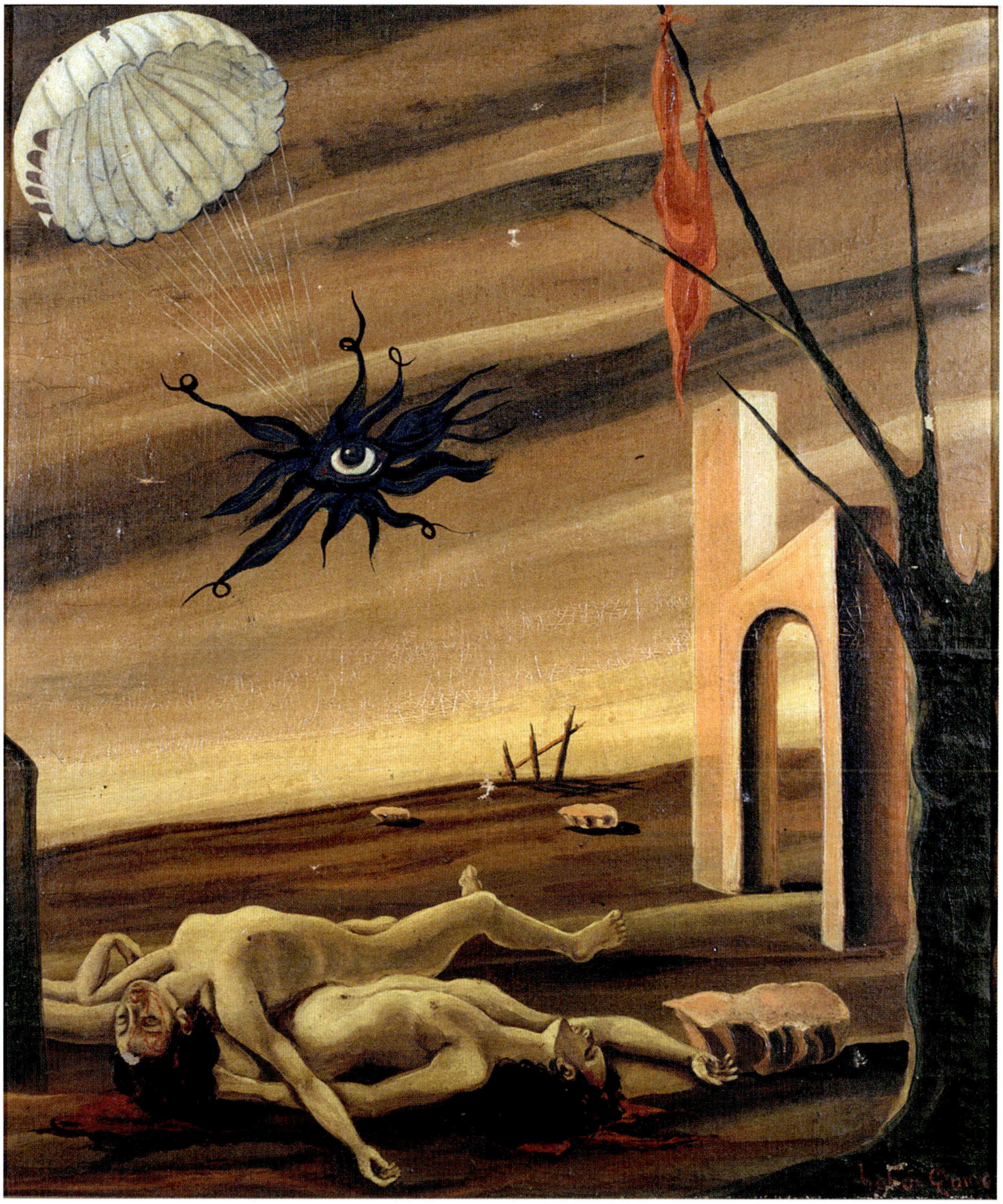

HELIOS GÓMEZ
(Seville, 1905 – Barcelona, 1956)
Airlifted Pain (Parachute with an Eye)
c. 1947-1948
Oil on canvas
55 × 46 cm
Collection of the Associació Cultural Helios Gómez, 2007
Museu Nacional d'Art de Catalunya

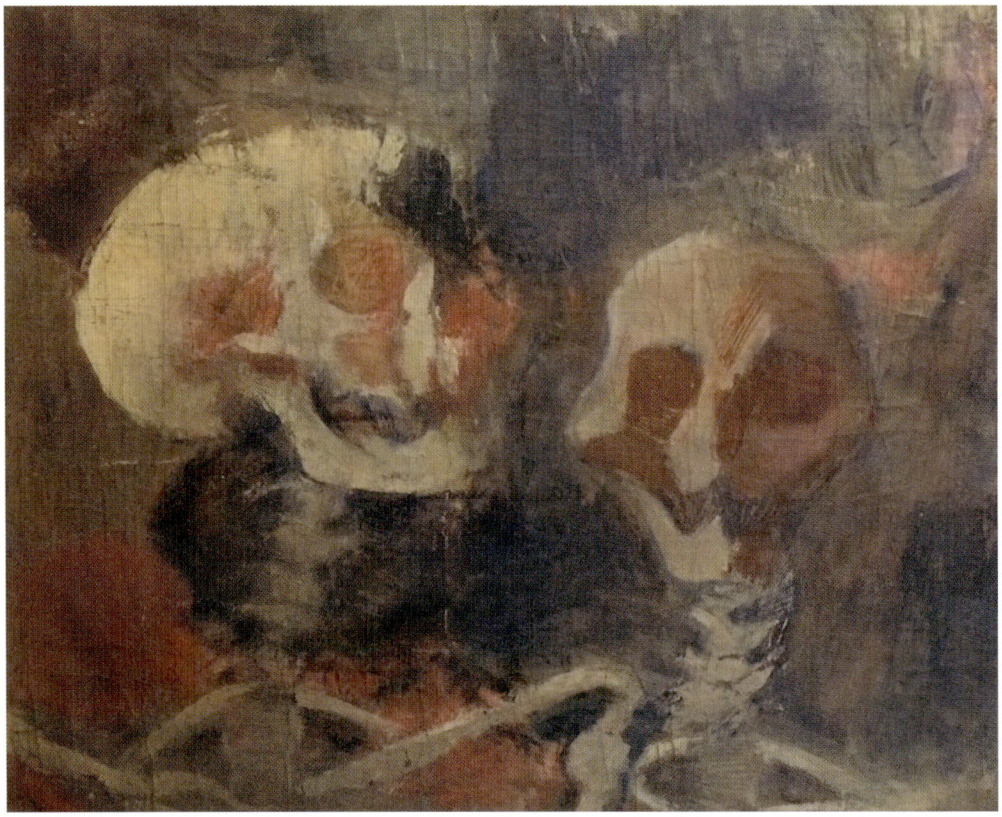

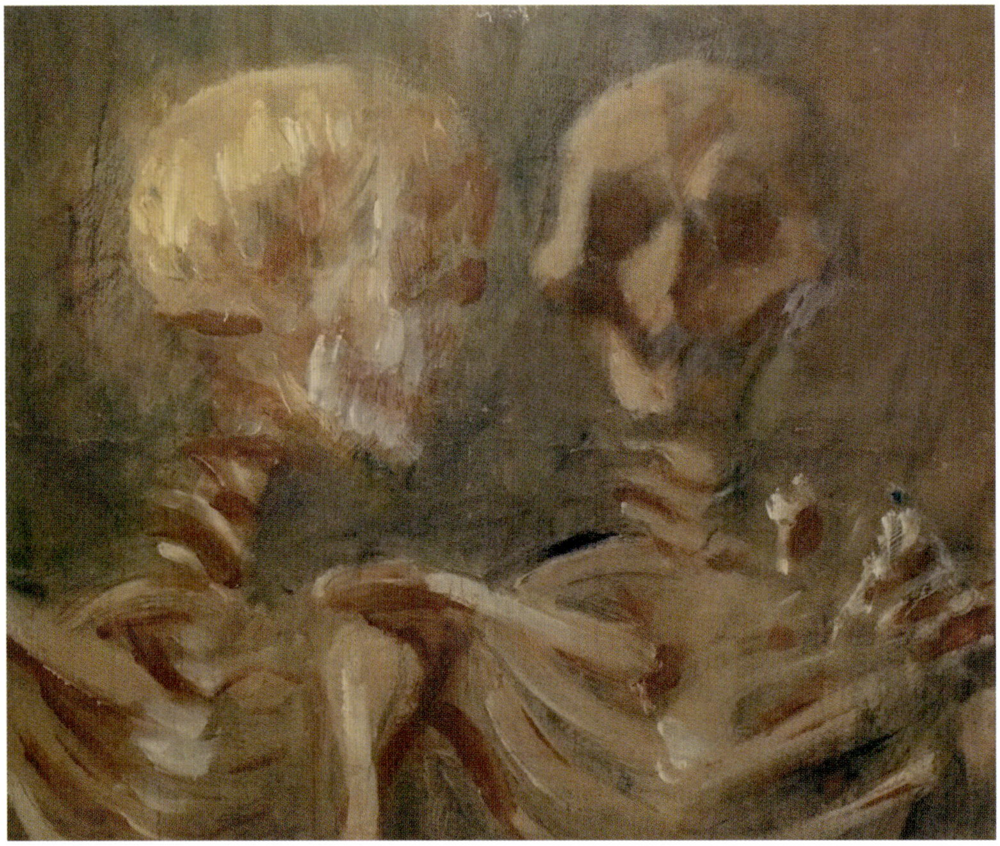

PERE GASTÓ
(Barcelona, 1908-1997)
Skulls
1950
Oil on canvas
46 × 55 cm
Gastó Collection

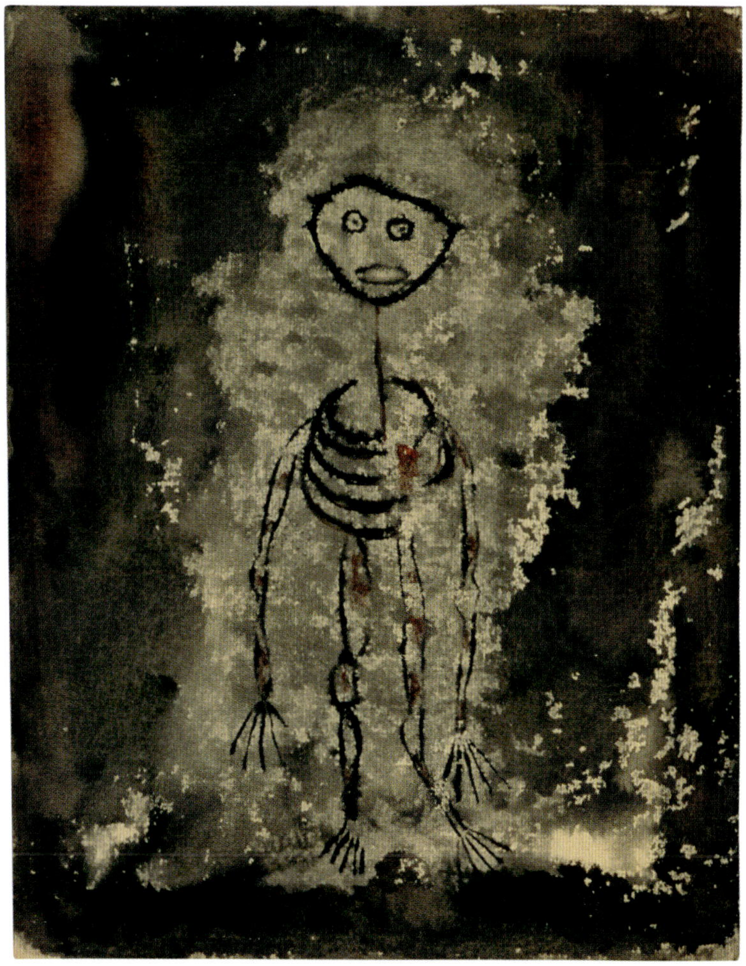

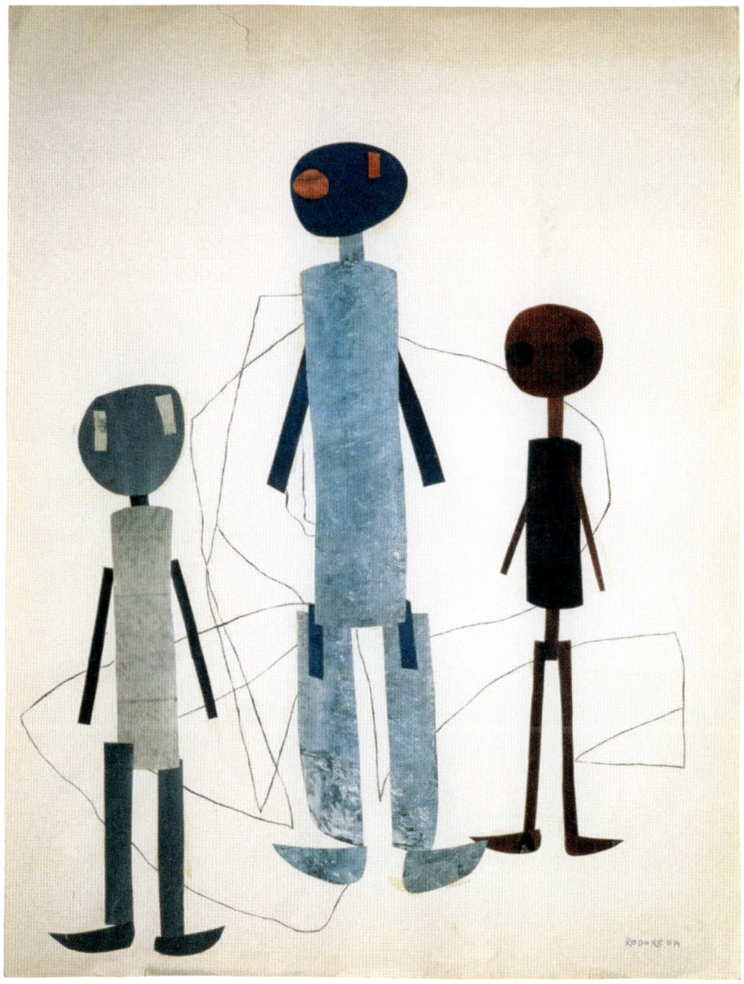

MERCÈ RODOREDA
(Barcelona, 1908 – Girona, 1983)
Untitled (Skeleton)
1950s
Watercolour on paper
32 × 24 cm
Fundació Mercè Rodoreda. Institut d'Estudis Catalans

MERCÈ RODOREDA
(Barcelona, 1908 – Girona, 1983)
Untitled (Three Personages)
1950s
Collage on paper
65 × 50 cm
Fundació Mercè Rodoreda. Institut d'Estudis Catalans

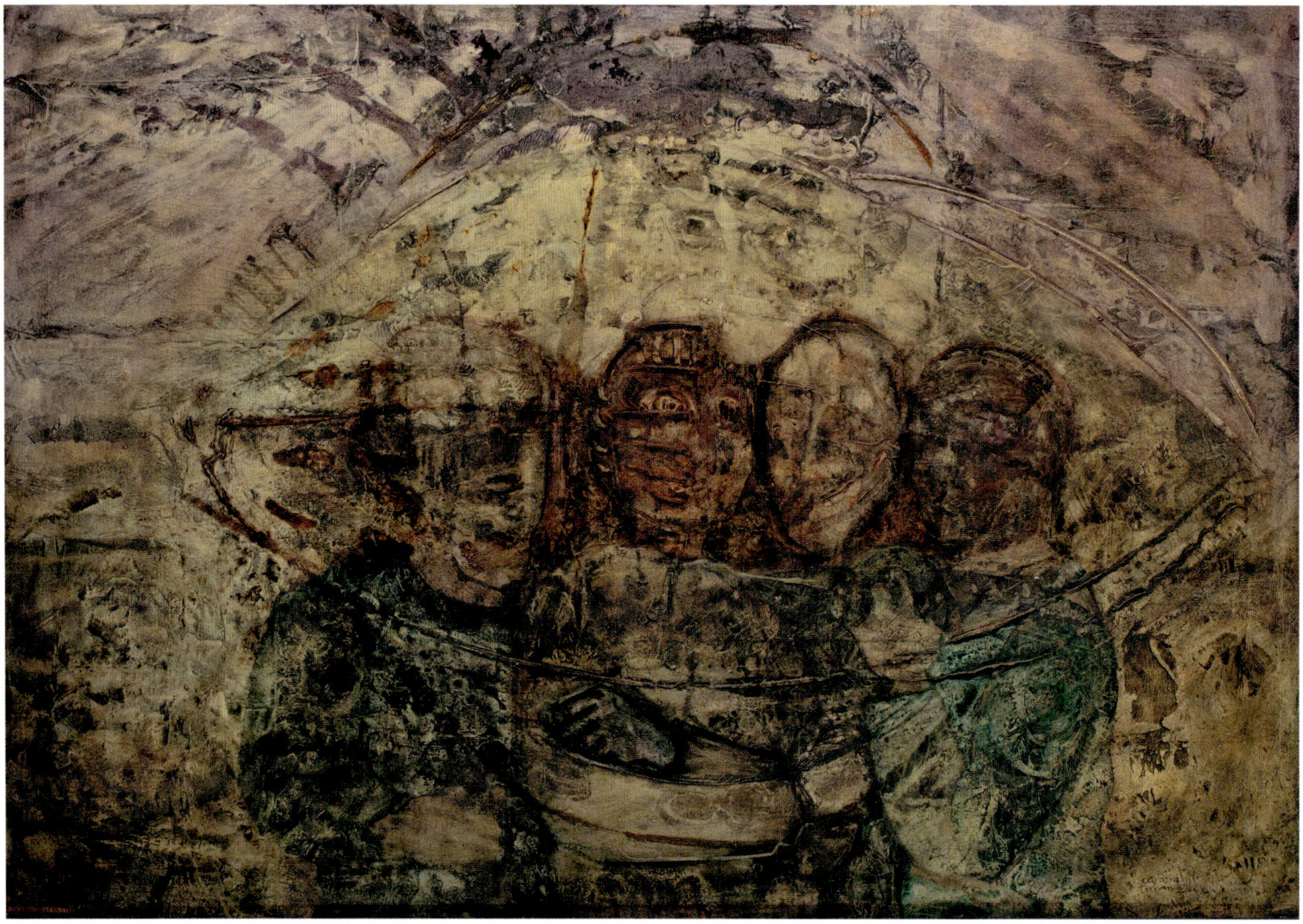

JOSEP MARIA SUBIRACHS
(Barcelona, 1927-2014)
Atomic bomb
1954
Ink on paper
30 × 60 cm
Espai Subirachs

ARMAND CARDONA TORRANDELL
(Barcelona, 1928 – Sant Pere de Ribes, 1995)
The Concentrationary Universe
1963
Oil on canvas
121 × 159 cm
Private collection, Vilanova i la Geltrú

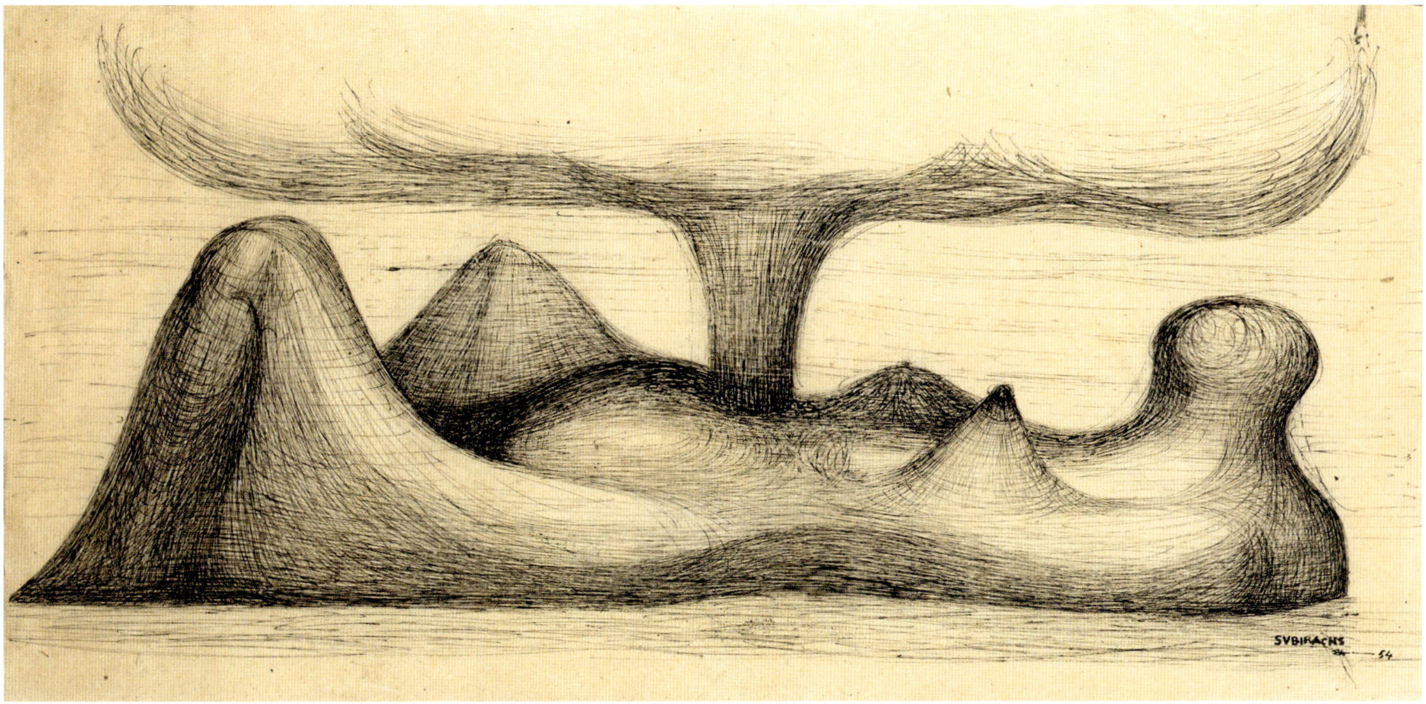

MODEST CUIXART
(Barcelona, 1925 – Palamós, 2007)
Children without Name
1963
Material collage and mixed technique on canvas
100 × 81 cm
Cuixart Estate

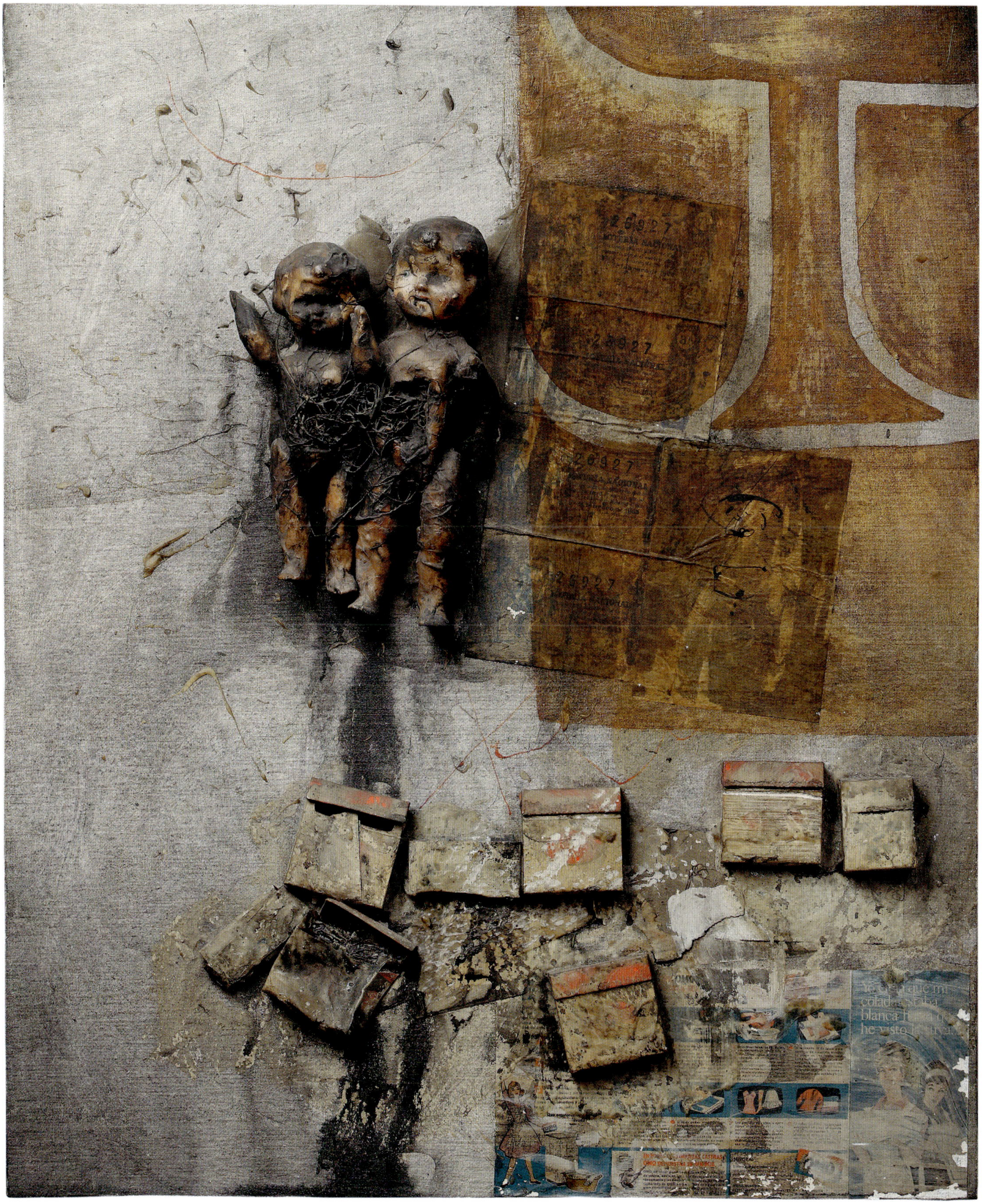

Some artists approached the figure of the victim from an anti-monumental attitude. They highlighted the anonymous, defenceless civilian who suffers aggression. The tortured body and the annihilated individual form a counterpoint to the rhetoric of the hero, power. As in Anton Prinner's *La femme tondue* ('Shaven-headed woman'), serenity and pain converge, the fact that their travails are recorded having the effect of subliming their humiliation and vindicating their dignity.

THE PLACE OF THE VICTIM

FRANCIS GRUBER
(Nancy, 1912 – Paris, 1948)
The Hostages
1946
Oil on canvas
88.5 × 100 cm
Privately owned, Daniel Blau, Salzburg, Austria

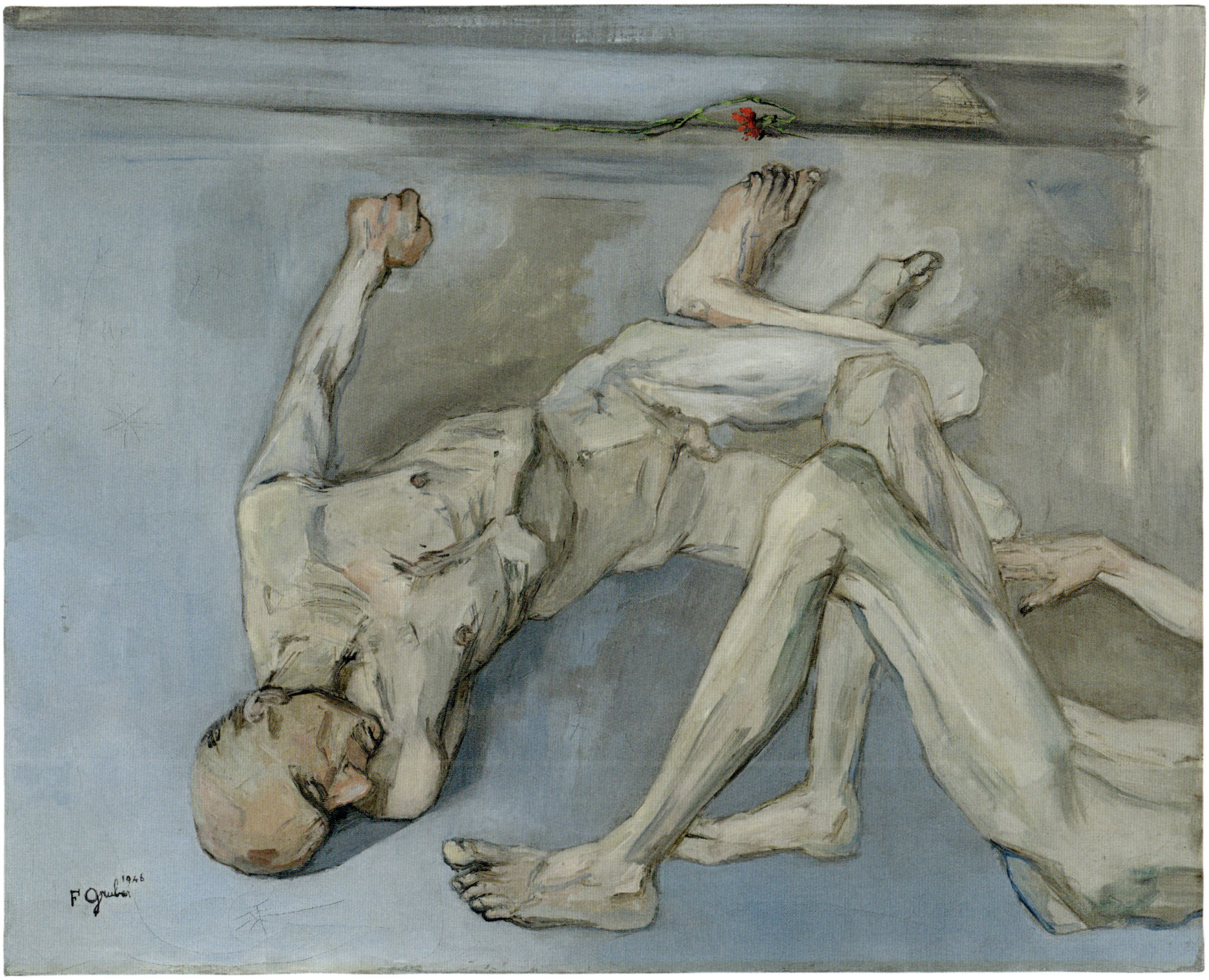

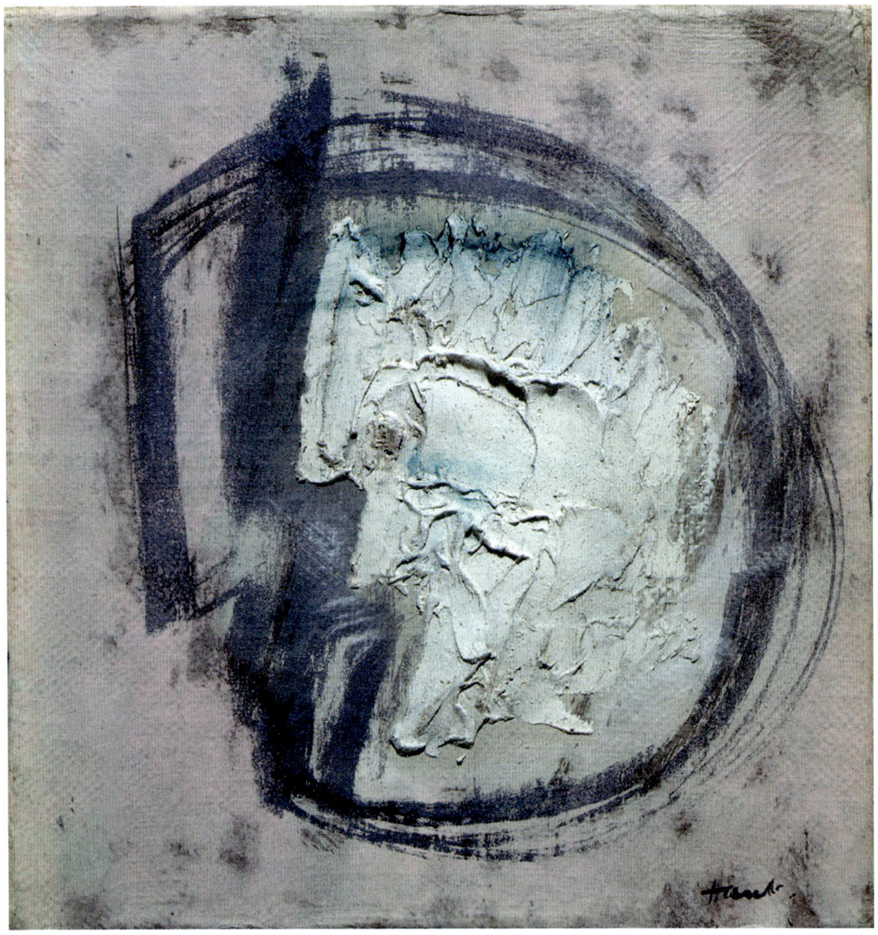

JEAN FAUTRIER
(Paris, 1898 – Châtenay-Malabry, France, 1964)
Untitled (Head of Partisan)
1956-1957
Mixed technique on paper glued to canvas
28.5 × 27 cm
Galleria Nazionale d'Arte Moderna
e Contemporanea, Rome

JOSEP BARTOLÍ
(Barcelona, 1910 – New York, 1995)
Drawings for the book *Campos de concentración 1939-1944*
1936-1944
Ink on paper
41 × 32.4 cm approx.
Ajuntament de Barcelona, Institut de Cultura de Barcelona

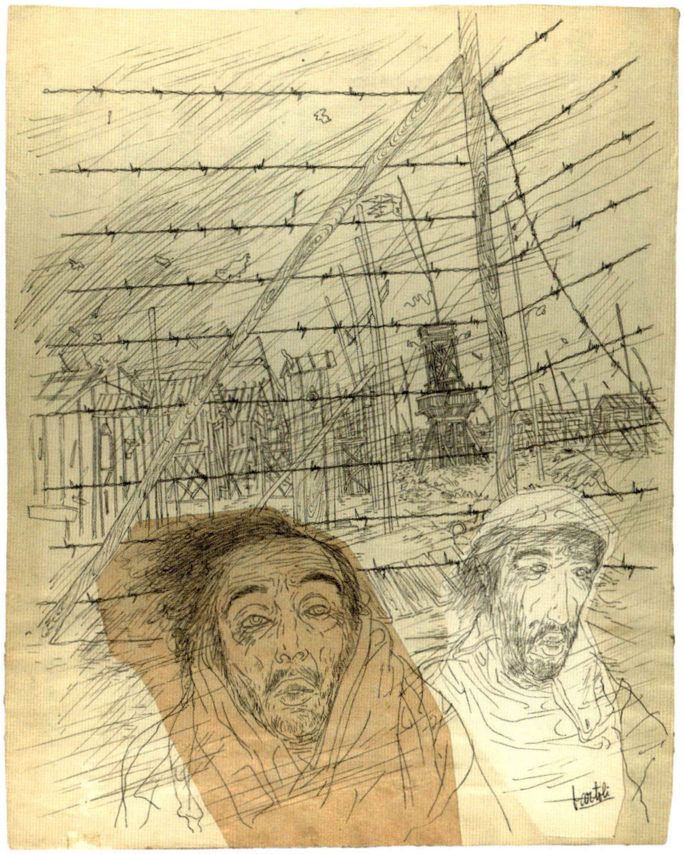
bartoli

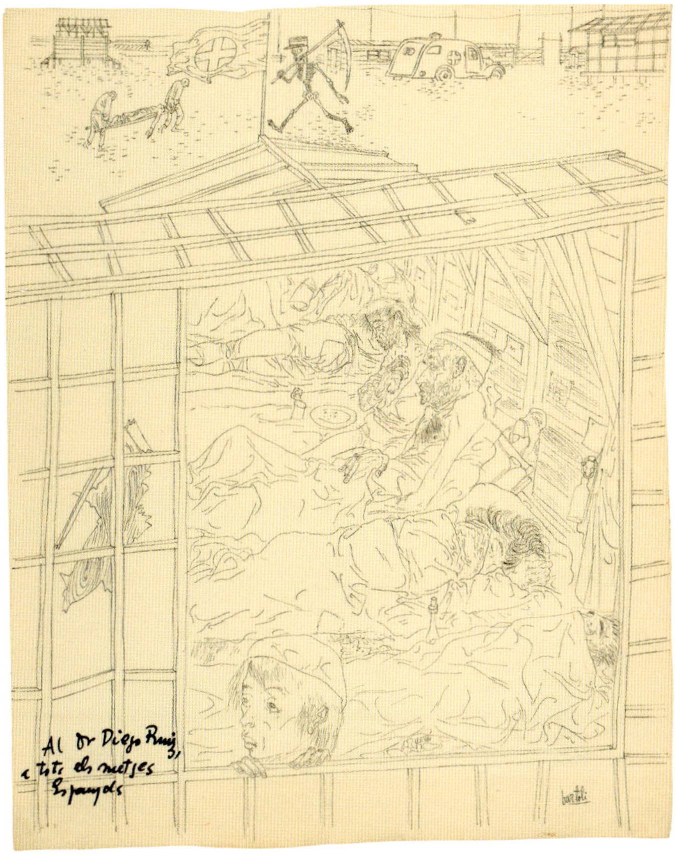
Al Dr Diego Ruiz,
a tots els metges
Espanyols
bartoli

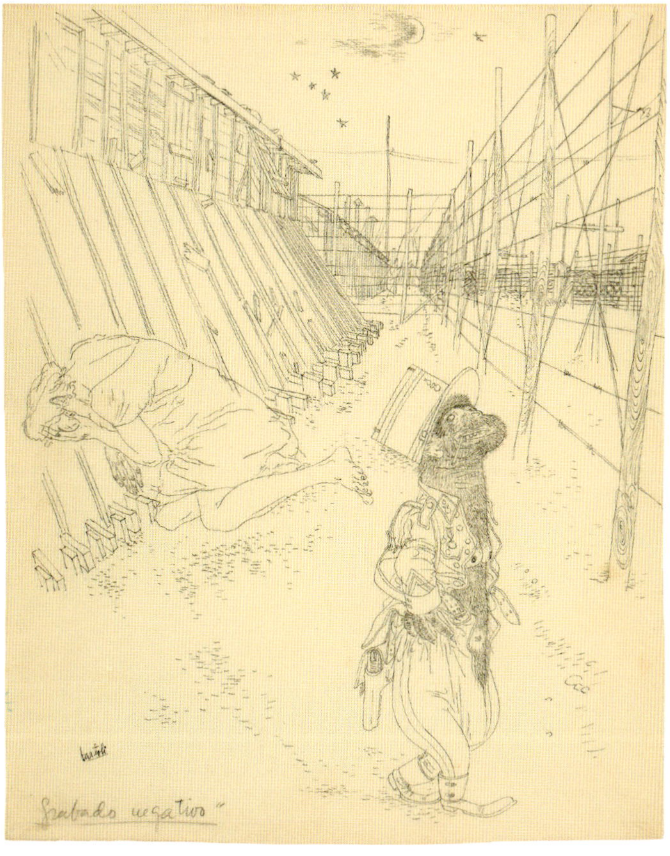
bartoli
"Grabado negativo"

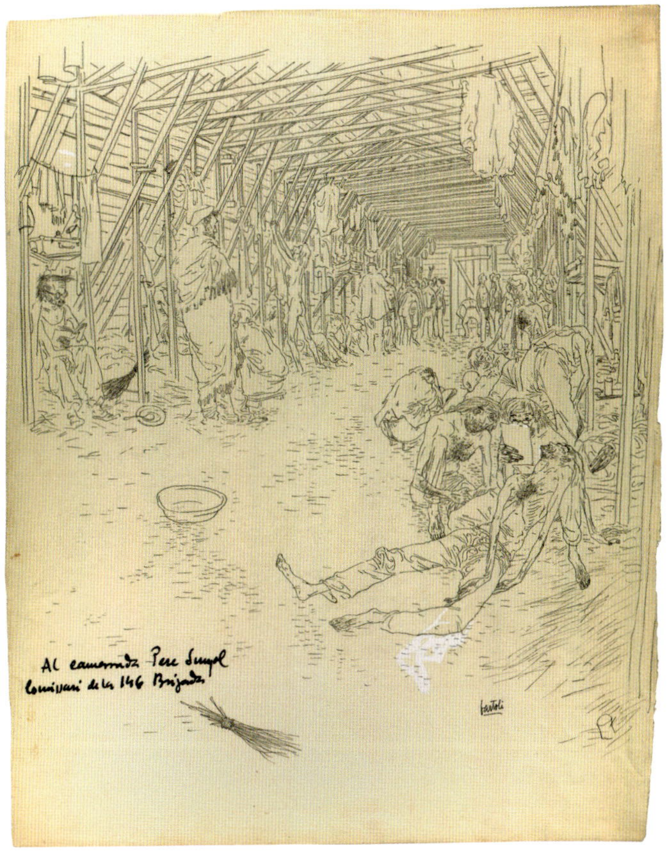
Al camarada Pere Sunyol
Comissari de la 146 Brigada
bartoli

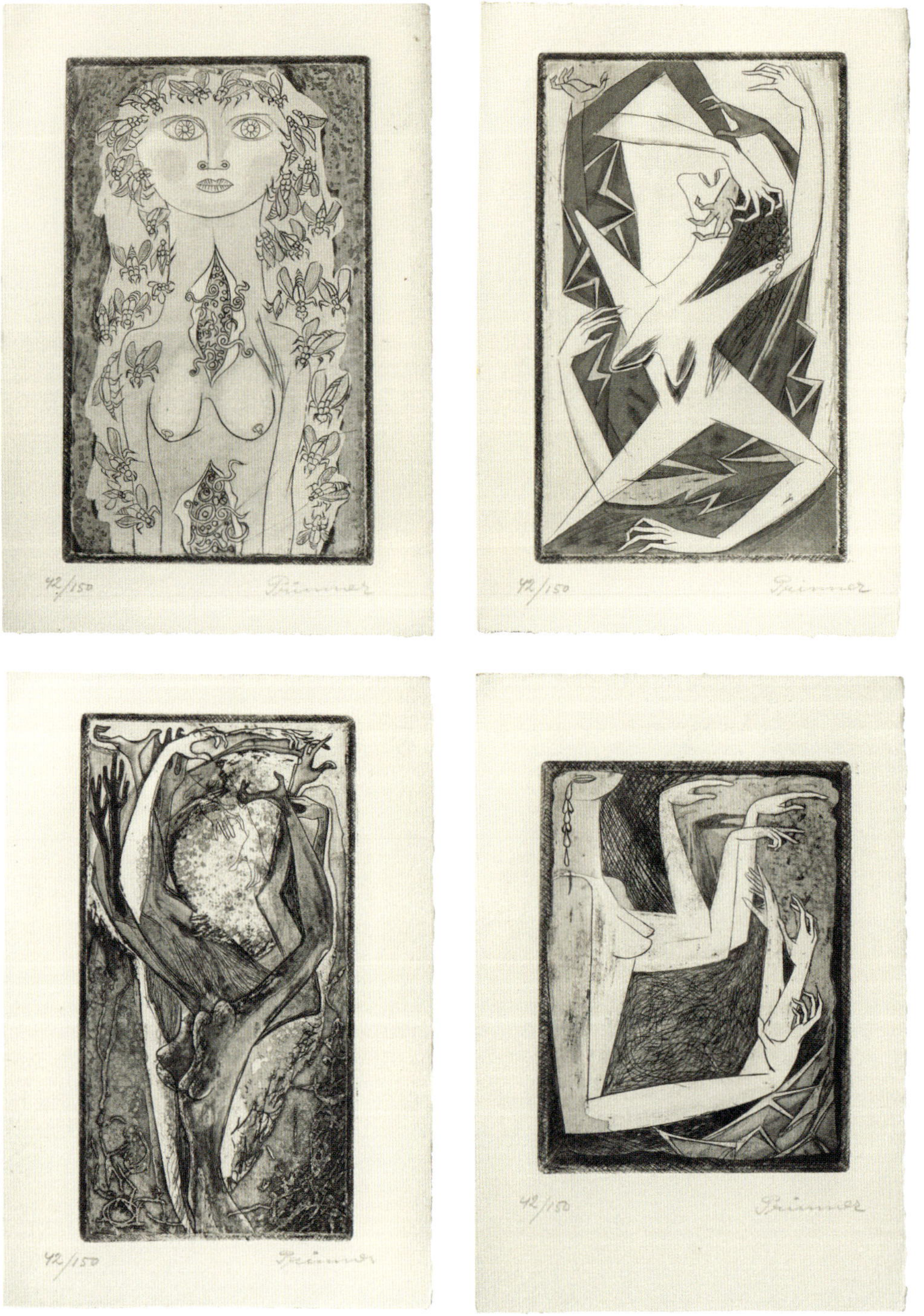

ANTON PRINNER
(Budapest, 1902 – Paris, 1983)
La femme tondue
1946
Etching on paper
19.2 × 13 cm
Biblioteca Folch i Torres. Acquisition, 2023
Museu Nacional d’Art de Catalunya

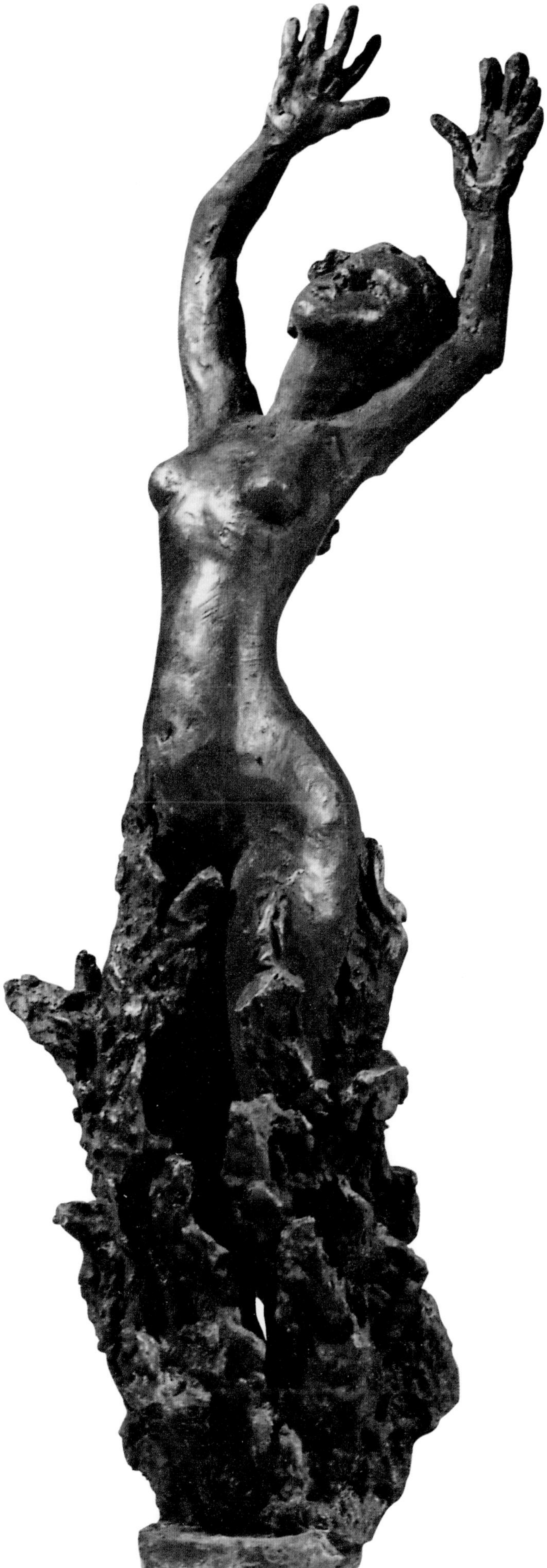

APEL·LES FENOSA
(Barcelona, 1899 – Paris, 1988)
Maquette for the *Monument to the Martyrs of Oradour-sur-Glane*
1944
Cast in bronze
118 × 35 × 30 cm
Deposit of the Generalitat de Catalunya
Museu de Valls

JULI GONZÁLEZ
(Barcelona, 1876 – Arcueil, France, 1942)
Raised Left Hand
c. 1942
Cast in bronze
37.2 × 19 × 15.2 cm
Donated by Roberta González,
the artist's daughter, 1972; acquisition, 1973
Museu Nacional d'Art de Catalunya

JULI GONZÁLEZ
(Barcelona, 1876 – Arcueil, France, 1942)
Raised Right Hand
c. 1942
Cast in bronze
44 × 15.2 × 12.6 cm
Donated by Roberta González,
the artist's daughter, 1972; acquisition, 1973
Museu Nacional d'Art de Catalunya

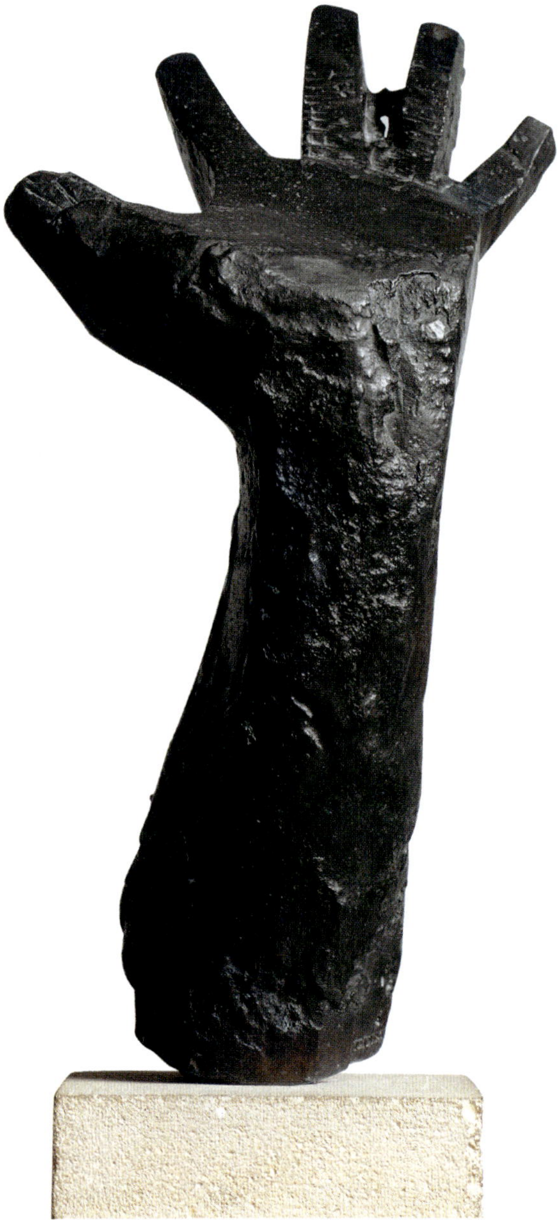

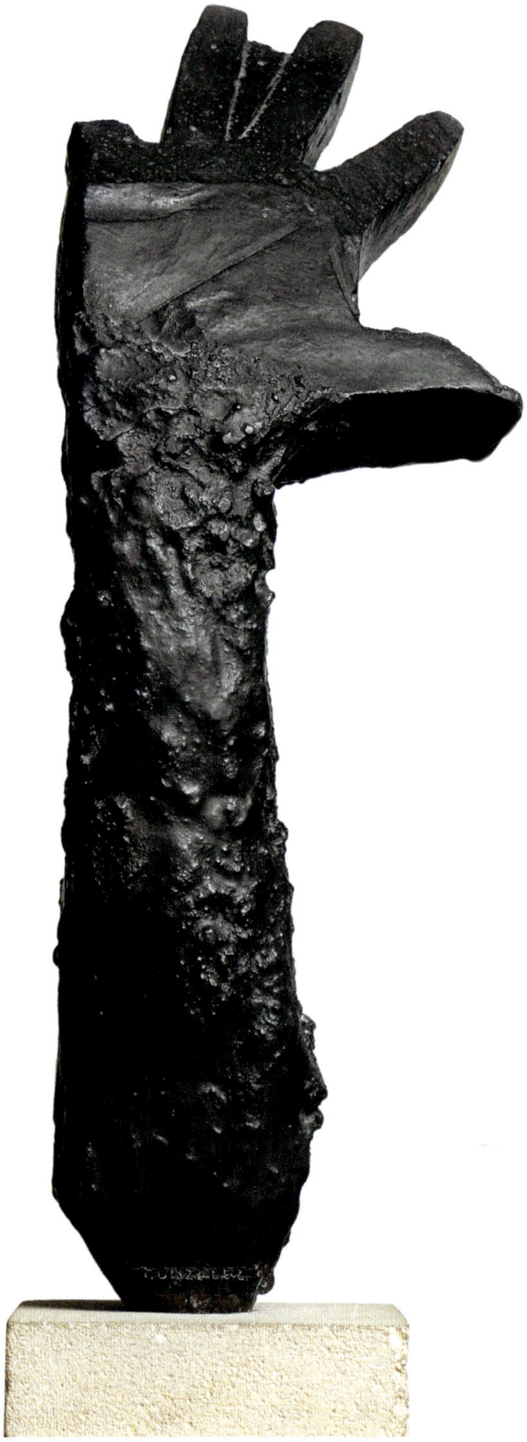

JULI GONZÁLEZ
(Barcelona, 1876 – Arcueil, France, 1942)
Head of Montserrat Shouting
c. 1942
Cast in bronze
31.5 × 19.8 × 29.3 cm
Donated by Roberta González,
the artist's daughter, 1972; acquisition, 1973
Museu Nacional d'Art de Catalunya

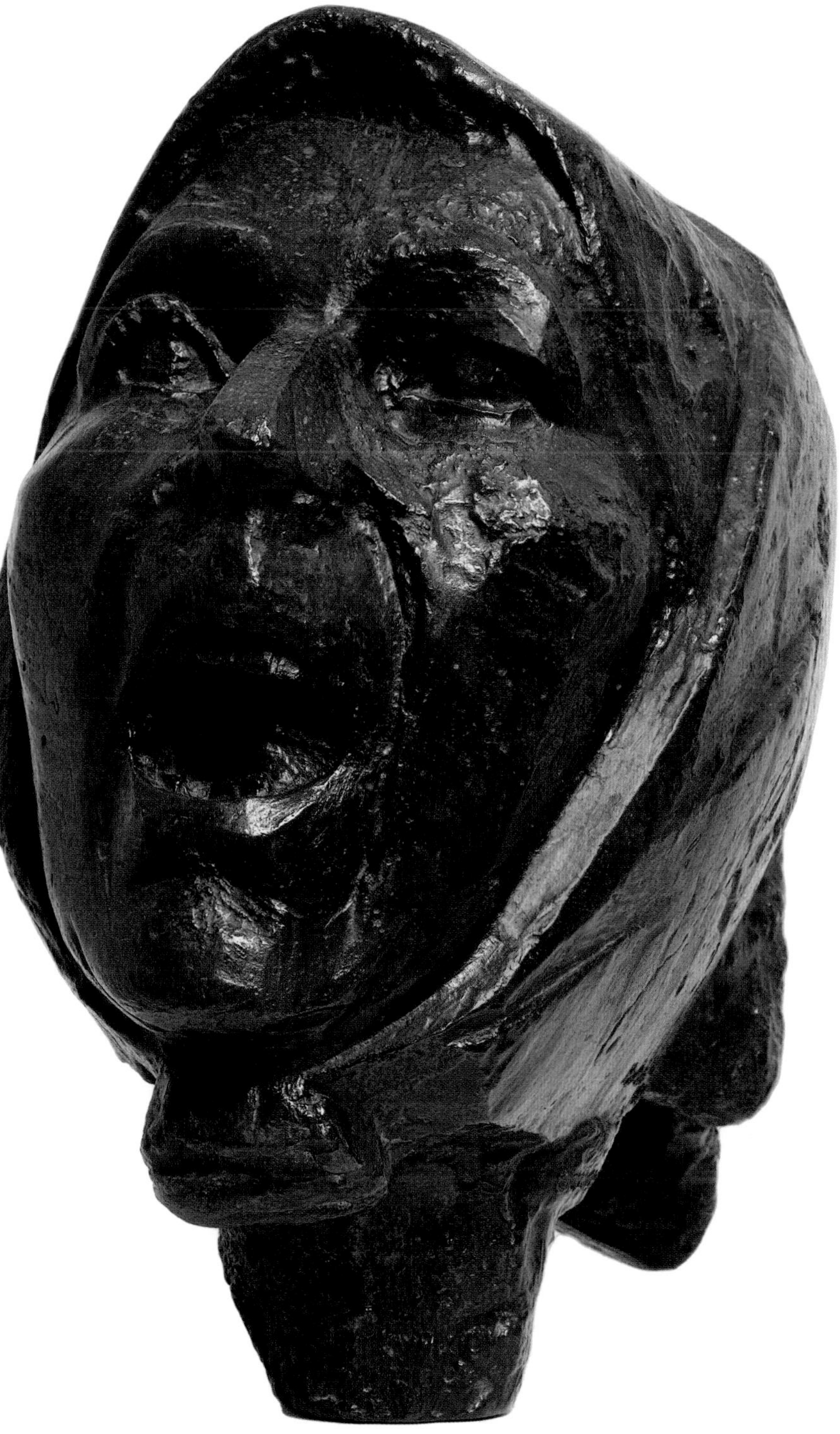

HENRY MOORE
(Castleford, UK, 1898 – Much Hadham, UK, 1986)
Falling Warrior
1957-1960
Bronze
67 × 154 × 85 cm
Kirklees Collection: Huddersfield Art Gallery

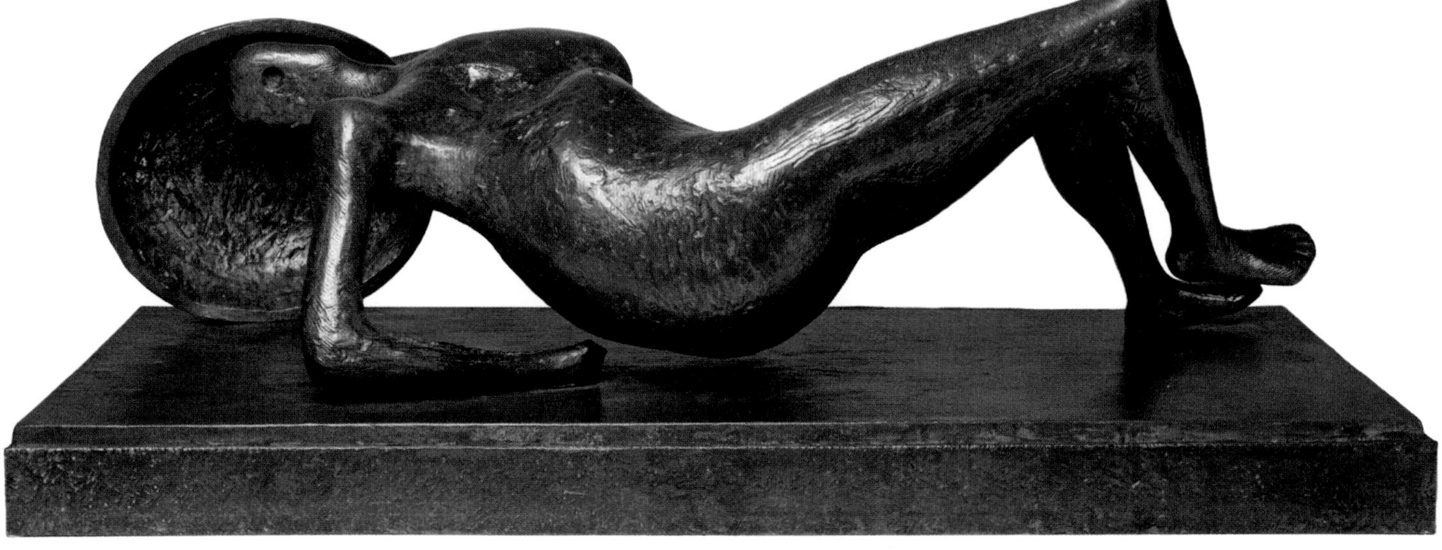

JOSEP MARIA SUBIRACHS
(Barcelona, 1927-2014)
Europe
1953
Bronze
21 × 54 × 19 cm
Espai Subirachs

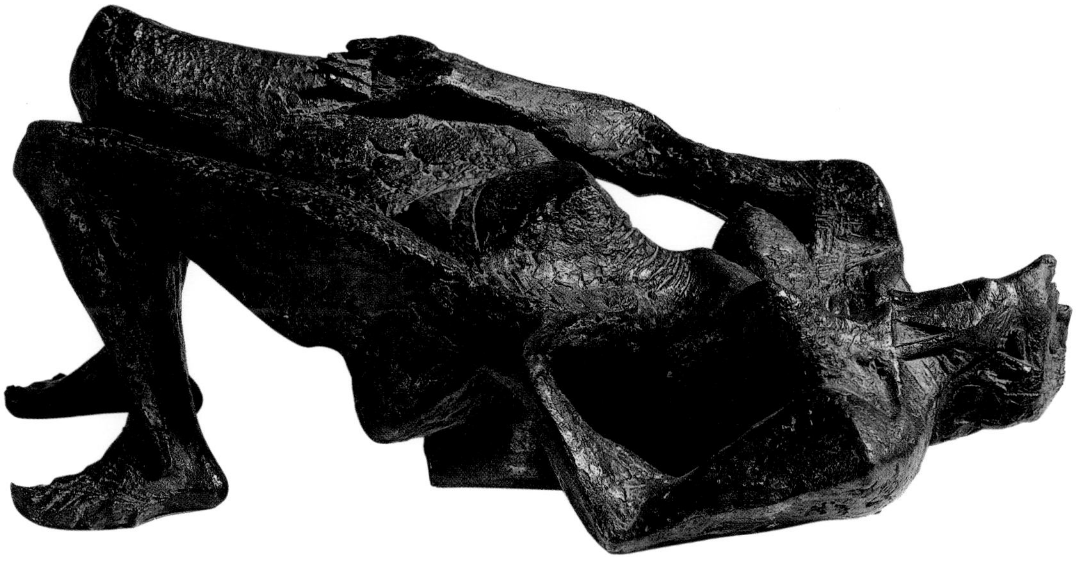

MARC ALEU
(Barcelona, 1922 – Cadaqués, 1996)
The Defeated
1956
Oil on canvas
193 × 160 cm
Deposit of the Generalitat de Catalunya
Col·lecció Nacional d'Art, 2019
Museu Nacional d'Art de Catalunya

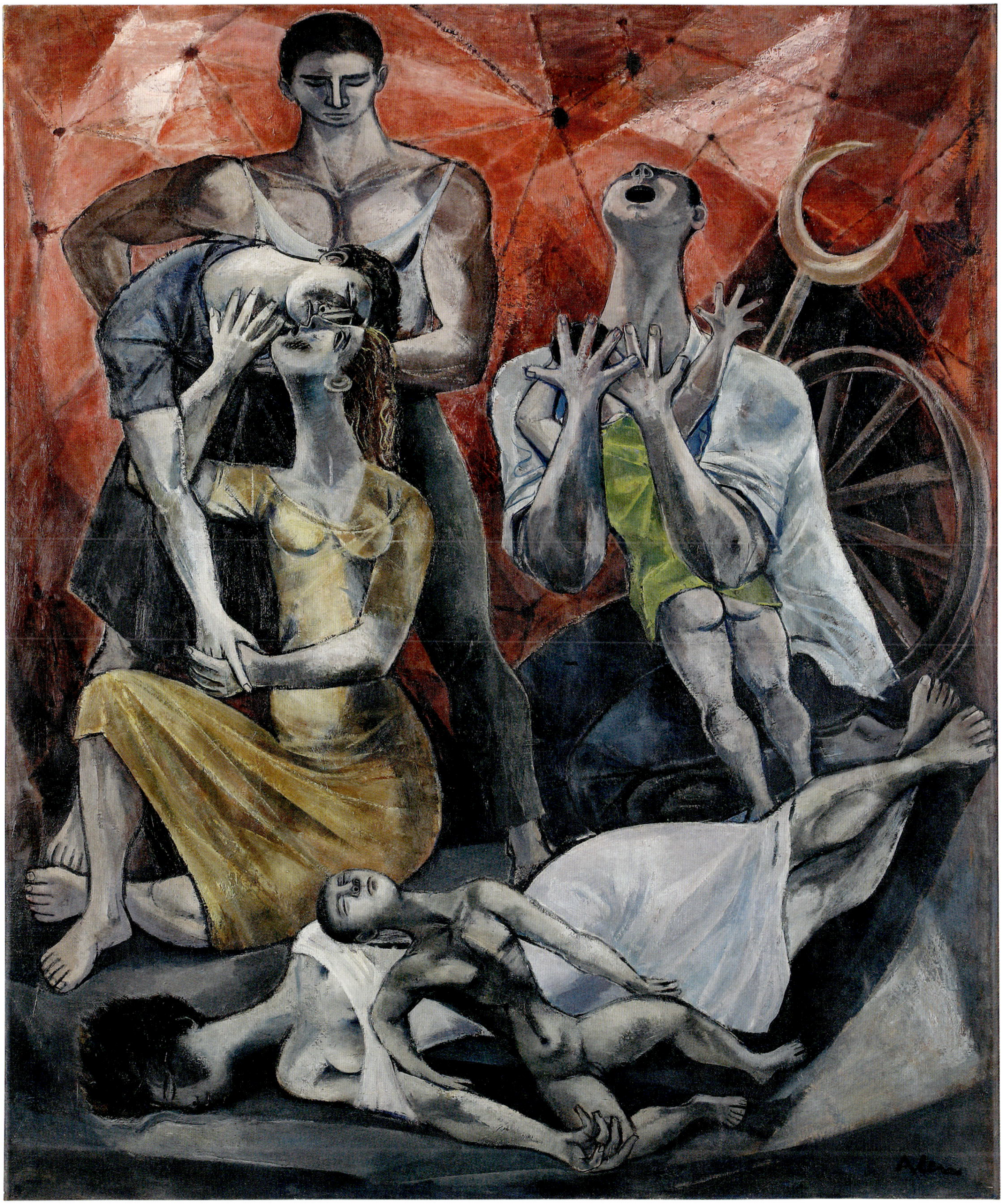

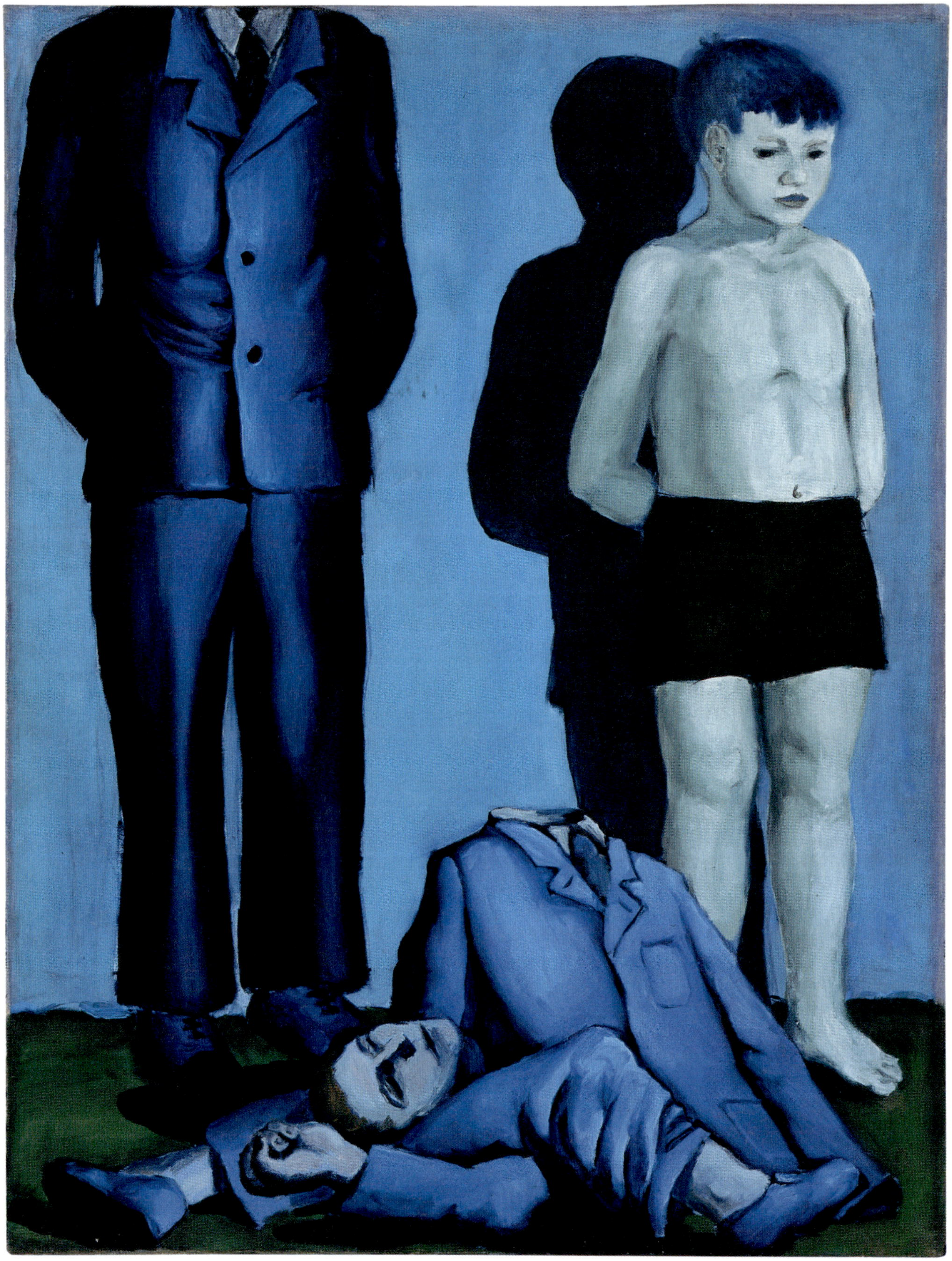

ANDRZEJ WRÓBLEWSKI
(Vilnius, Lithuania, 1927 - Tatra Mountains, Poland, 1957)
Execution with a Boy
1949
Oil on canvas
120 × 90 cm
National Museum in Poznań

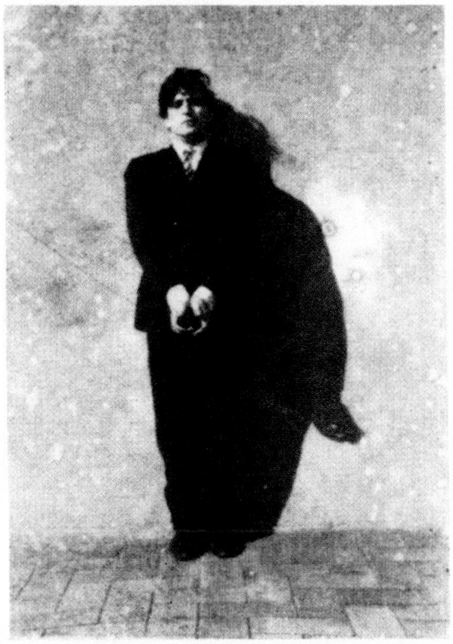

Posició **A**

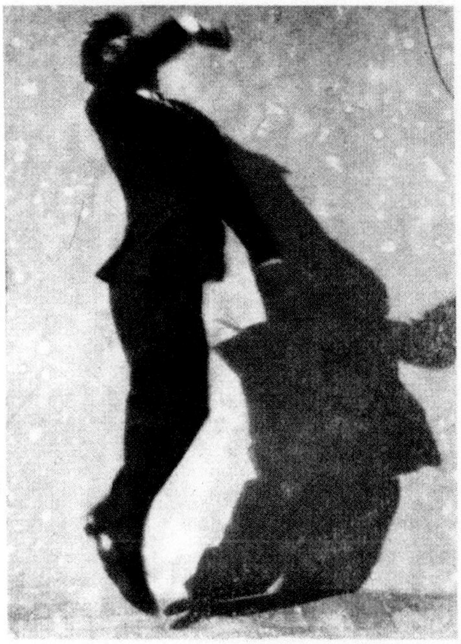

Posició **B**

DANSA DEL AFUSELLAMENT

GONÇAL SOBRER
(Barcelona, 1932)
Execution Dance
1966 (2023 edition)
Photoengraving (2/3)
57 × 40 cm (plate 27 × 20)
Artist donation. Museu Nacional d'Art de Catalunya

The horror caused by all this cruelty generated disturbing images (that is to say, icons) of monstrous, grotesque, disgusting humanity, recreating its sickening perversity. In contrast, the desperate humanist crisis of the postwar period also led to the emergence of a tragic religiousness that eschewed traditional pomp and ceremony. The figure of the martyrdom of Christ was revived within the framework of a severe, tragic expressionism that acquired a certain timeless dimension.

THE MONSTER AND THE SAINT

FRANCIS BACON
(Dublin, 1909 – Madrid, 1992)
Fragment of a Crucifixion
1950
Oli and cotton on canvas
140 × 108.5 cm
Van Abbemuseum Collection, Eindhoven

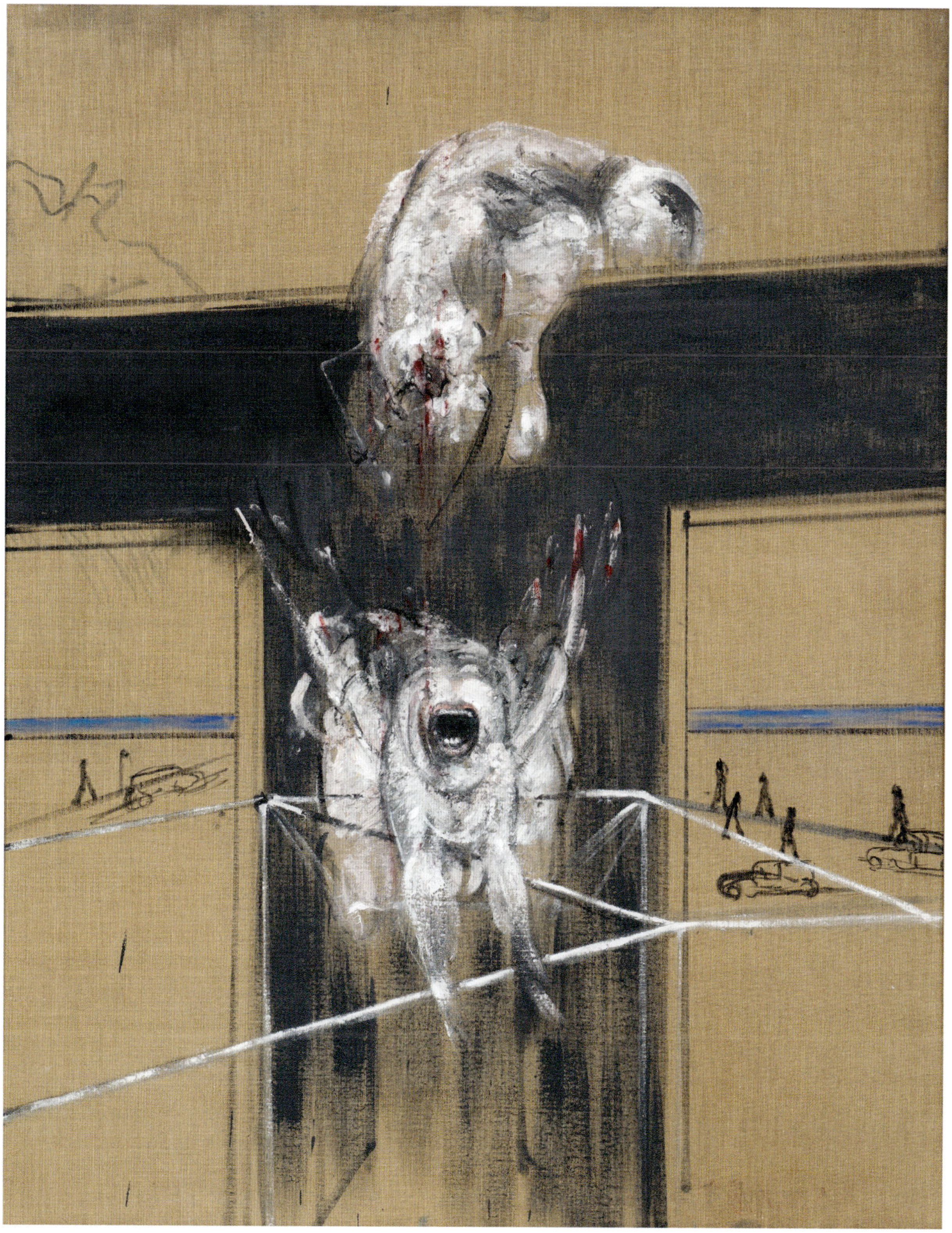

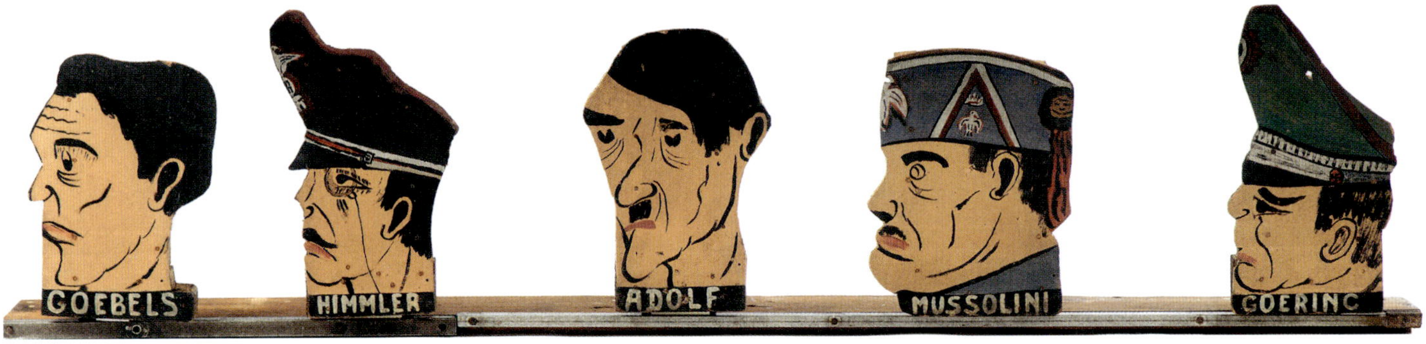

UNKNOWN ARTIST
Bang-bang-bang (shooting gallery)
1945
Polychromed wood
32 × 145 × 11.5 cm
Fundación "La Mirada Ingenua"

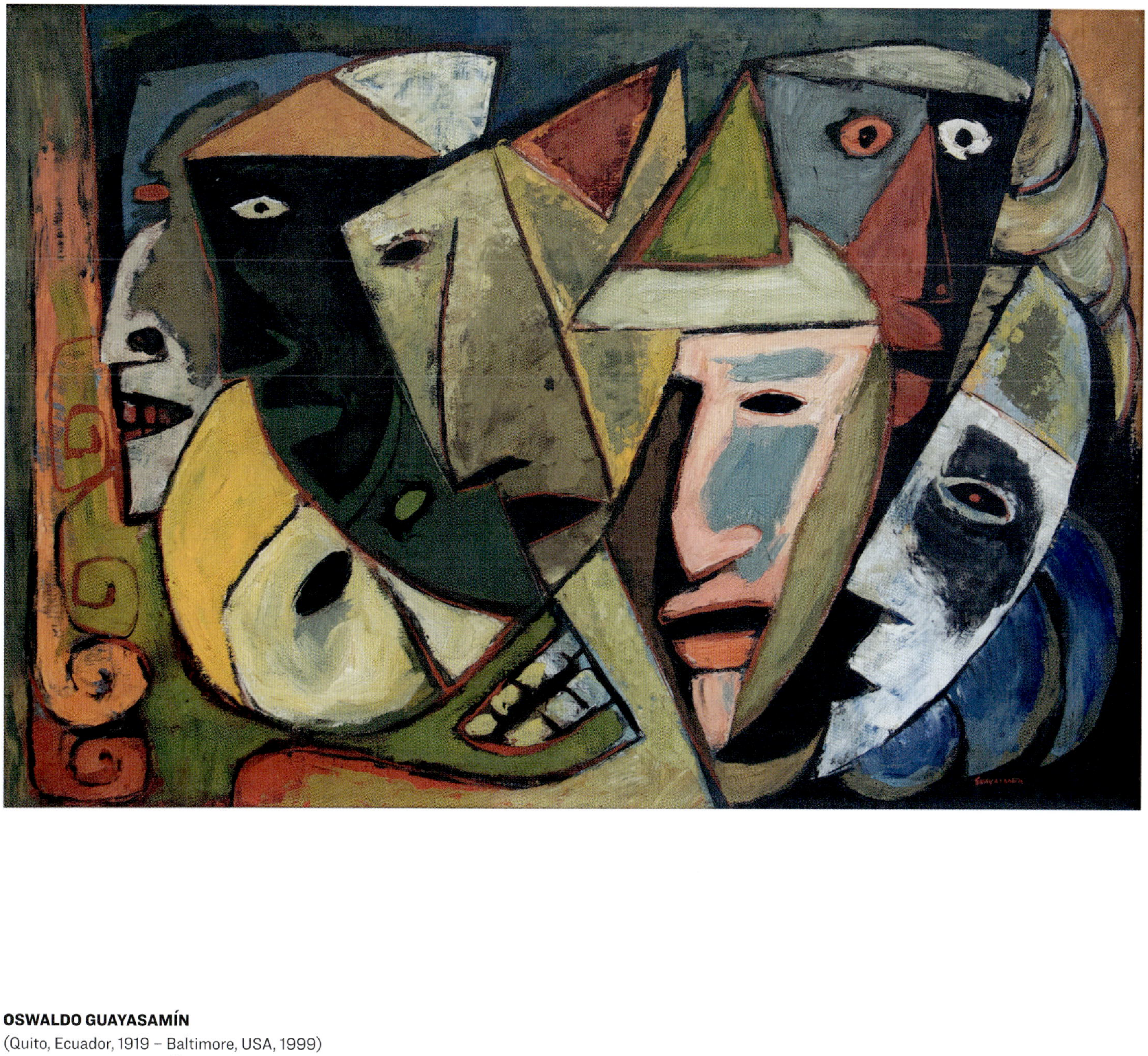

OSWALDO GUAYASAMÍN
(Quito, Ecuador, 1919 – Baltimore, USA, 1999)
Masks. Cruelty. Huacay-Ñan series
1950-1953
Oil on canvas
66 × 92 cm
Private collection, Madrid

FRANCIS NEWTON SOUZA
(Goa, India, 1924 – Bombay, India, 2002)
Untitled (Head)
1962
Oil on canvas
81.9 × 61.3 cm
Private collection c/o Grosvenor Gallery, London

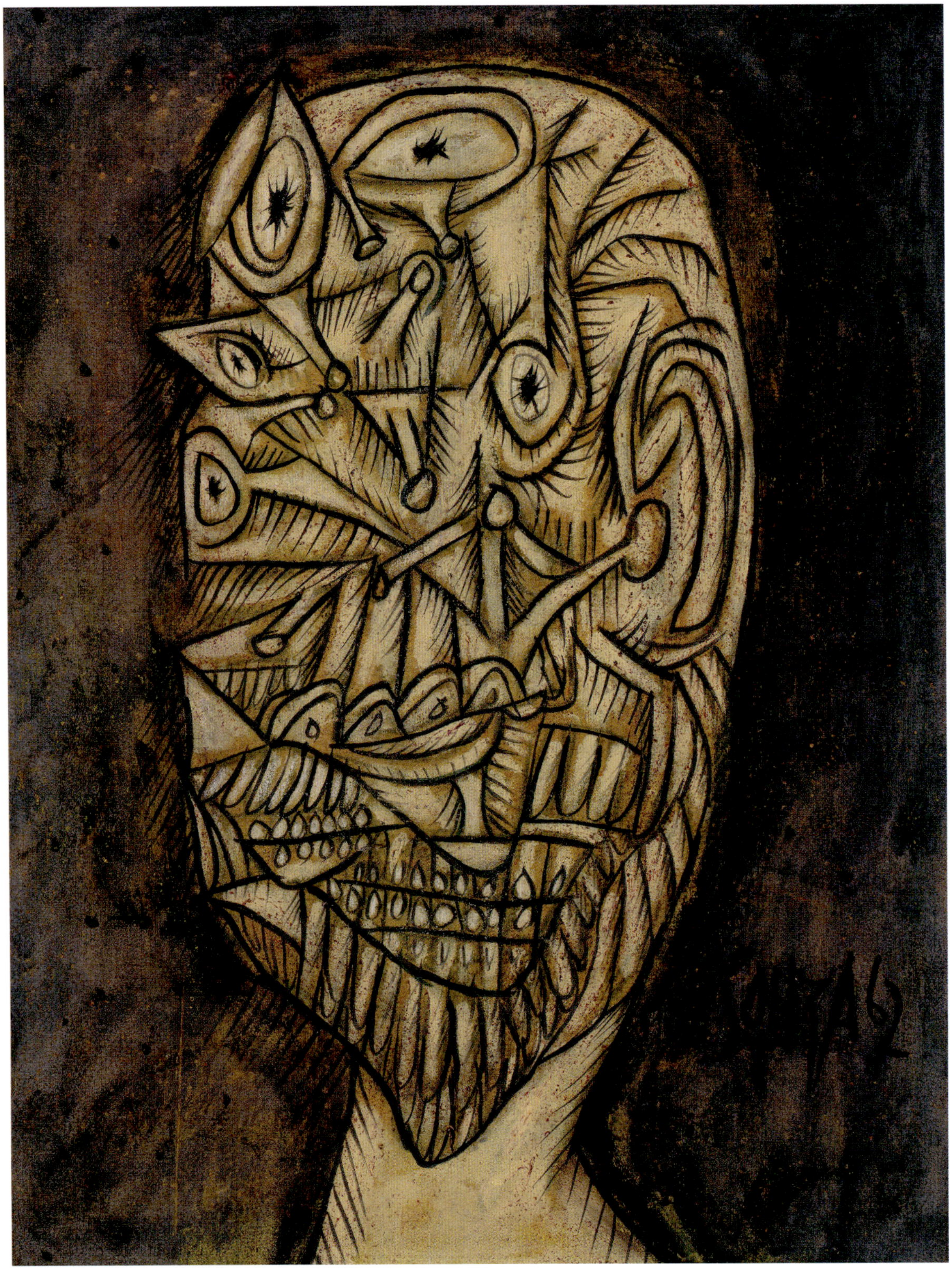

JOSEP GUINOVART
(Barcelona, 1927-2007)
Head I
1954
Gouache on board
67 × 50 cm
Fundació Espai Guinovart Agramunt

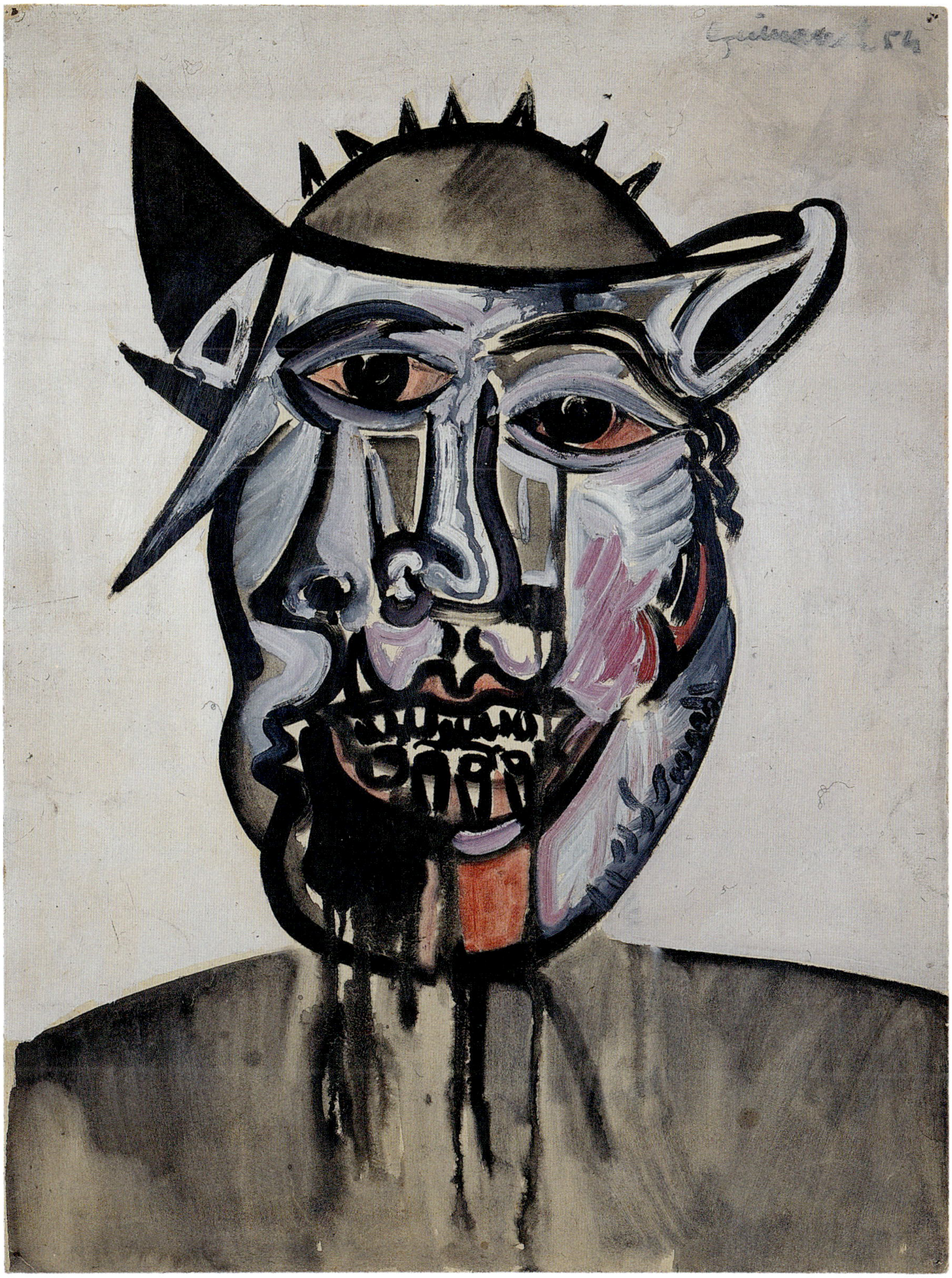

BERNARD BUFFET
(Paris, 1928 – Tourtour, France, 1999)
The Stoning
1948
Oil and graphite pencil on canvas
202 × 96 cm
LaM – Lille Métropole Musée d'art moderne, d'art contemporain et d'art brut

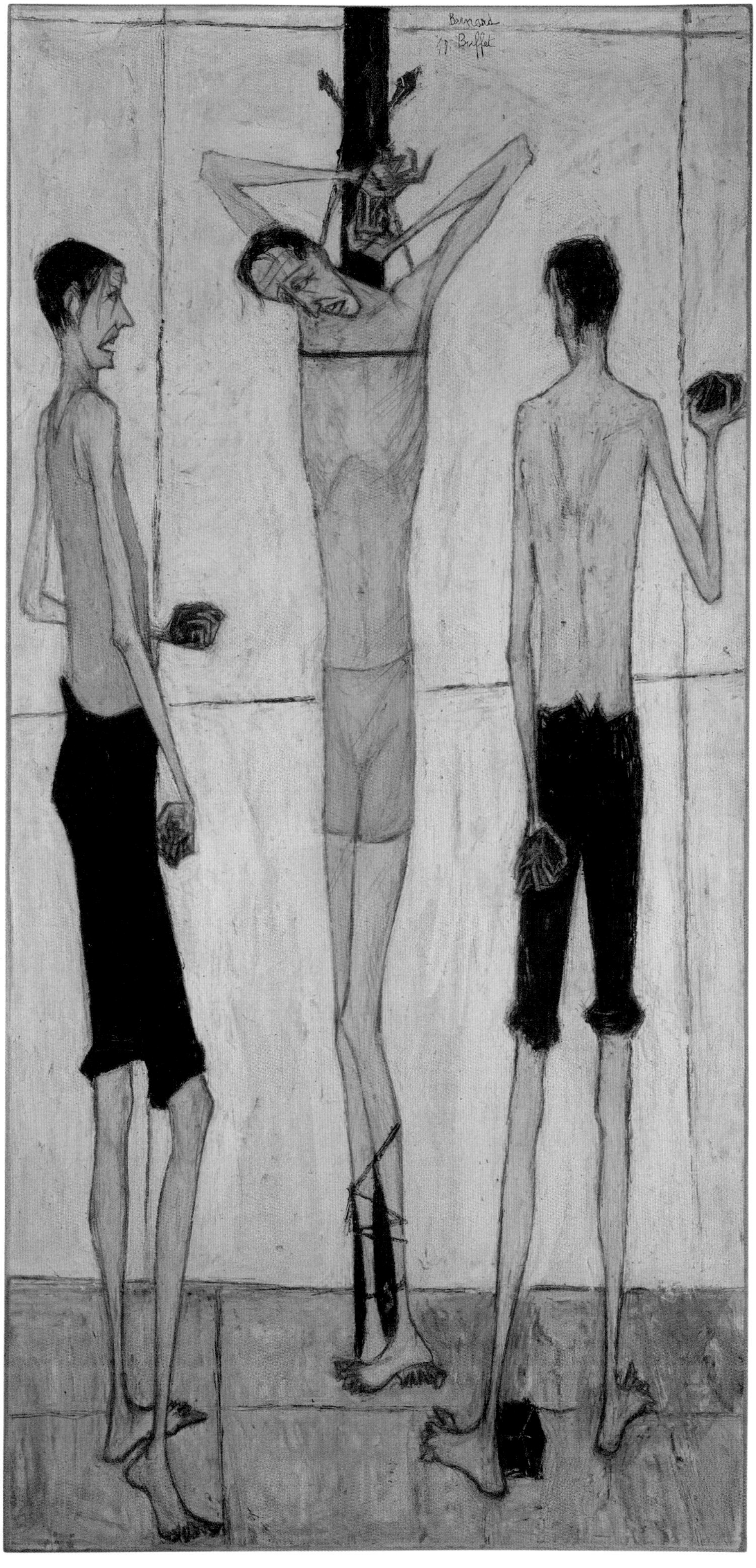

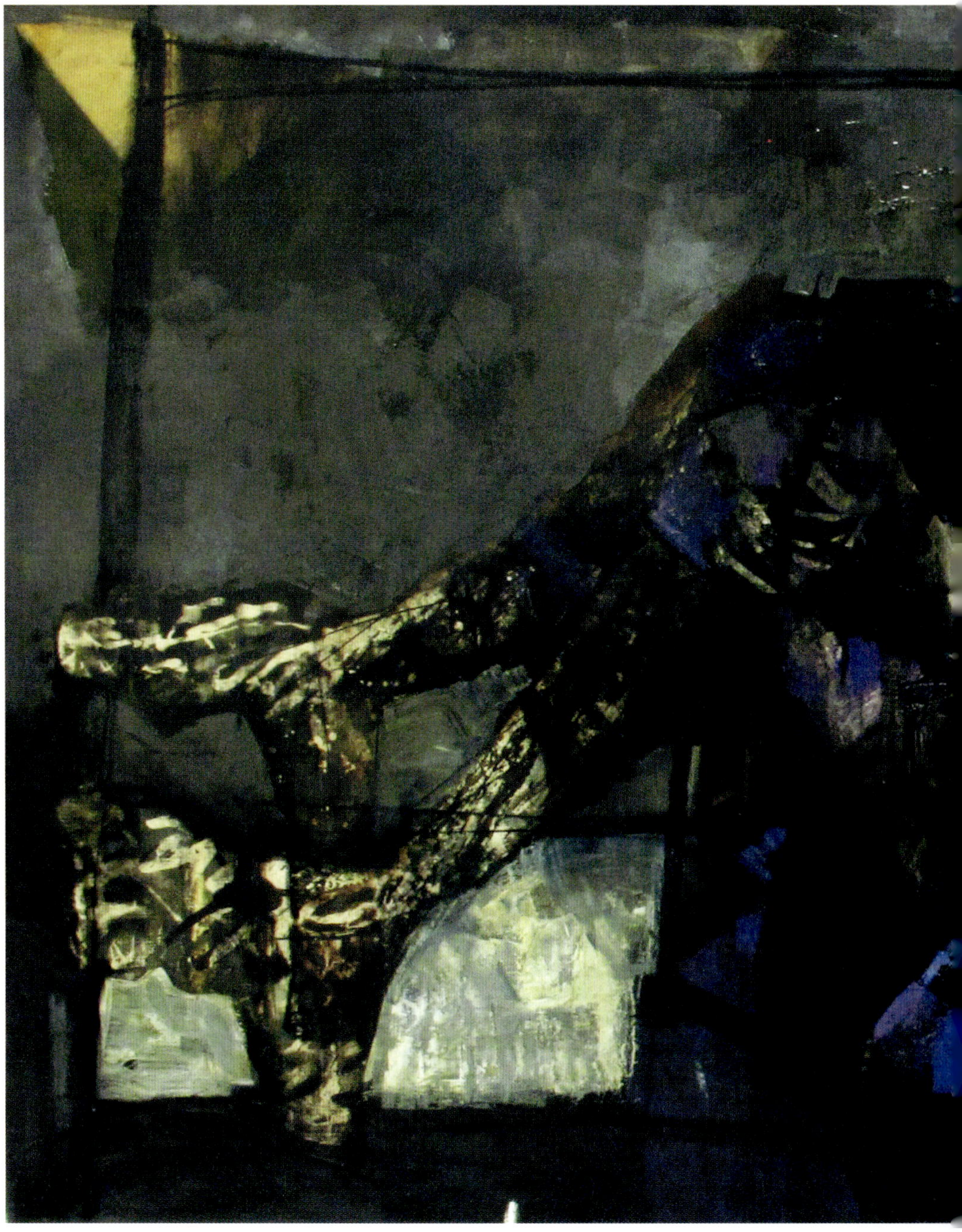

ANTONI CLAVÉ
(Barcelona, 1913 – Saint-Tropez, France, 2005)
Christ of Alba de Tormes
1954
Oil on canvas
117 × 222 cm
Private collection, Barcelona

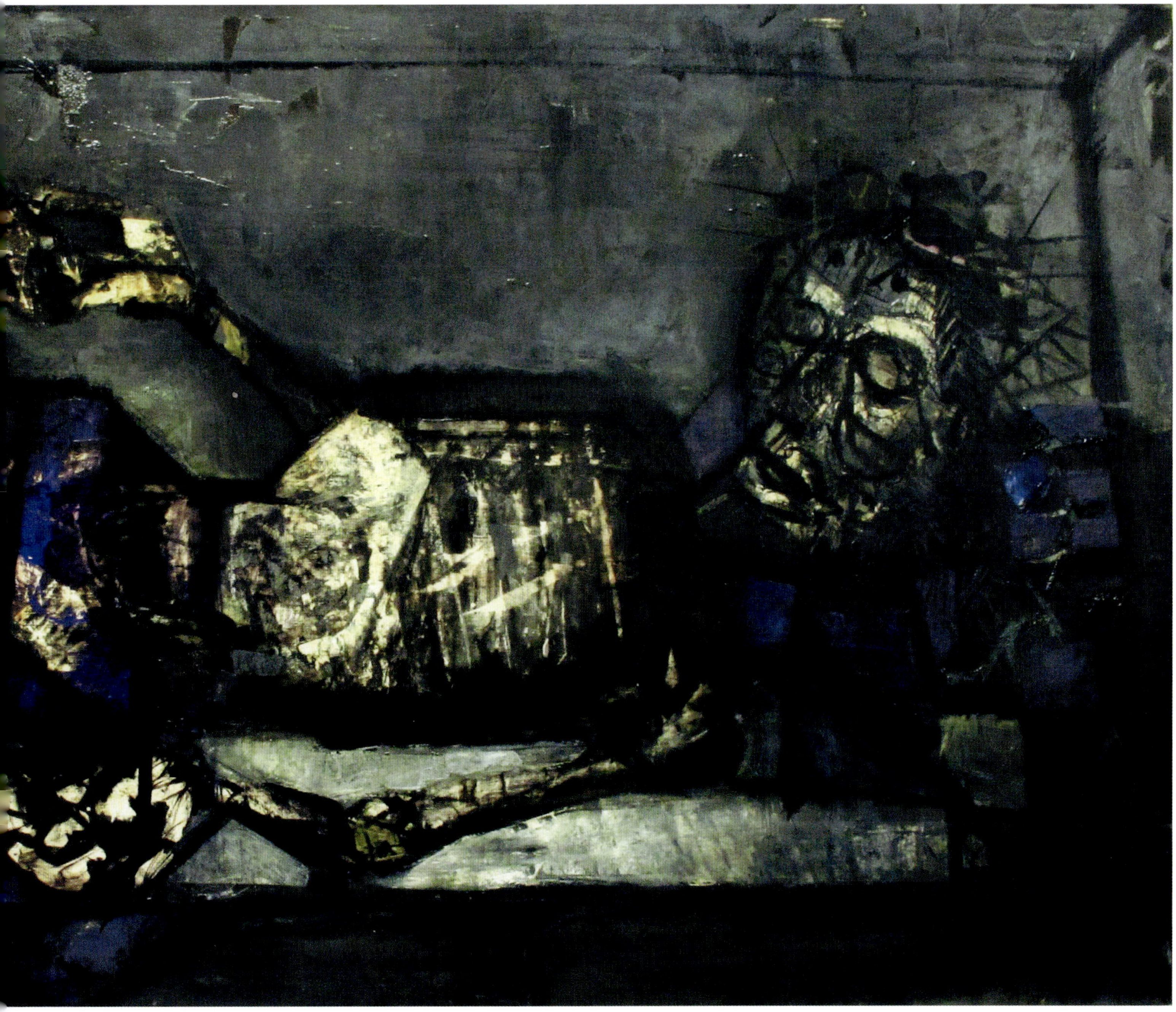

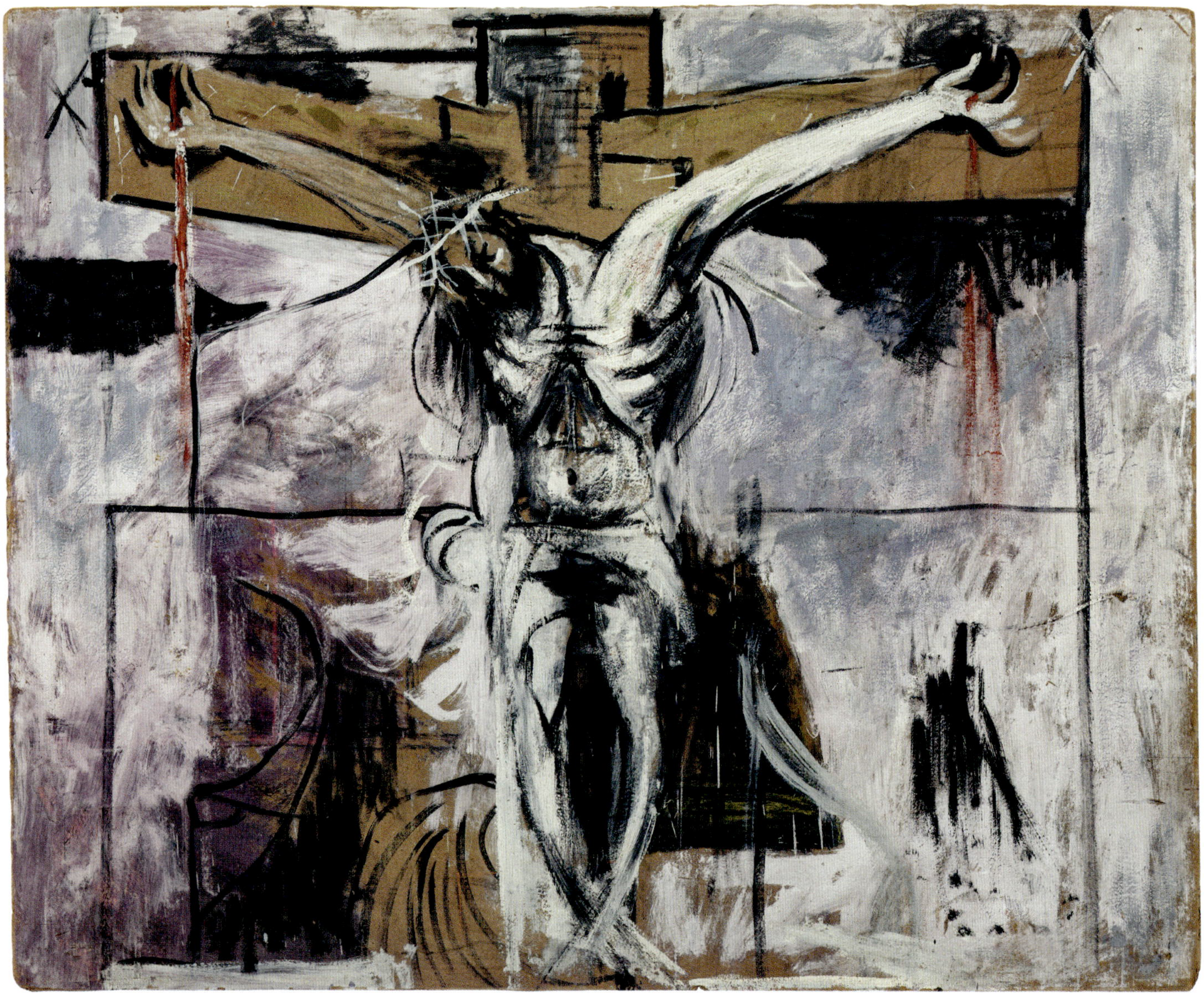

GRAHAM SUTHERLAND
(London, 1903 – Kent, UK, 1980)
Study for Crucifixion
1947
Oil on masonite
97 × 118 cm
Musei Vaticani, Vatican City

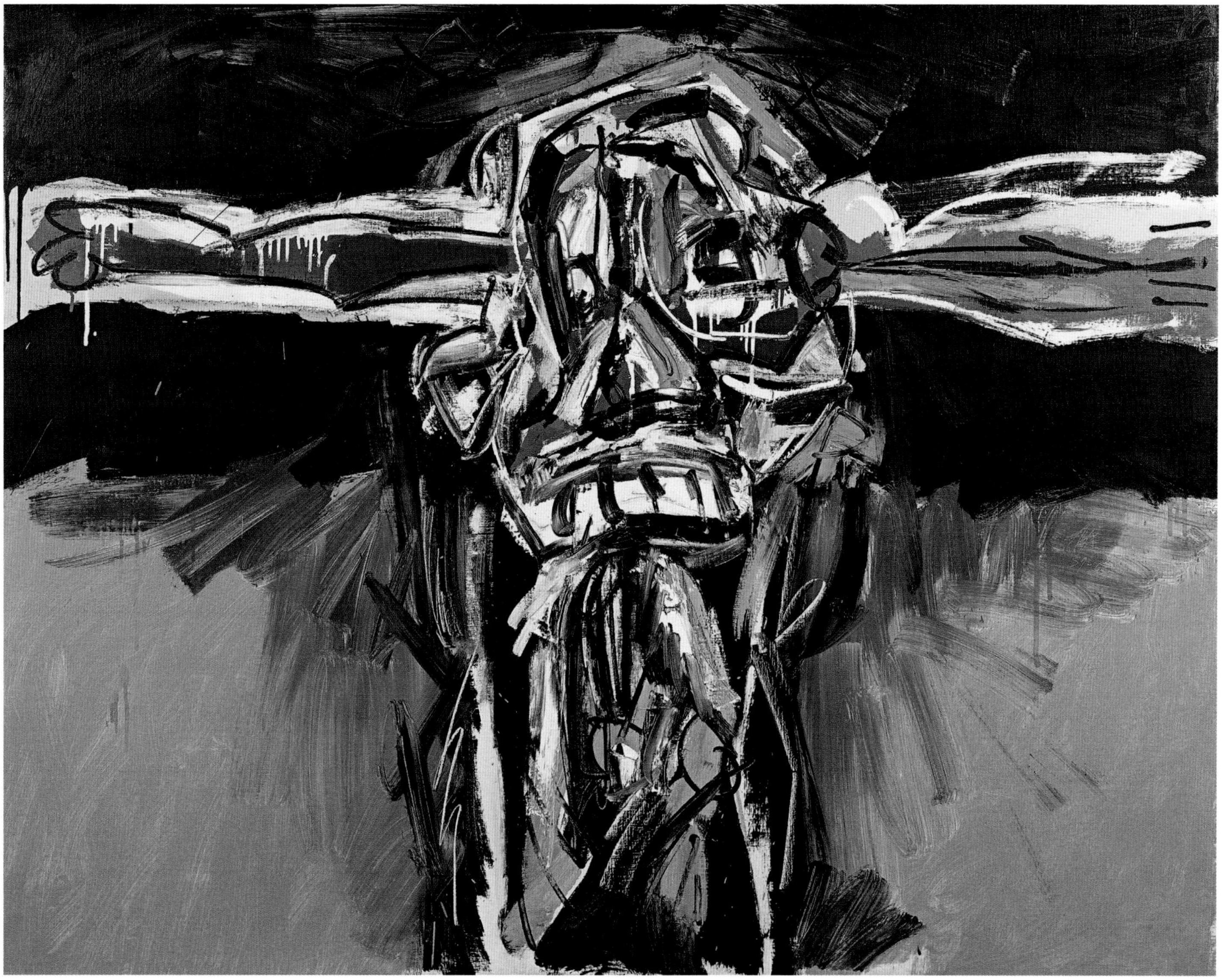

ANTONIO SAURA
(Huesca, 1930 – Cuenca, 1998)
Crucifixion
1959-1963
Oil on canvas
133 × 164.6 cm
Guggenheim Bilbao Museoa

JORGE OTEIZA
(Orio, Guipúzcoa, 1908 – San Sebastián, 2003)
Heads of the Apostles nos. 8 (Peter), 9 (Paul) and 1
1953
Bronze
40 × 40 × 37.5 cm, 41 × 31 × 30 cm and 42 × 31 × 32 cm
Fundación Museo Jorge Oteiza Fundazio Museoa, Alzuza (Navarre)

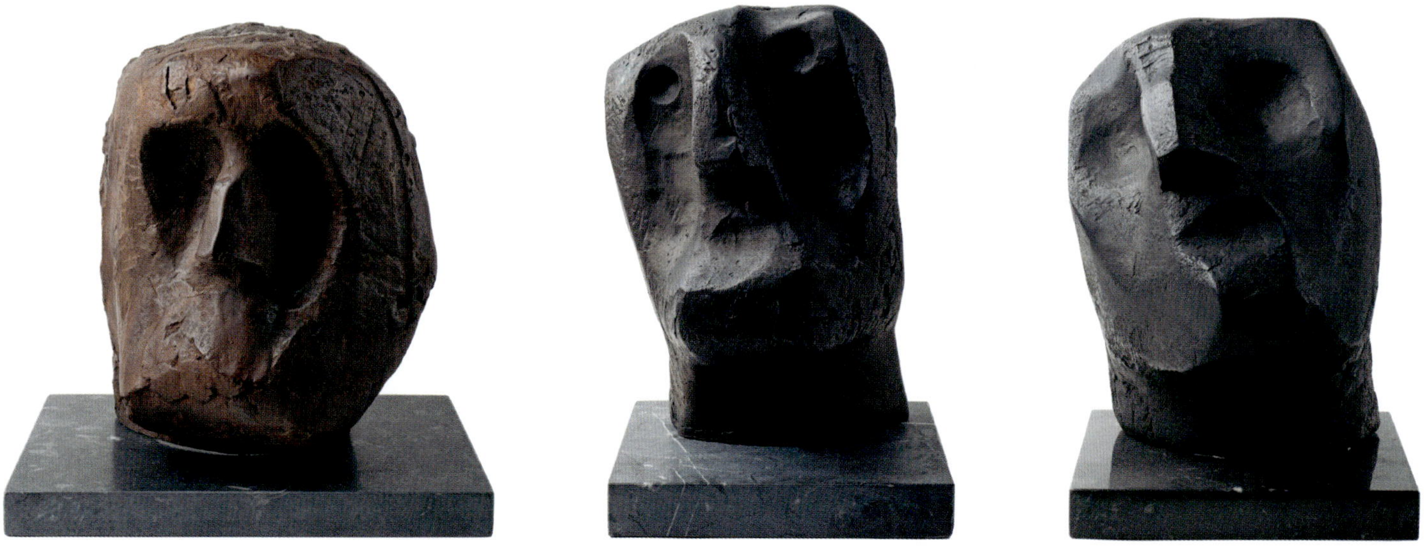

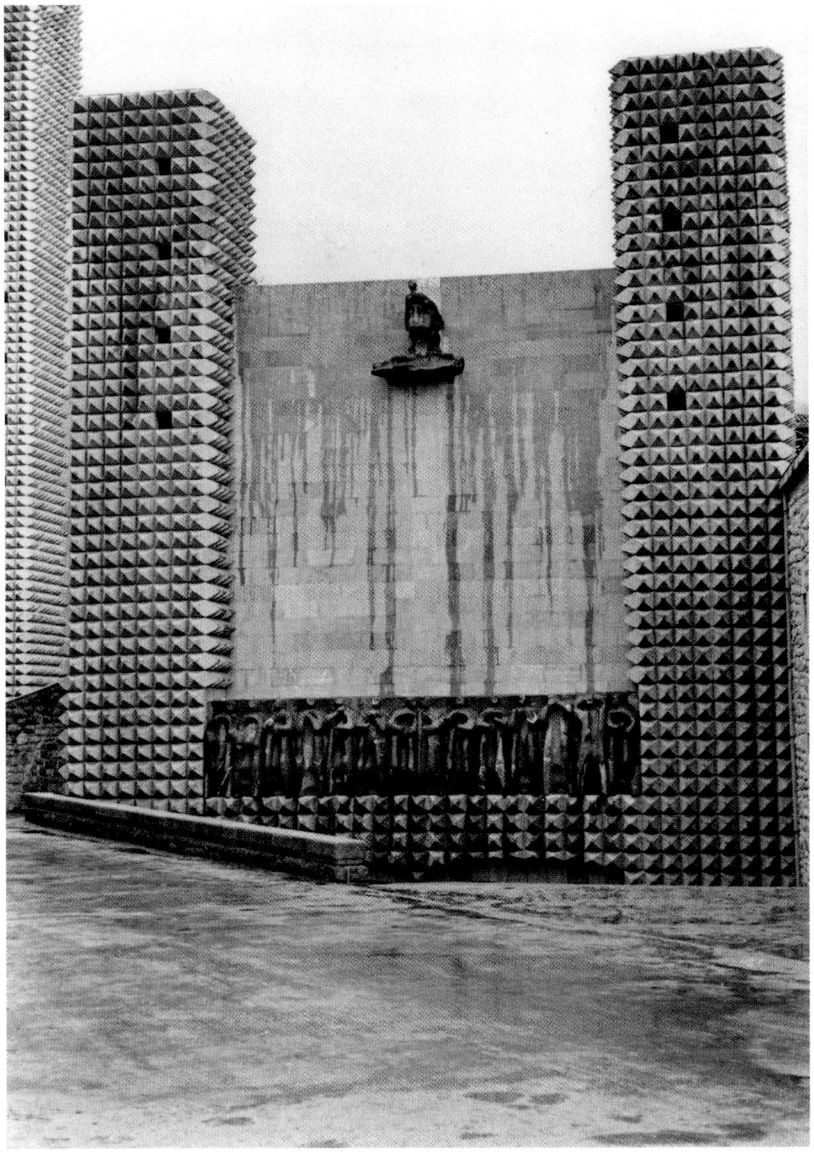
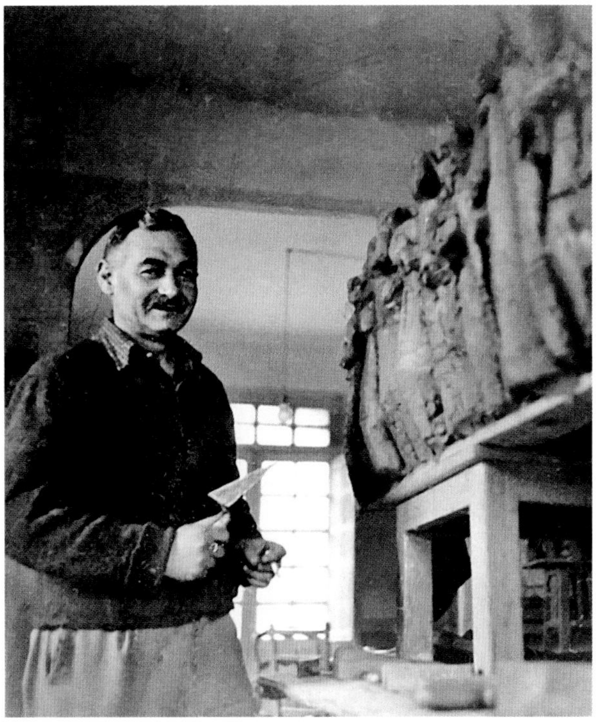
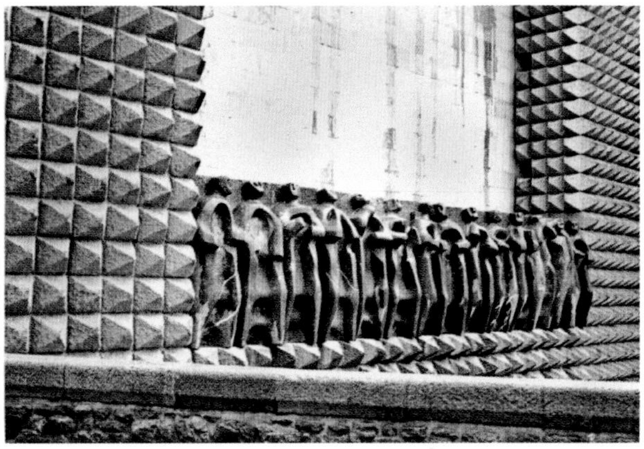
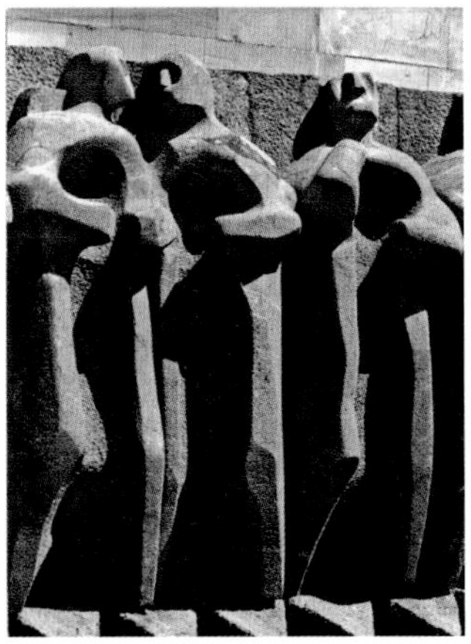
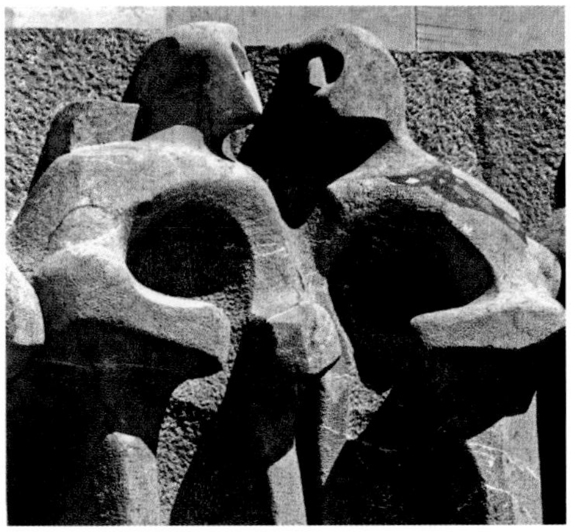
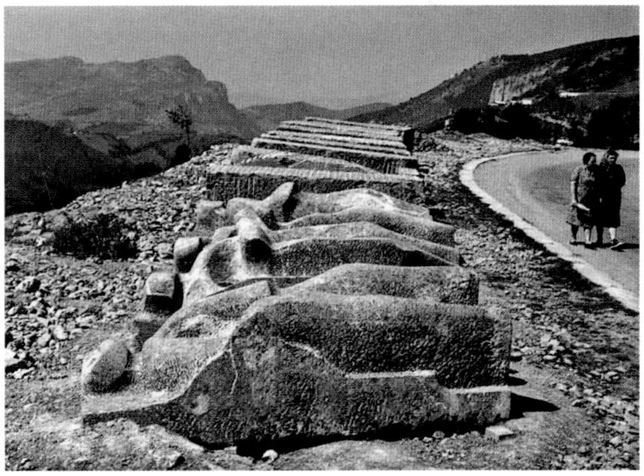

Sculptures by Jorge Oteiza for the Basilica
of Arantzazu (Bizcaya)
1950-1969
Photographs by Ricardo Ugarte Zubiarraín, Benigno
Plazaola Goronaeta and Antton Elezegi Beloki

Modern copy, 2023
Archivo de la Fundación Museo Jorge Oteiza
Fundazio Museoa, Alzuza (Navarre)

PACO GÓMEZ
(Pamplona, 1918 – Madrid, 1998)
Josep Maria Subirachs before the Apostle Saint Peter
Report, 1960
Modern copy, 2023
Archivo Paco Gómez / Fundación Foto Colectania

Sculptures by Josep Maria Subirachs for the Basilica of the Virgen del Camino of León
1960
Photographs by Miquel Badia
Modern copy, 2023
Arxiu Subirachs

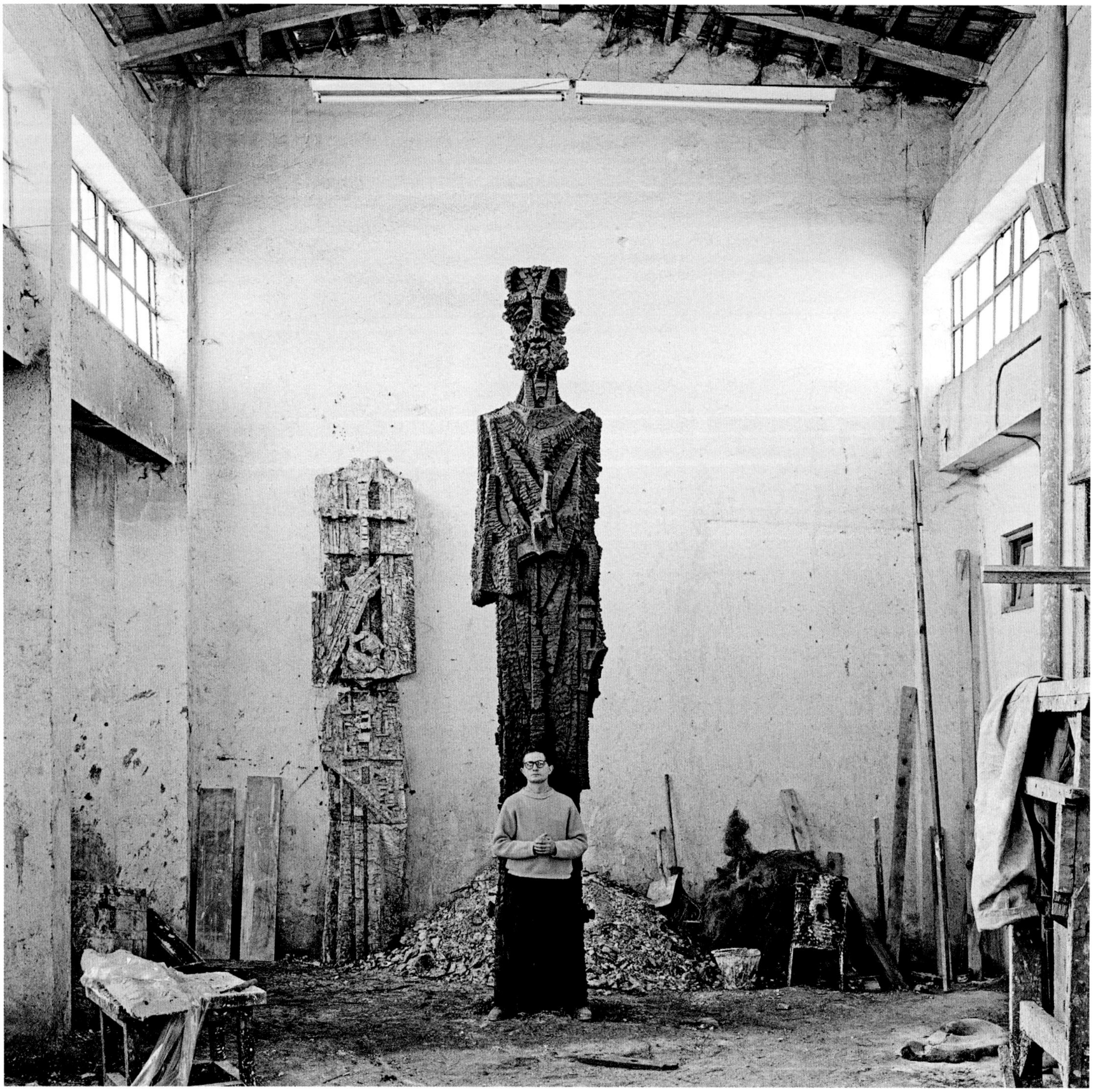

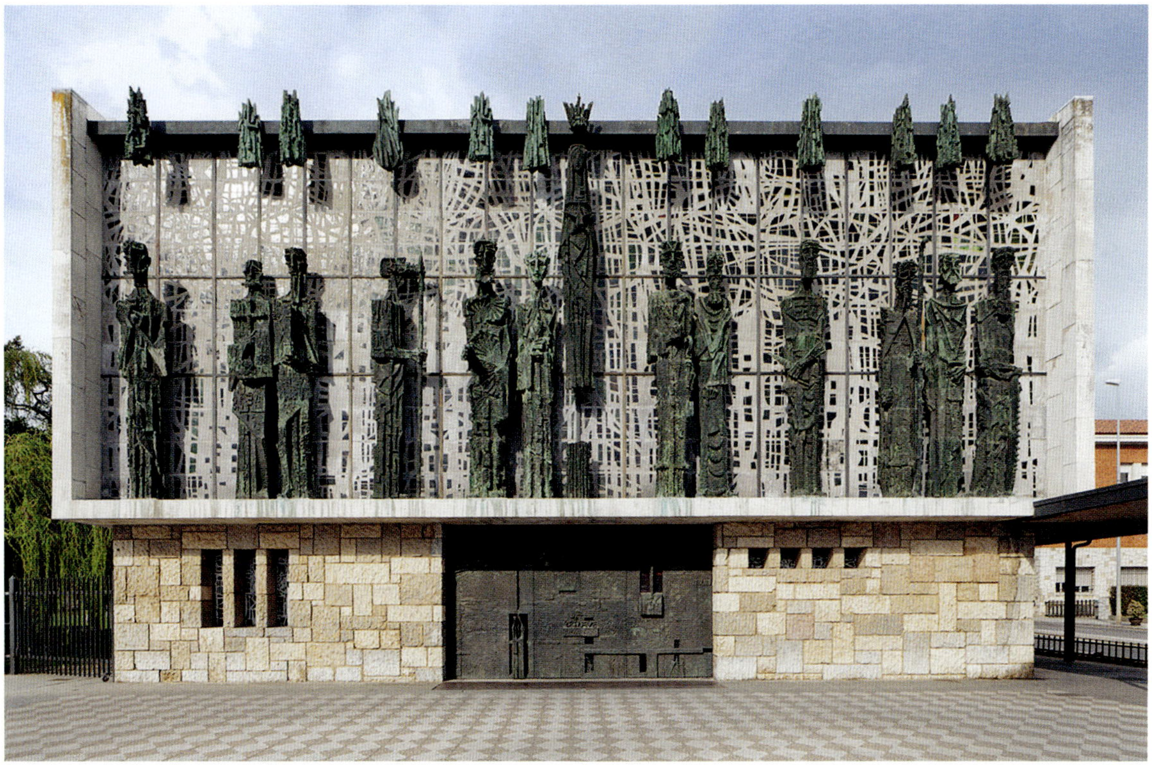

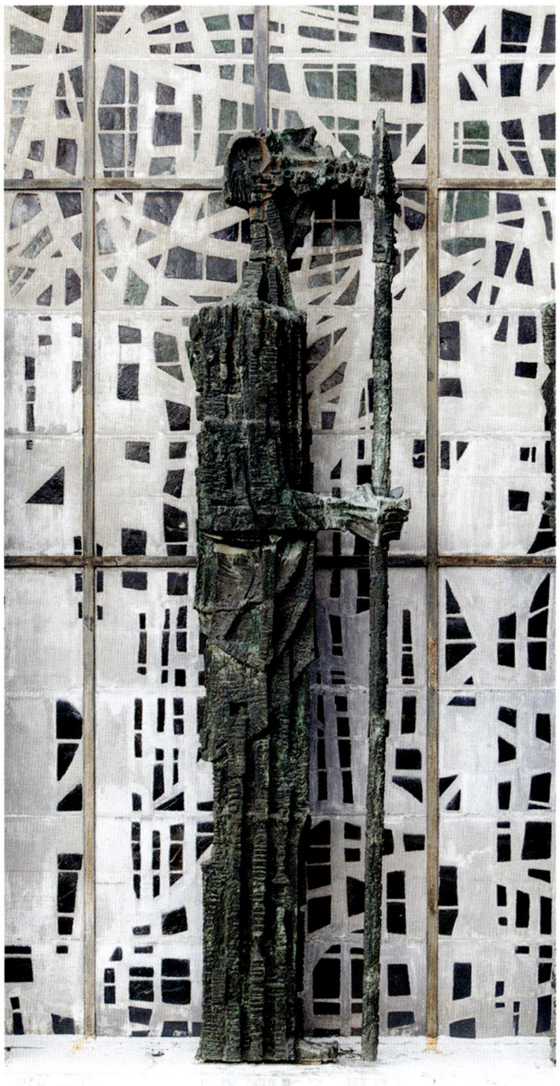

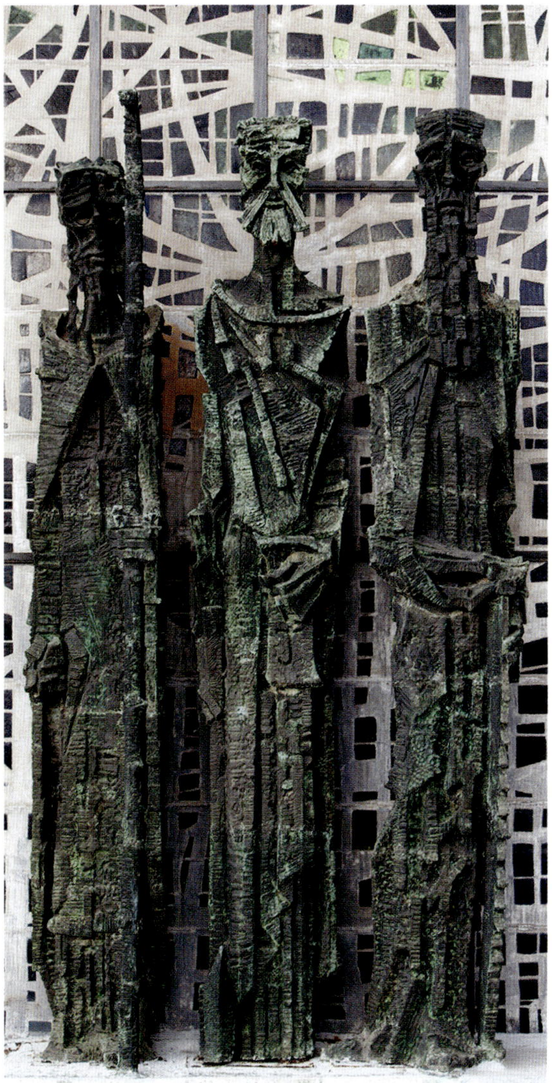

Regarding the human condition, the idea and image of a full, serene, well-balanced humanity, seemed destined to oblivion. The dissolution of the body, its practical disappearance, was a symptom of a humanity wounded to the point of destruction. But, at practically the same time, whether in the context of the victory over fascism or moral and philosophical determination, the figure recovers and rises once more, often fragile, battered and beaten, to present itself once again as precarious potential, moving towards an uncertain but possible future.

FROM DISSOLUTION TO UPRISING

FRANCISZKA THEMERSON
(Warsaw, 1907 – London, 1988)
Why is the mind in the head?
1954
Oil on canvas
100 × 75 × 7.5 cm
Collection of the Themerson Estate

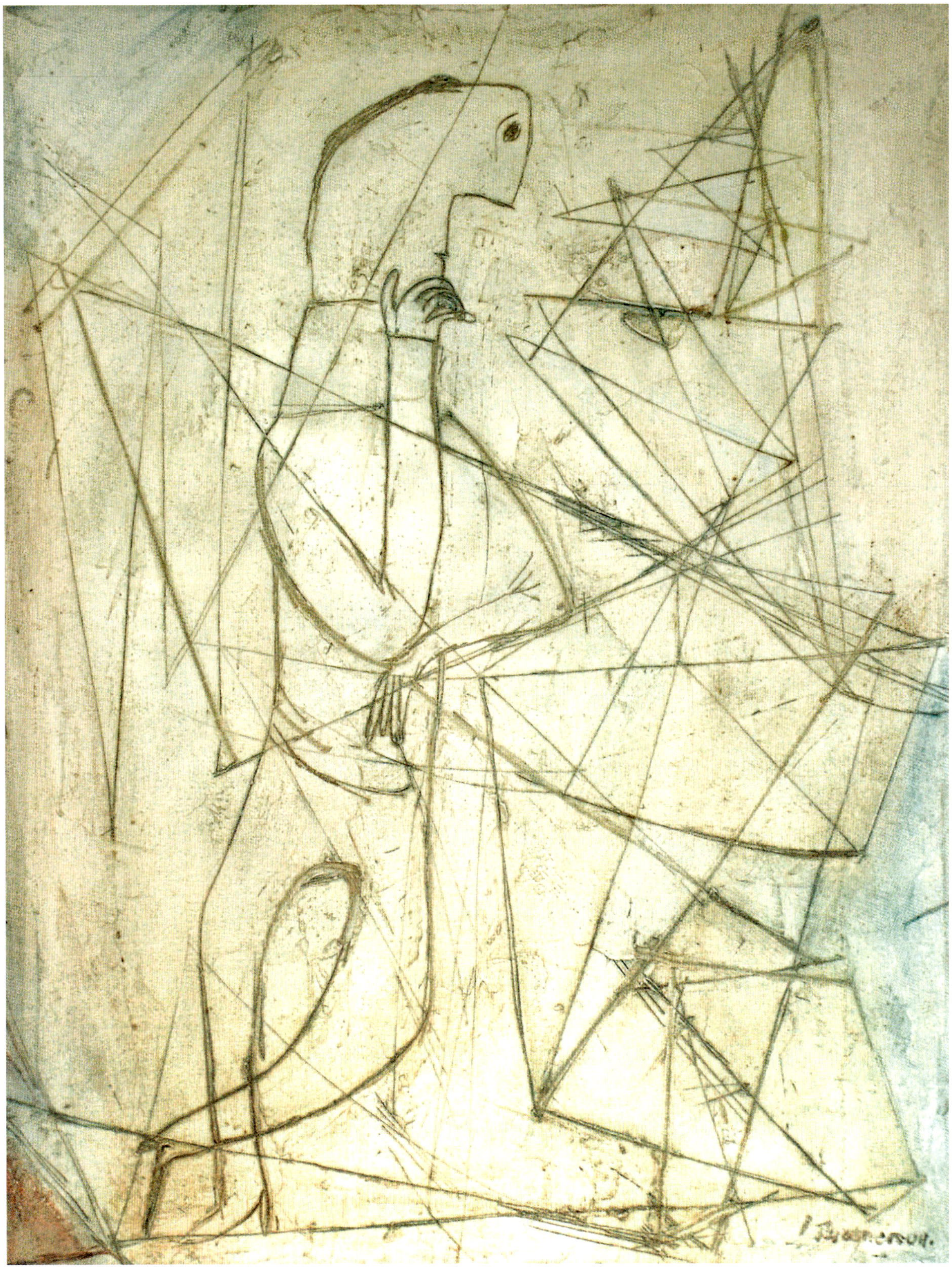

PIERRE TAL-COAT
(Clohars-Carnoët, France, 1905 – Saint-Pierre-de-Bailleul, France, 1985)
Precisions (Profile Under Water)
1949
Oil on canvas
100 × 81 cm
Private collection, Paris

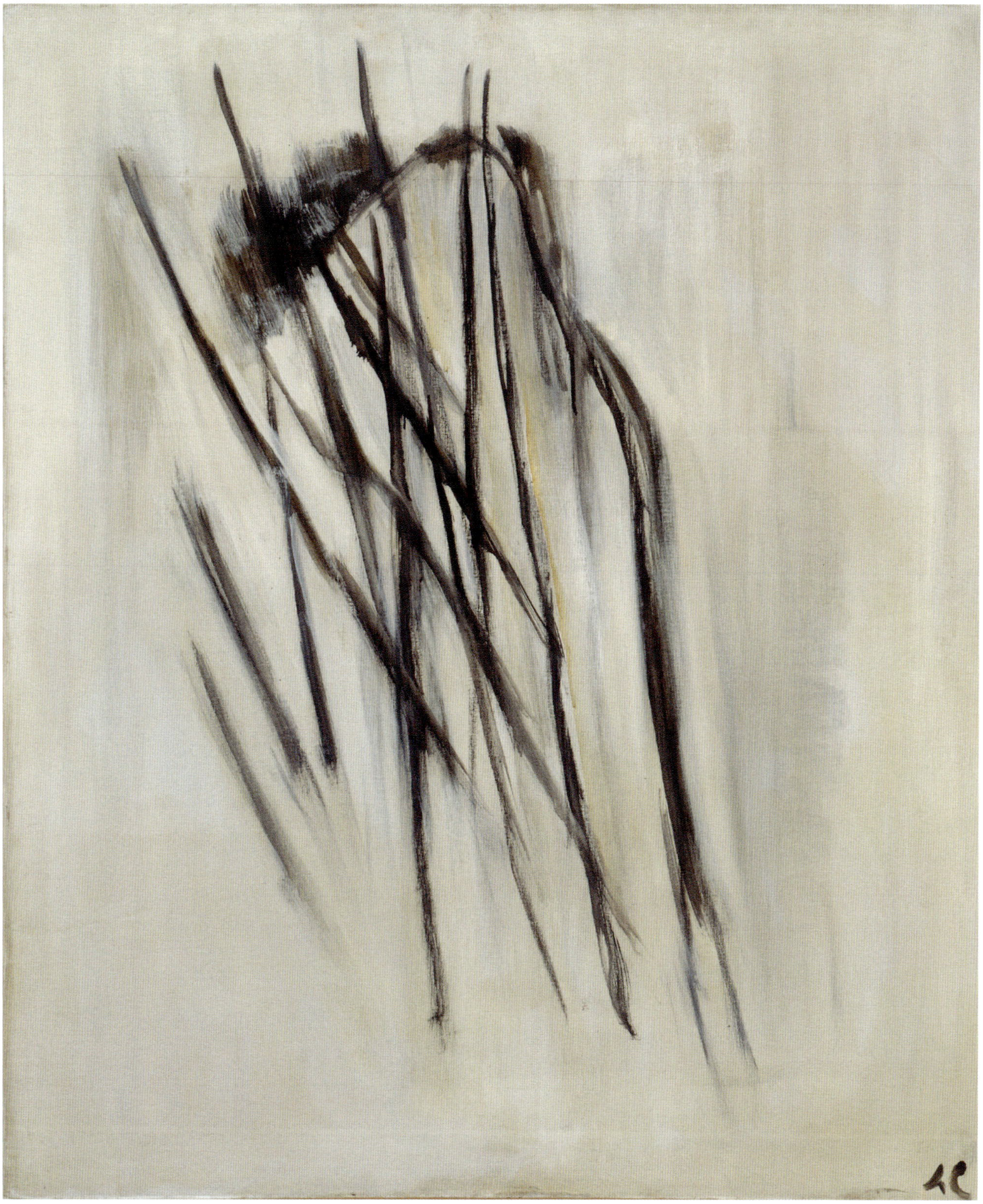

ANTONI TÀPIES
(Barcelona, 1923-2012)
Hand
1945
Paris pencil on paper
28.5 × 21.5 cm
Fundació Antoni Tàpies, Barcelona

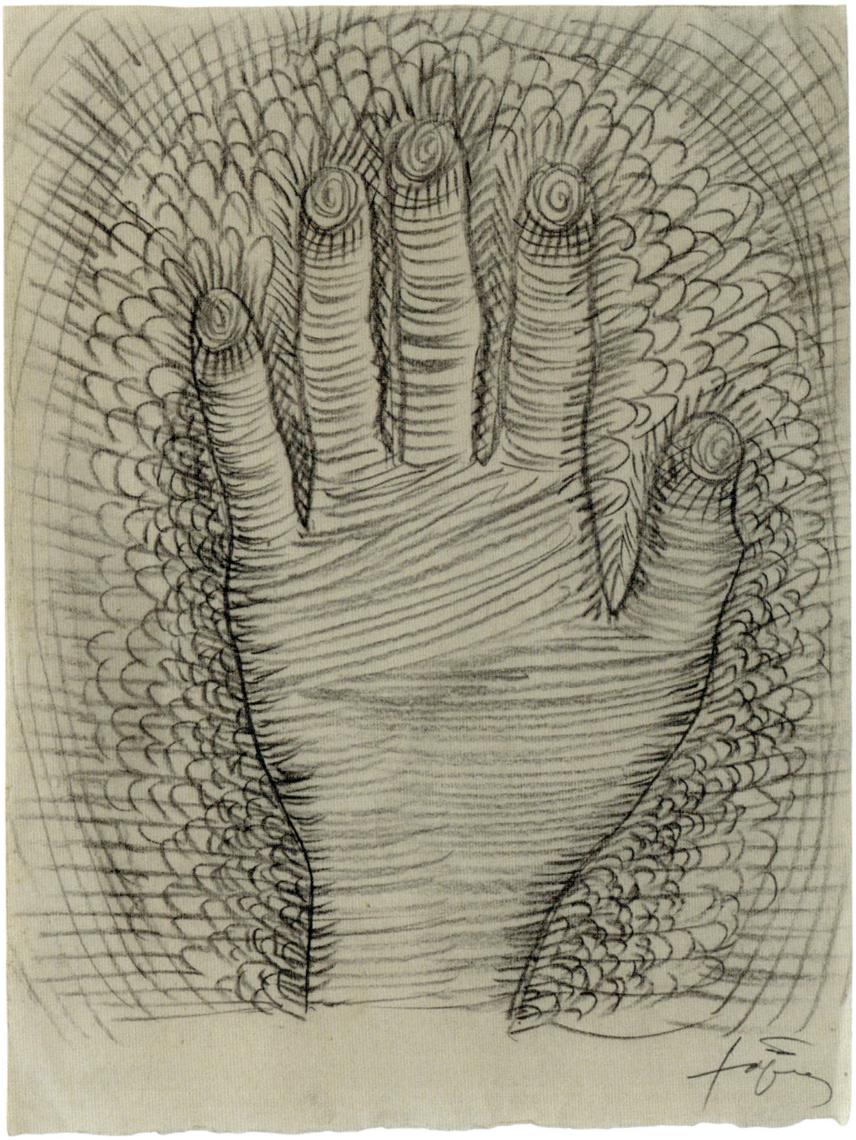

ANTONI TÀPIES
(Barcelona, 1923-2012)
Black Form on Grey Square
1960
Mixed technique on canvas
162 × 162 cm
Fundació Antoni Tàpies, Barcelona

MANOLO MILLARES
(Las Palmas de Gran Canaria, 1926 – Madrid, 1972)
Homúnculo
1960
Mixed technique on hessian
200 × 200 cm
Banco Santander Collection

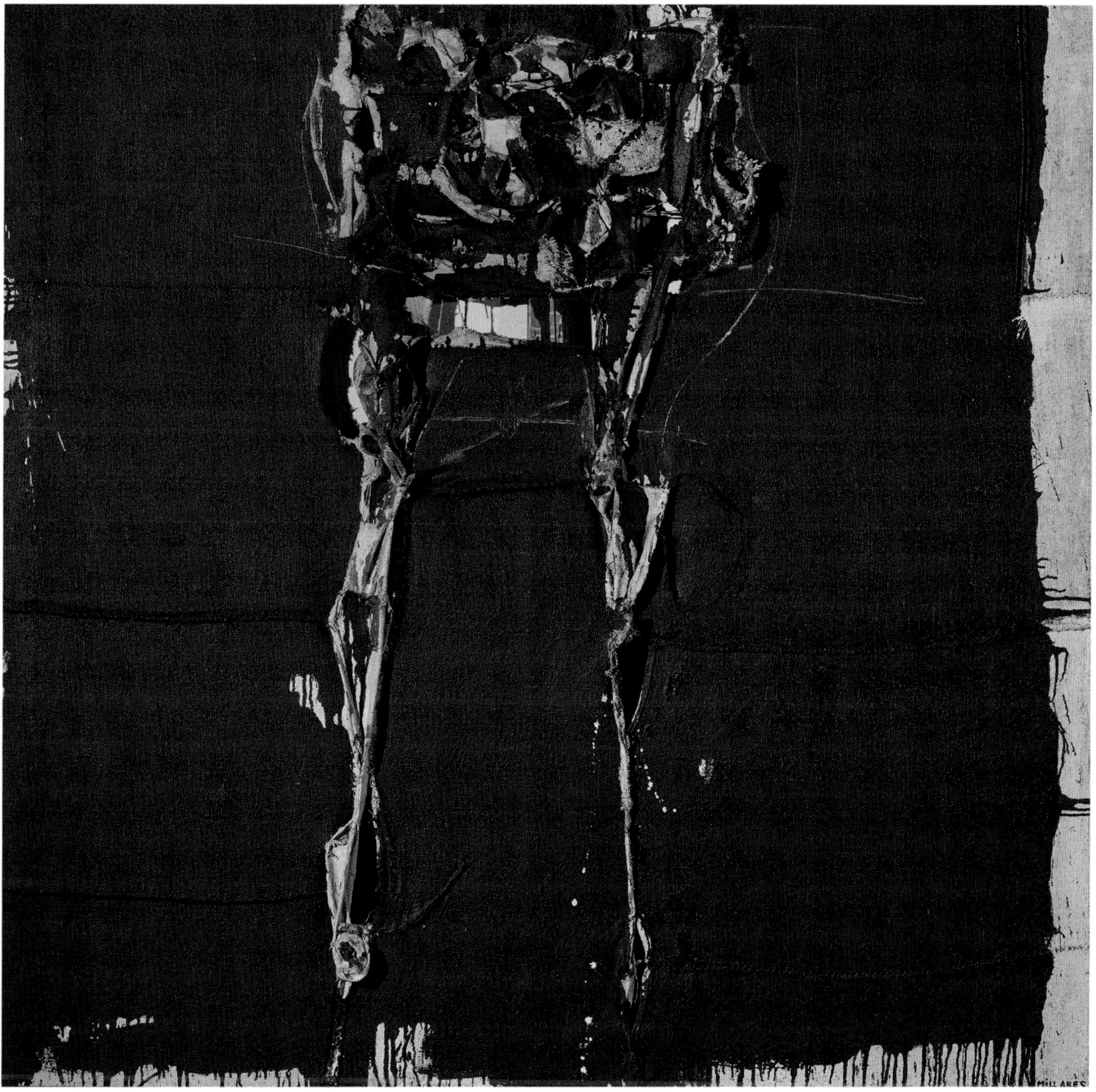
MILLARES

ALBERTO GIACOMETTI
(Borgonovo, Switzerland, 1901 – Chur, Switzerland, 1966)
Bust of a man on plinth
1947
Bronze
54.3 × 11.4 × 10.1 cm
Fondation Giacometti

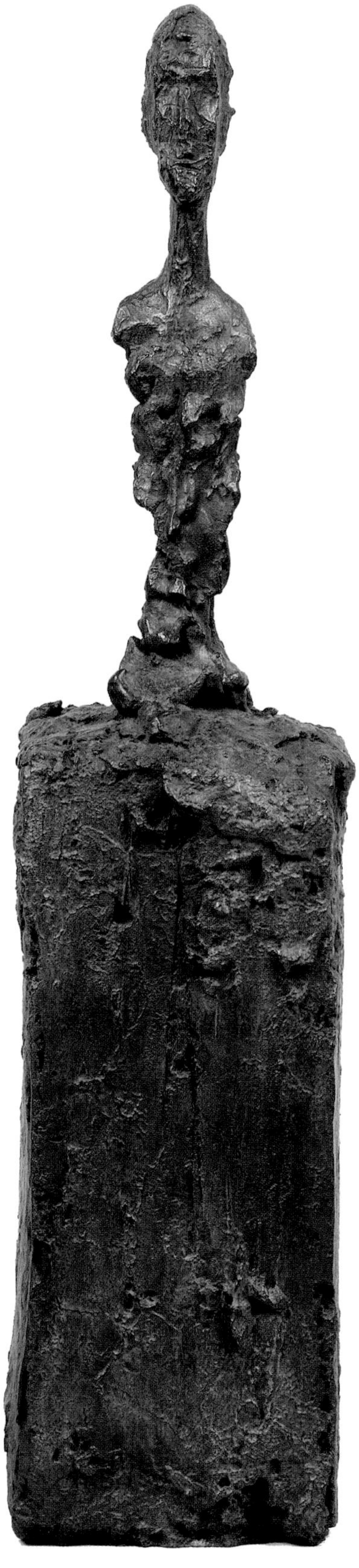

GERMAINE RICHIER
(Grans, France, 1902 – Montpellier, France, 1959)
The Ogre
1949
Bronze
83 × 45 × 40 cm
Galleria Nazionale d'Arte Moderna e Contemporanea, Rome

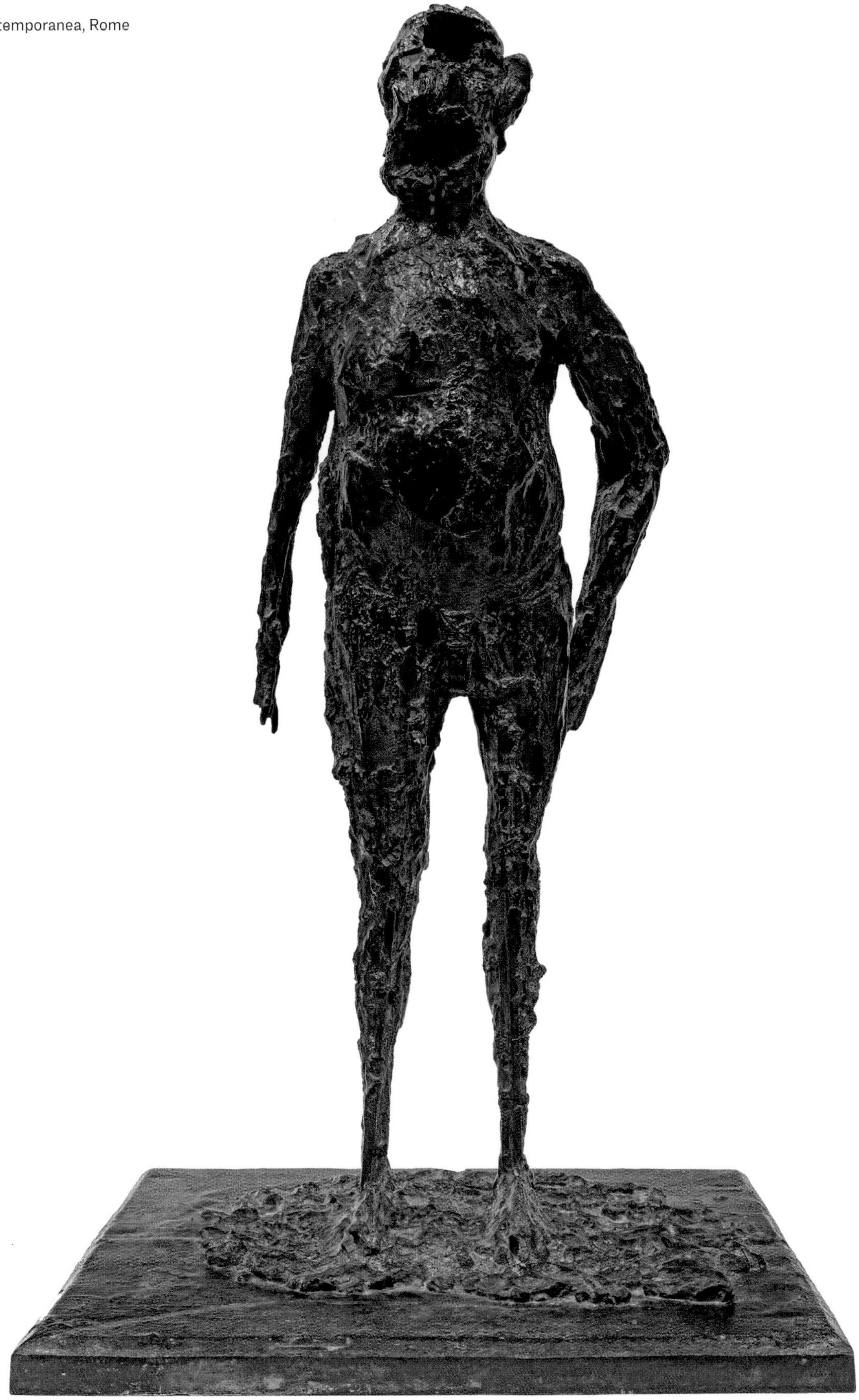

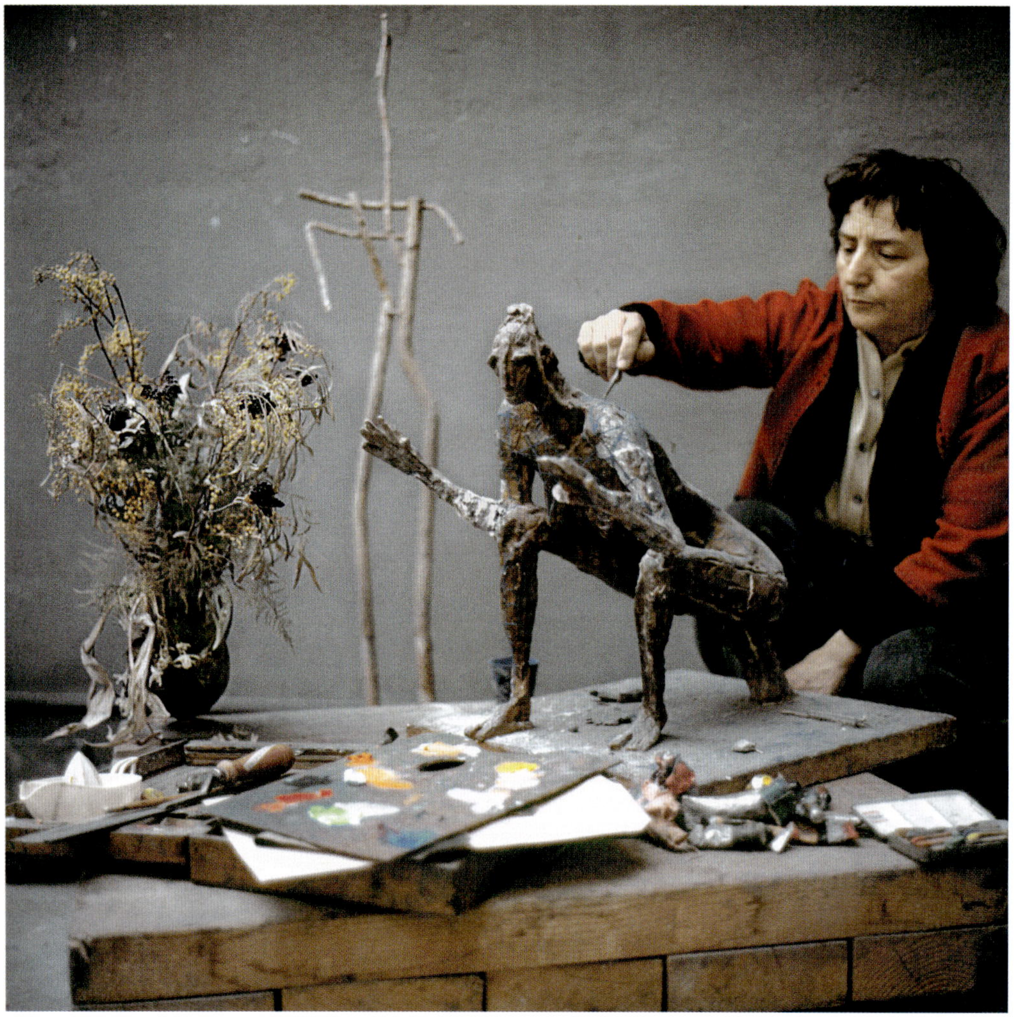

AGNÈS VARDA
(Ixelles, Belgium, 1928 – Paris, 2019)
Germaine Richier in her studio with La Sauterelle
c. 1945
Chromogenic print on Kodak RC satin photo paper, 2021
30 × 30 cm
Galerie Nathalie Obadia, Paris/Brussels

LOUISE BOURGEOIS
(Paris, 1911 – New York, 2010)
Figure
1960
Bronze, black patina with highlights
37.5 × 13.5 × 11.5 cm
Private Collection, Belgium

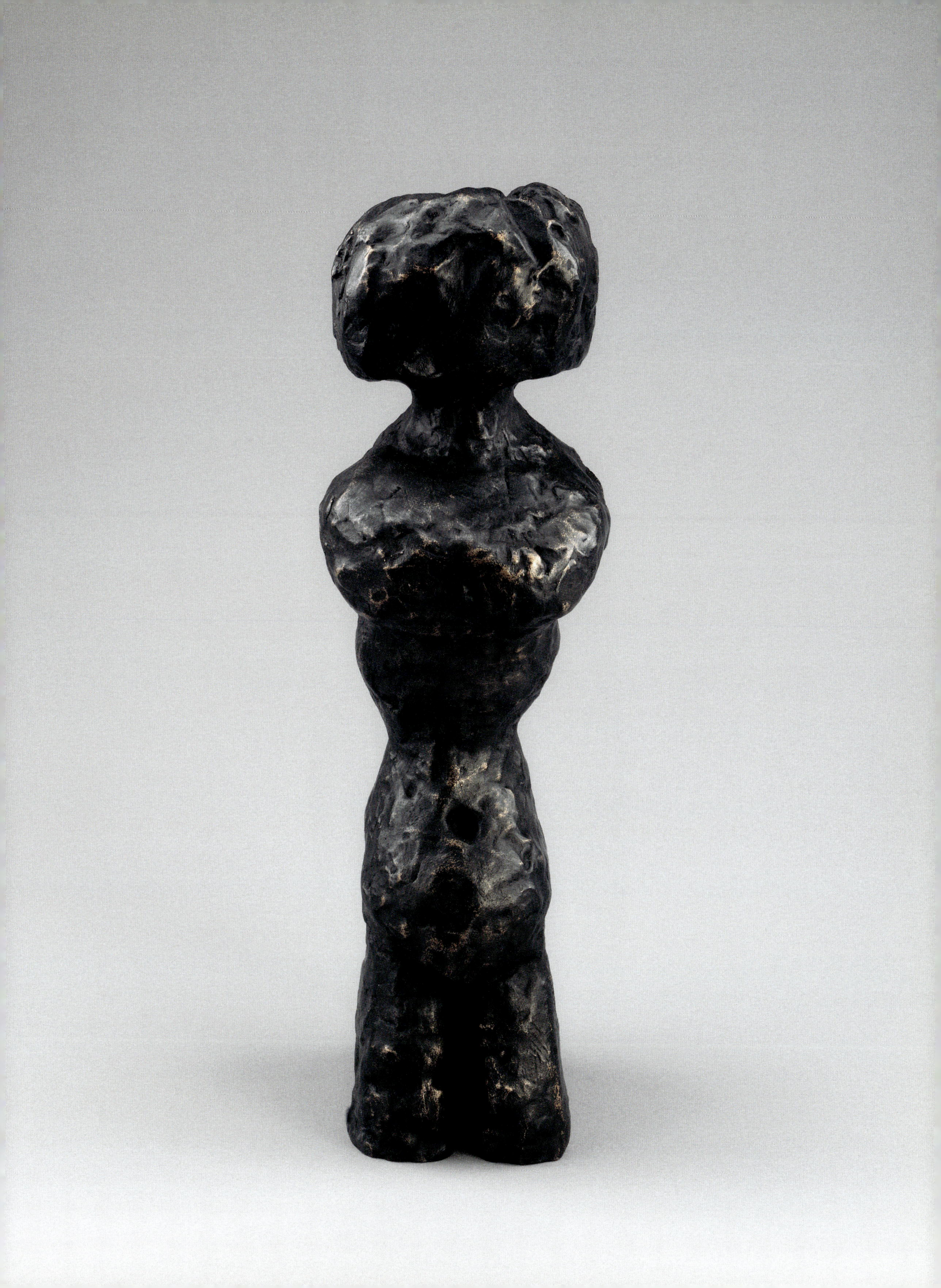

LLUÍS MARIA SAUMELLS
(Gironella, 1915 – Tarragona, 1999)
Stylite
1952
Lost wax casting
31 × 14.5 × 20 cm
Diputació de Tarragona. Museu d'Art Modern

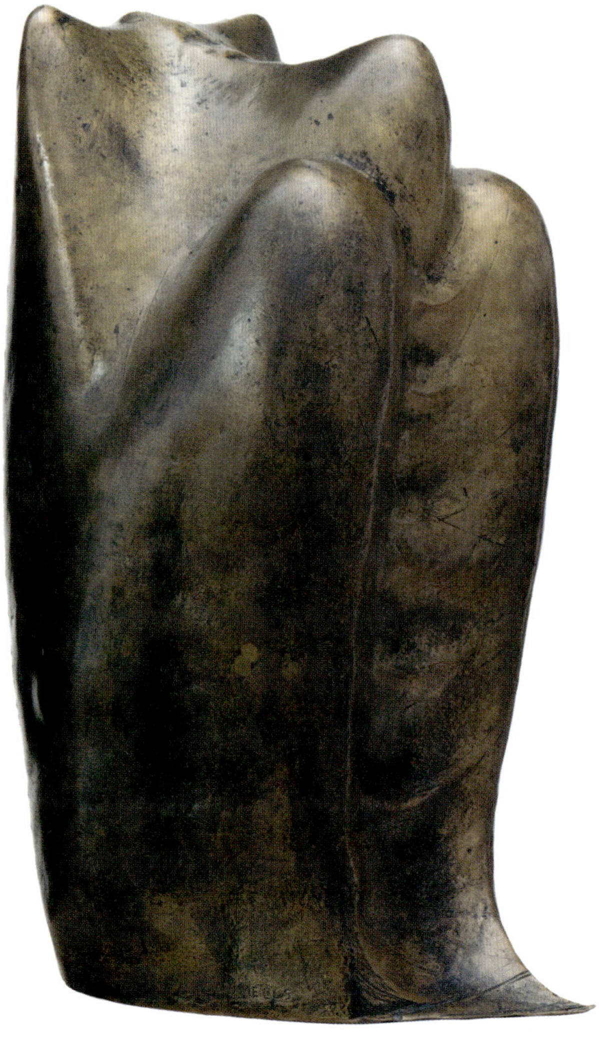

REG BUTLER
(Buntingford, UK, 1913 – Berkhamsted, UK, 1981)
Figure in Space
1956
Bronze
51 × 24 × 30.5 cm
Osborne Samuel Ltd.

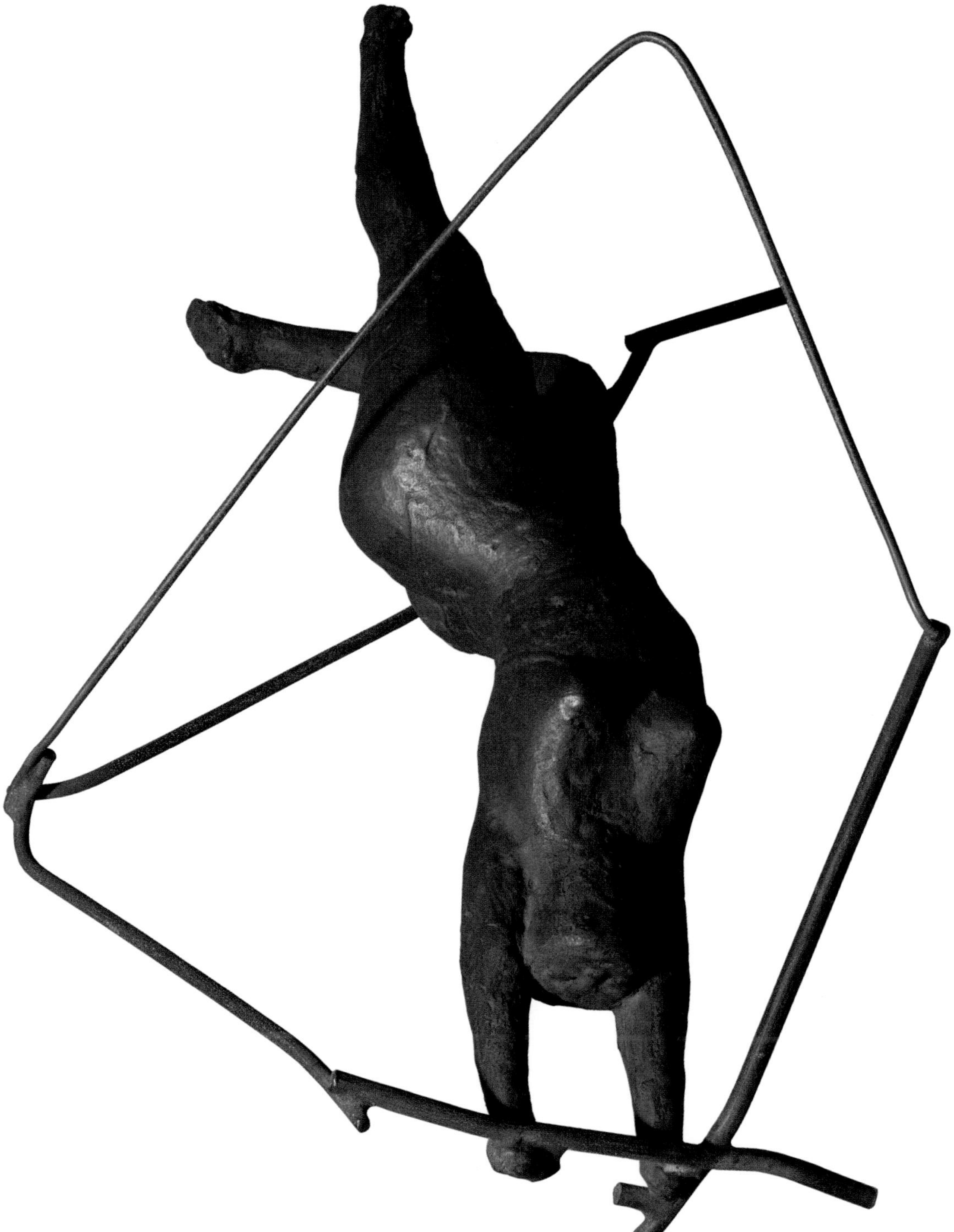

EDUARDO GREGORIO
(Las Palmas de Gran Canaria, 1903-1974)
Torsos
c. 1950
Alabaster
123.4 × 44 × 40 cm
Galeries Laietanes, 1958
Museu Nacional d'Art de Catalunya

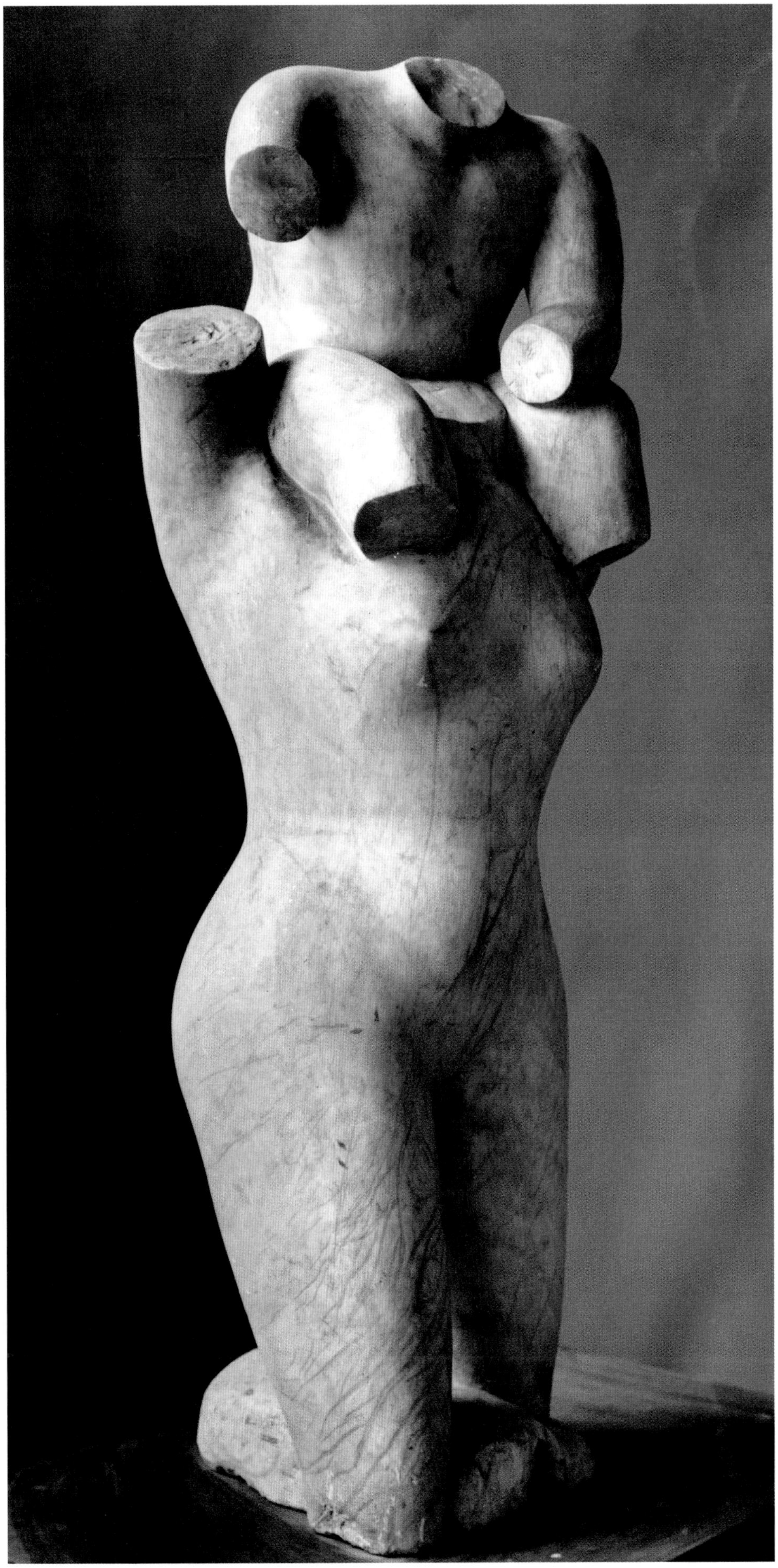

Despite the progressive optimism that was taking hold in those societies that celebrated victory, and the economic growth in Western countries, some countries and groups found themselves in a prolonged situation of precariousness and oppression. Exile and survival generated feelings of melancholy otherness, of split identities. The era and the revolts of the existentialists are imbued with a deep sense of solitude. The losers in the Spanish Civil War were haunted by banishment and despair in a tormented, suffocating period that meted out the worst punishment to the working classes and women.

INTERIOR EXILE

INGE MORATH
(Graz, Austria, 1923 – New York, 2002)
Saul Steinberg
(Râmnicu Sărat, Romania 1913 – New York, 1999)
Saul Steinberg with Mask; New York
1959
Gelatin silver print, 60,4 × 50,5 cm
Centre Pompidou, Paris
Musée national d'art moderne-Centre de création industrielle

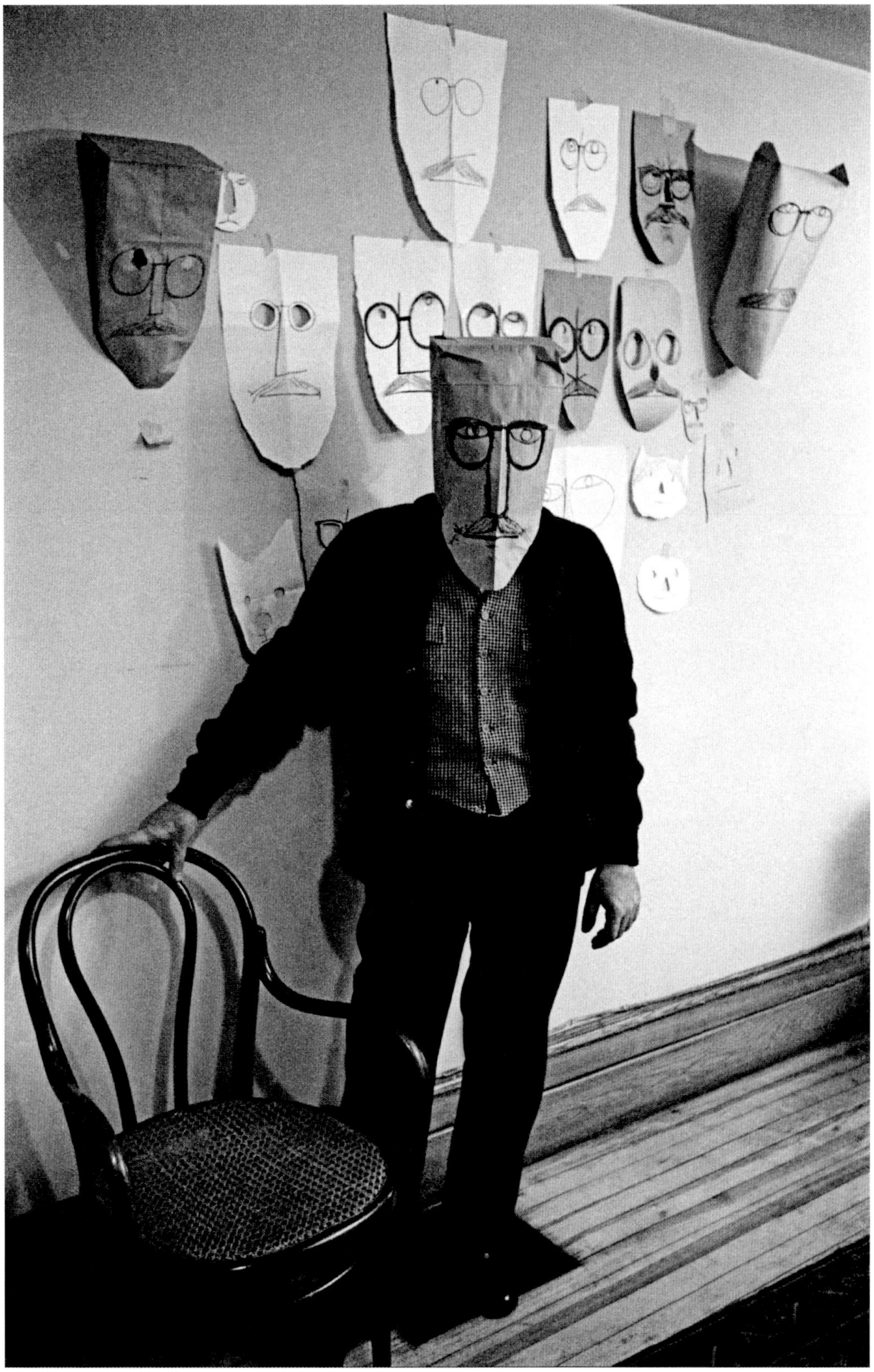

EDOUARD PIGNON
(Bully-les-Mines, France, 1905 –
La Couture-Boussey, France, 1993)
Catalan Woman
1946
Oil on canvas
81 × 65.5 cm
Private collection, Paris

ROBERTA GONZÁLEZ
(Paris, 1909 – Arcueil, France, 1976)
Portrait of Aunt Lola
1943
Oil on wood
32 × 18 cm
Donated by the artist, 1972; acquisition, 1973
Museu Nacional d'Art de Catalunya

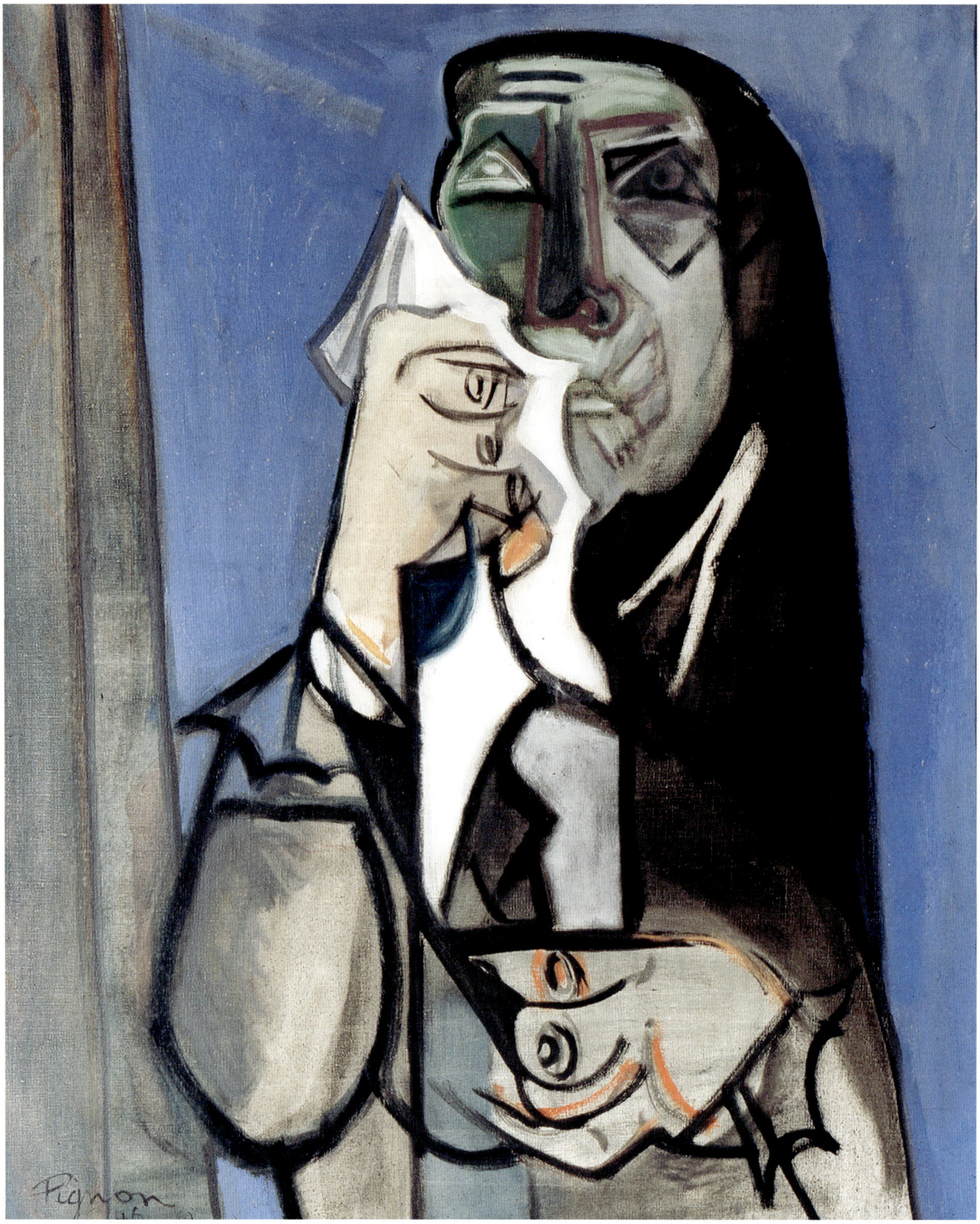

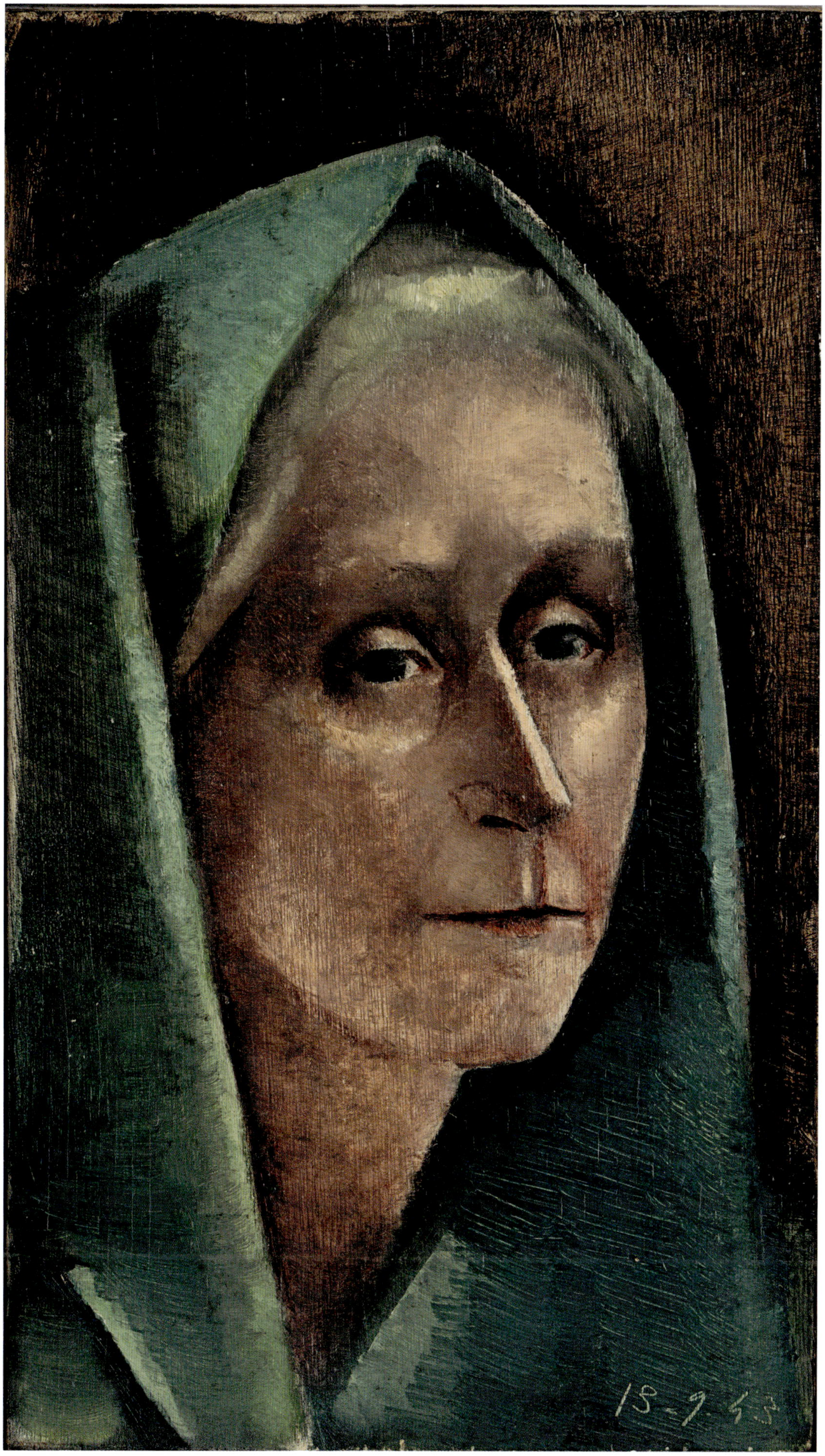
15-9-53

JUANA FRANCÉS
(Alicante, 1924 – Madrid, 1990)
Silence
1953
Oil on Tablex
72 × 52 cm
Studiolo Candela A. Soldevila Collection

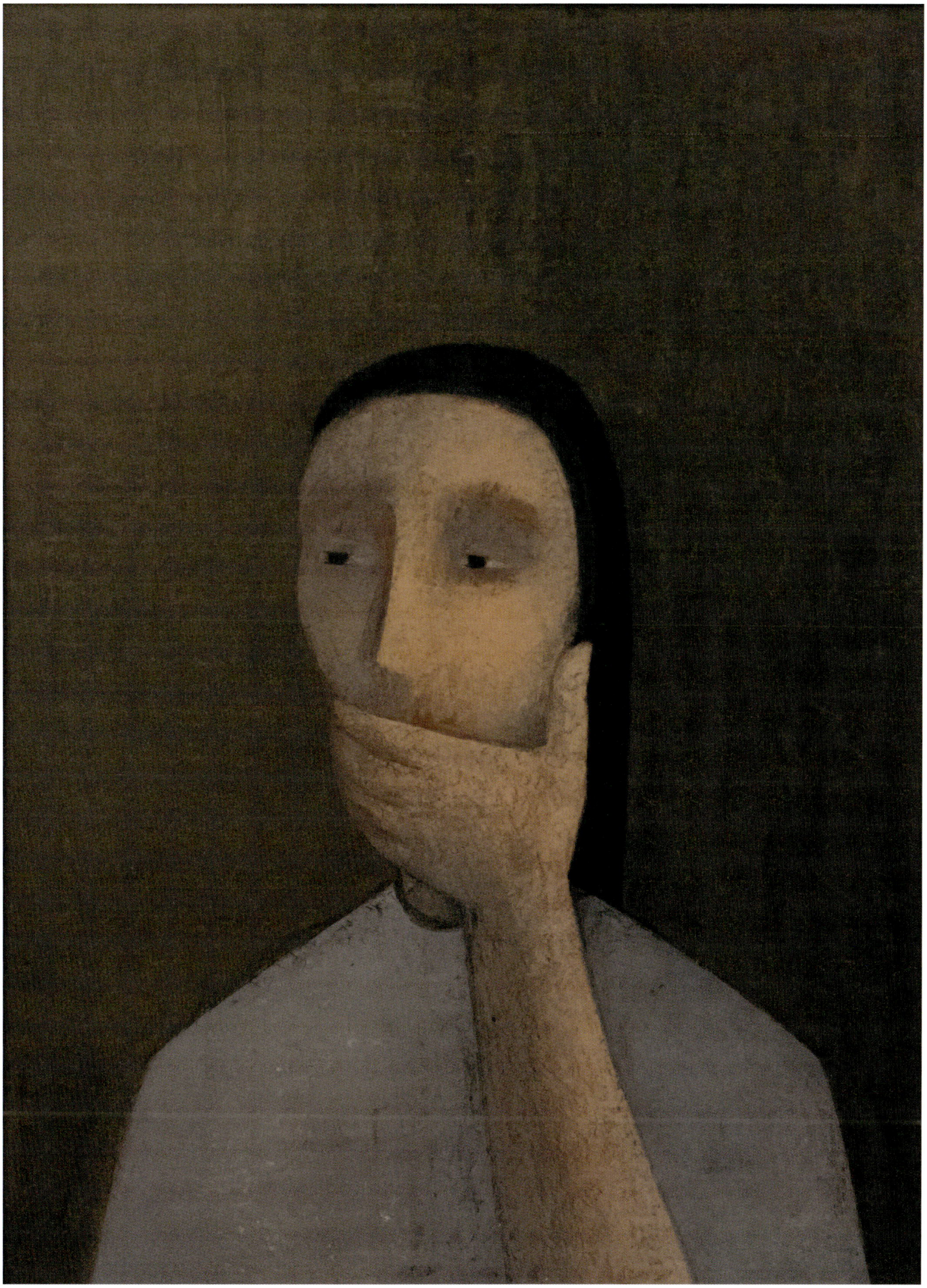

JOAN PONÇ
(Barcelona, 1927 – Saint-Paul-de-Vence, France, 1984)
Portrait of Roser
1950
Oil on canvas
162 × 97.5 cm
MACBA Collection. Deposit of the Generalitat de Catalunya
Former Salvador Riera Collection

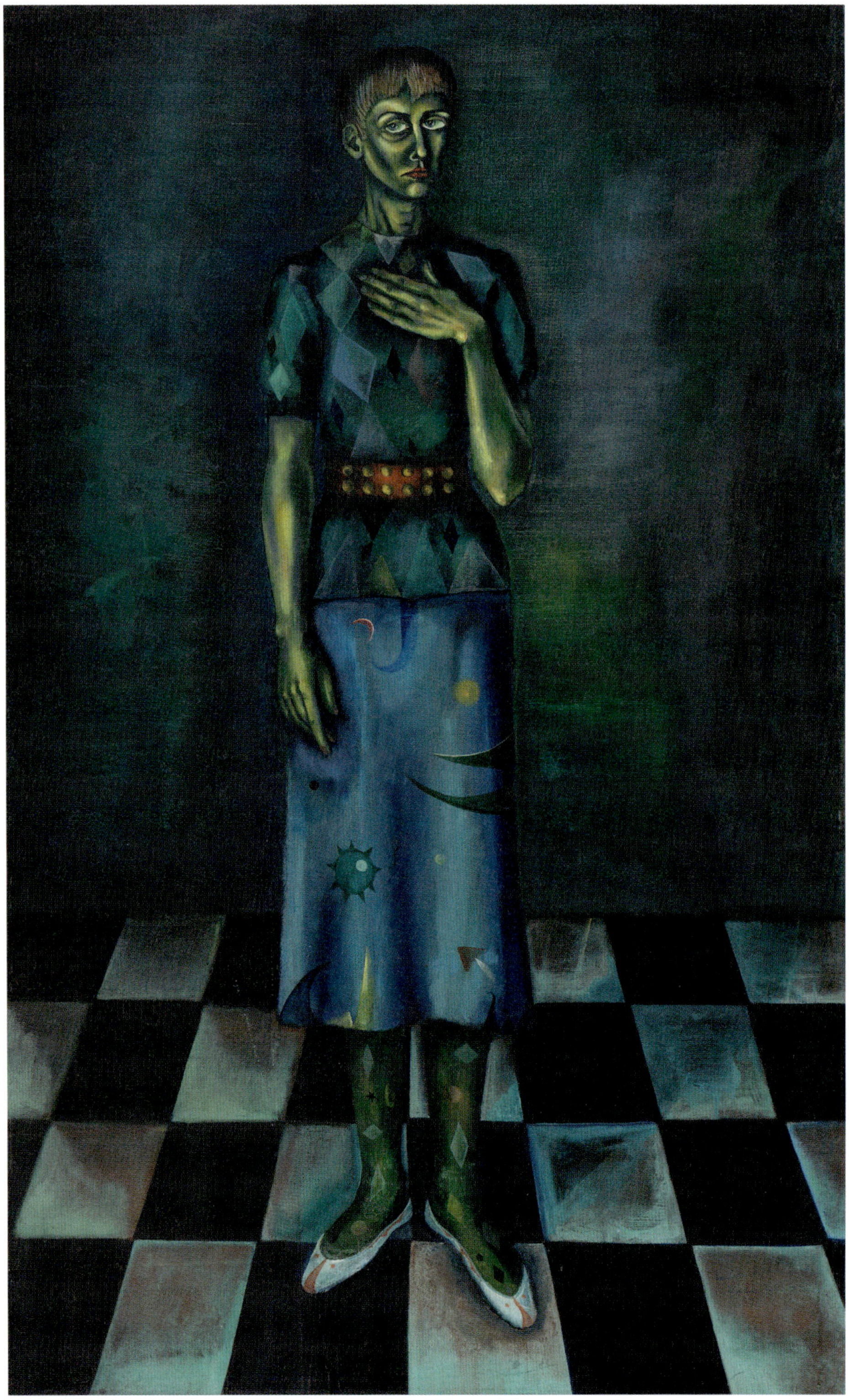

JOAN PONÇ
(Barcelona, 1927 – Saint-Paul-de-Vence, France, 1984)
The Prison
1950
Gouache, pastel and ink on paper
62 × 42.5 cm
MACBA Collection. Deposit of the Generalitat de Catalunya
Former Salvador Riera Collection

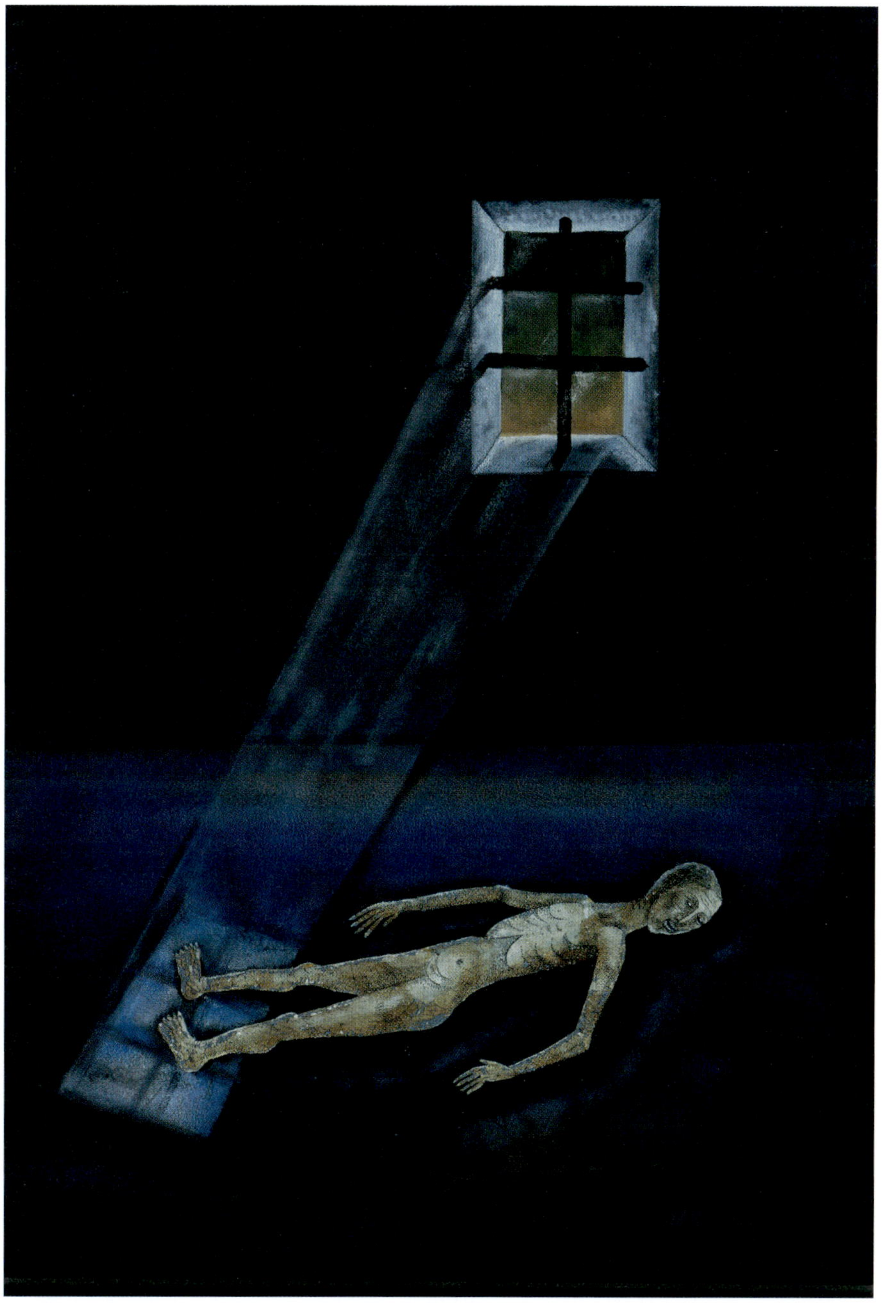

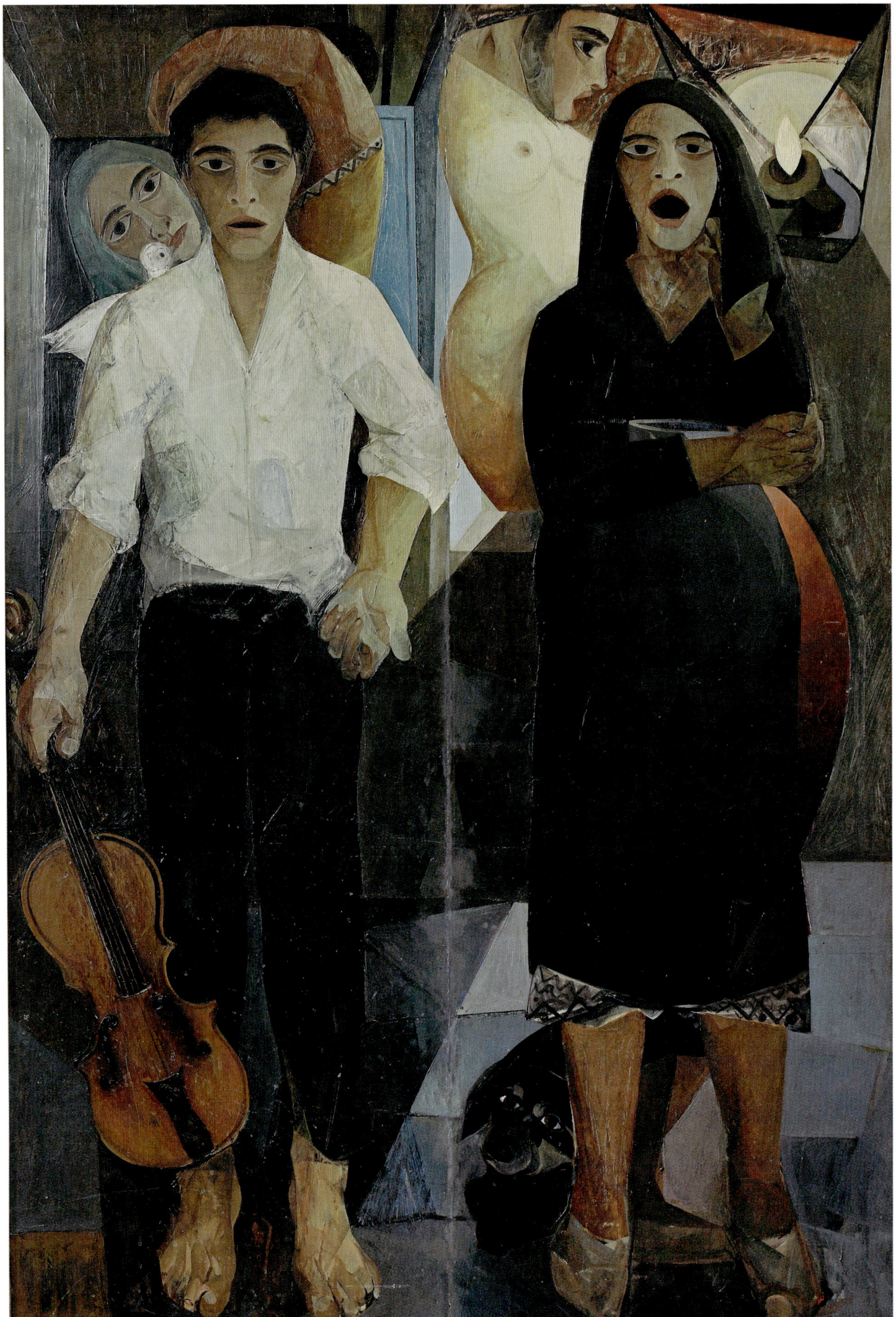

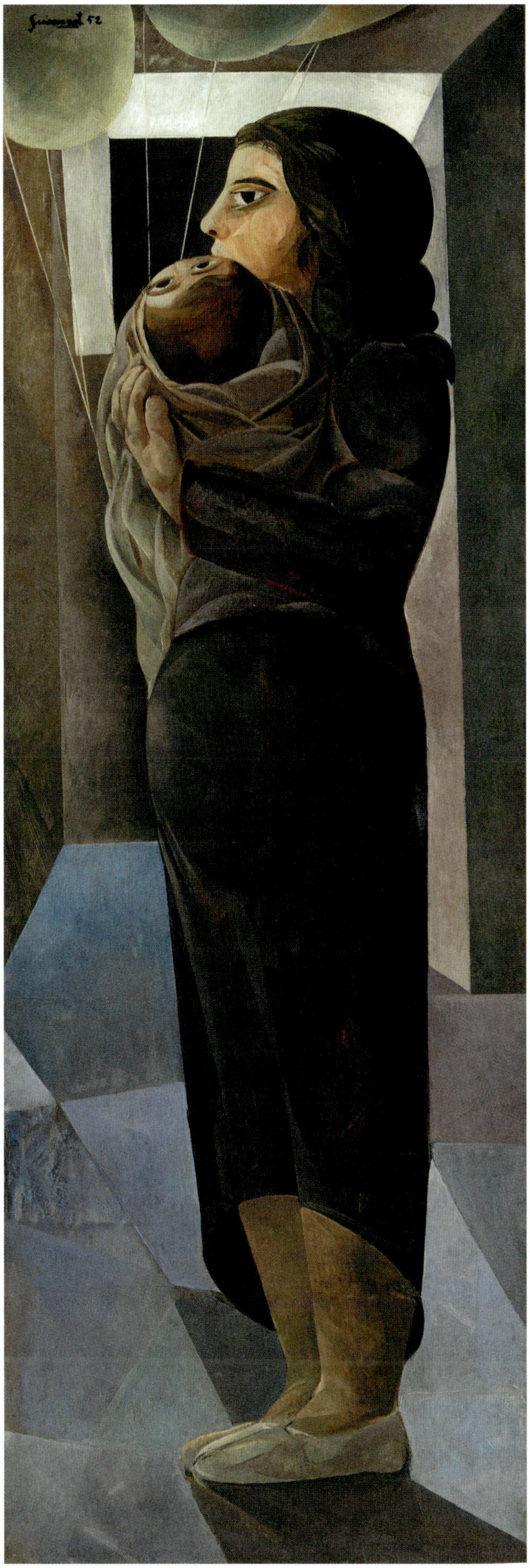

JOSEP GUINOVART
(Barcelona, 1927-2007)
Family
1951
Oil on panel
153 × 100 cm
Rodríguez-Aguilera Collection

JOSEP GUINOVART
(Barcelona, 1927-2007)
Family
1952
Oil on panel
156 × 51 cm
Bassat Collection
Fundació Privada Carmen & Luis Bassat

RAMON LLOVET
(Barcelona, 1917-1987)
Mask Sellers
1952
Oil on canvas
130 × 97 cm
Donated by the Llovet family, 2019
Museu Nacional d'Art de Catalunya

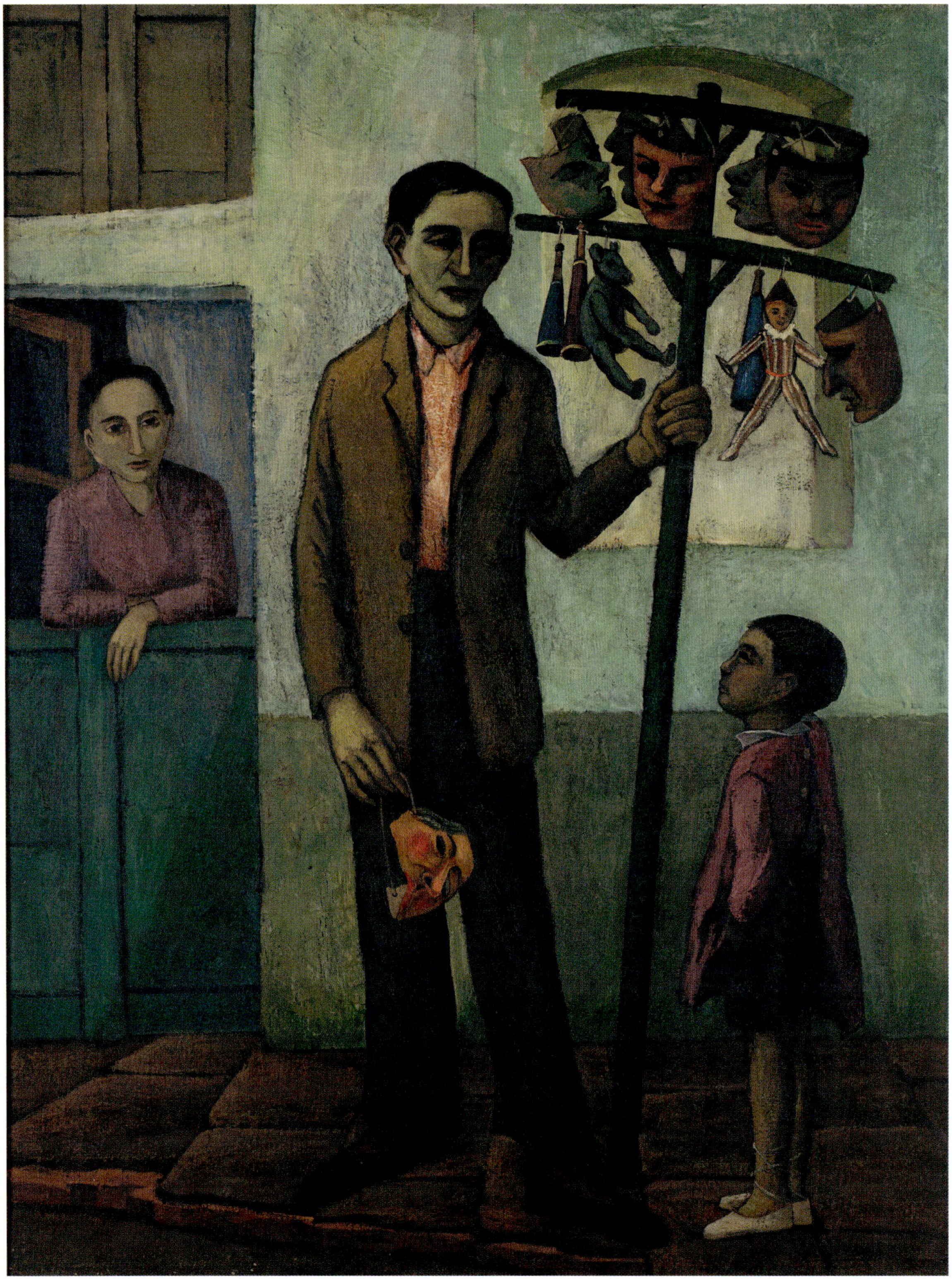

CARLOS MENSA
(Barcelona, 1936-1982)
Heads with Large Ball
1964
Oil on canvas
130 × 97 cm
Private collection

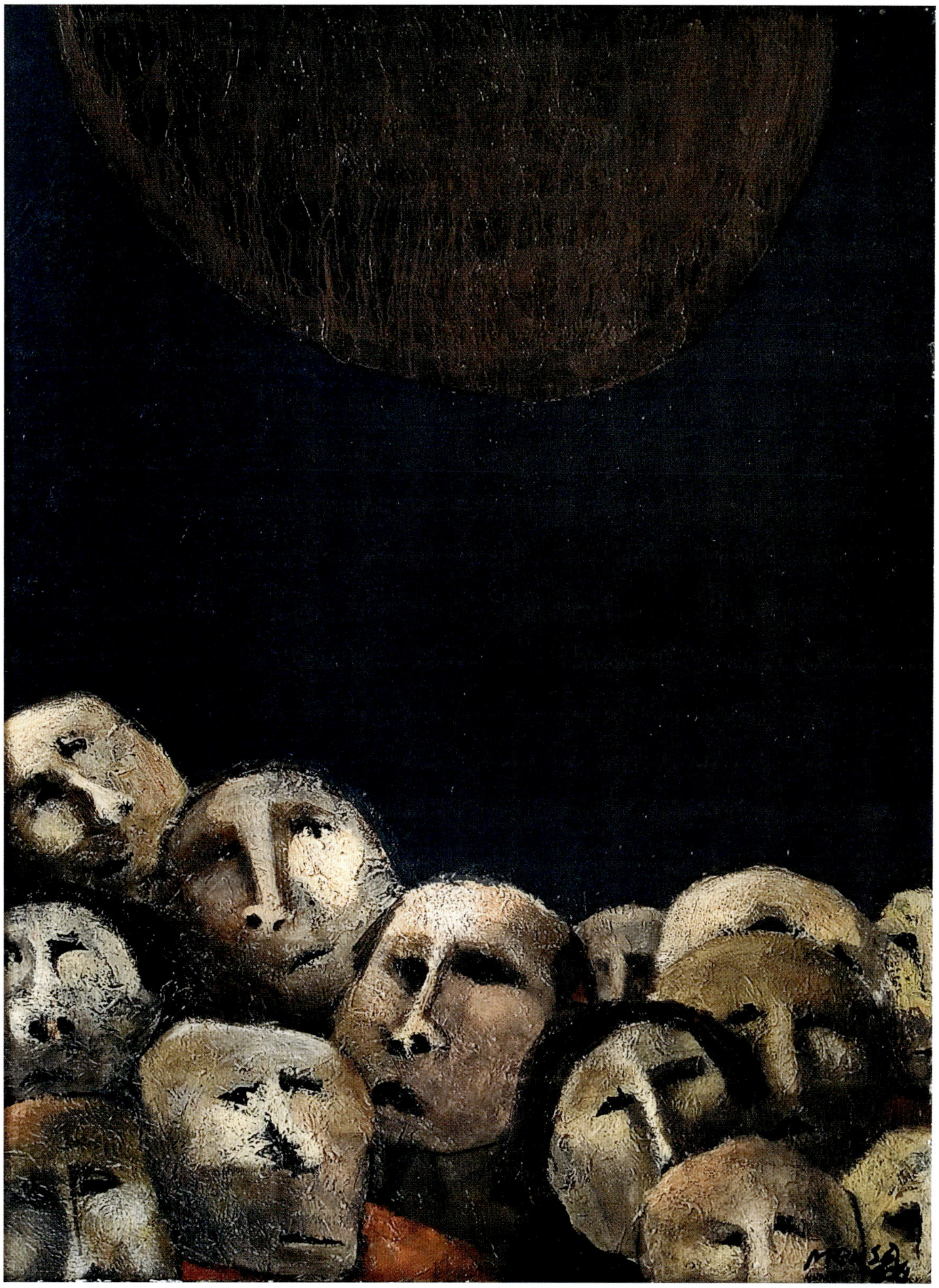

JOAN BROTAT
(Barcelona, 1920-1990)
The Passions
1954
Originally, poster with 12 *gouaches*
24 × 30.5 cm
Bassat Collection
Carmen & Luis Bassat Private Foundation

Rage	Anguish
Anger	Avarice
Love	Envy

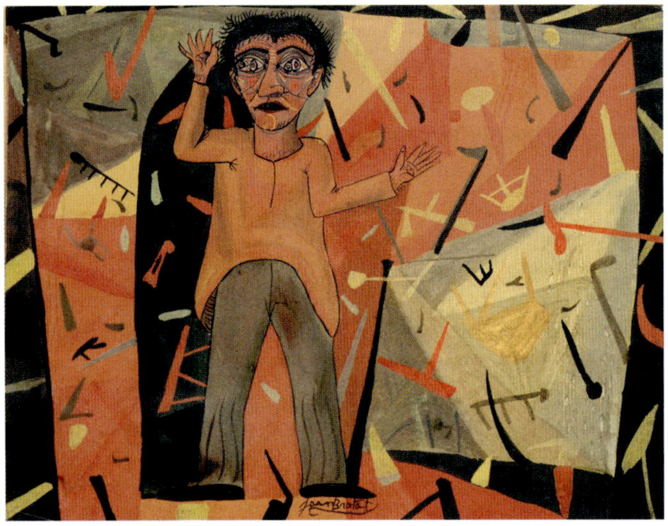

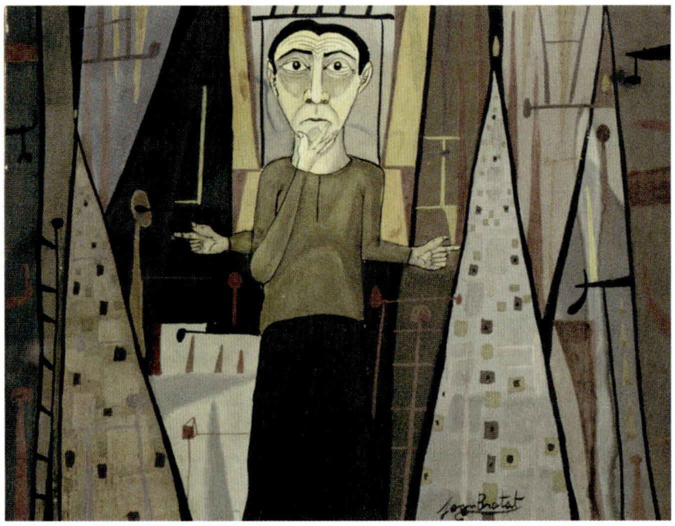

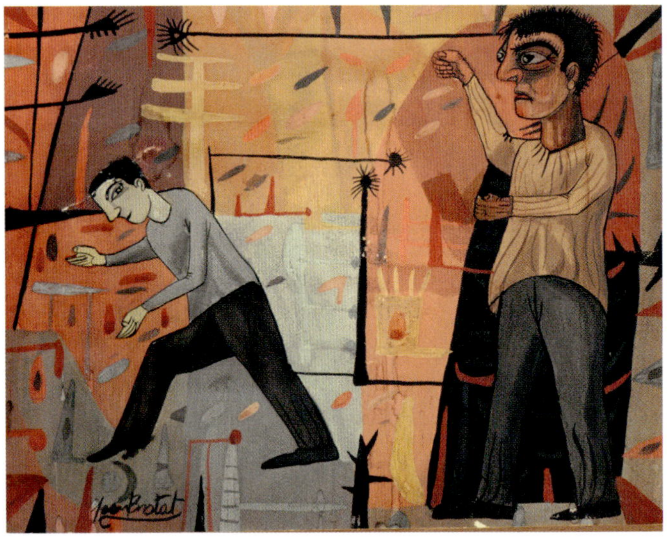

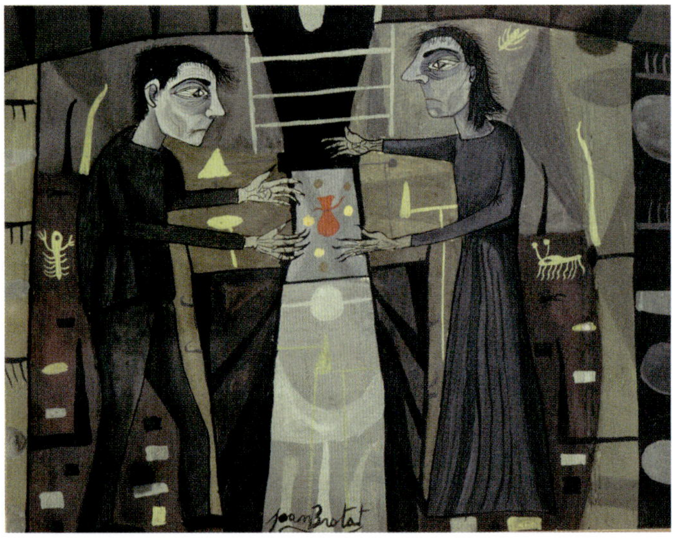

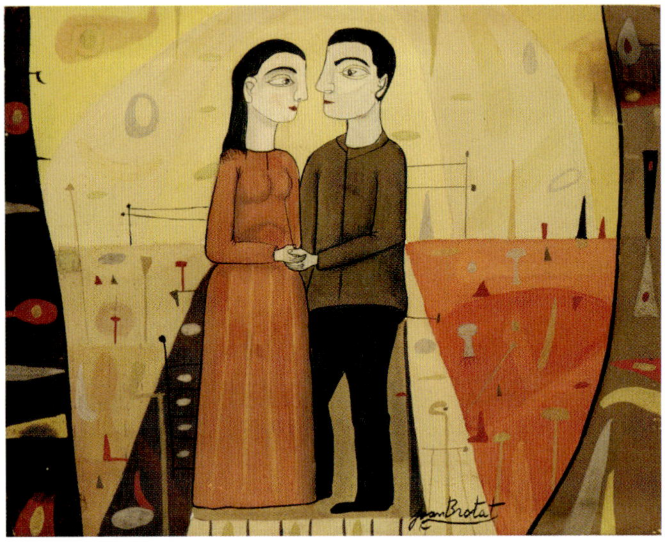

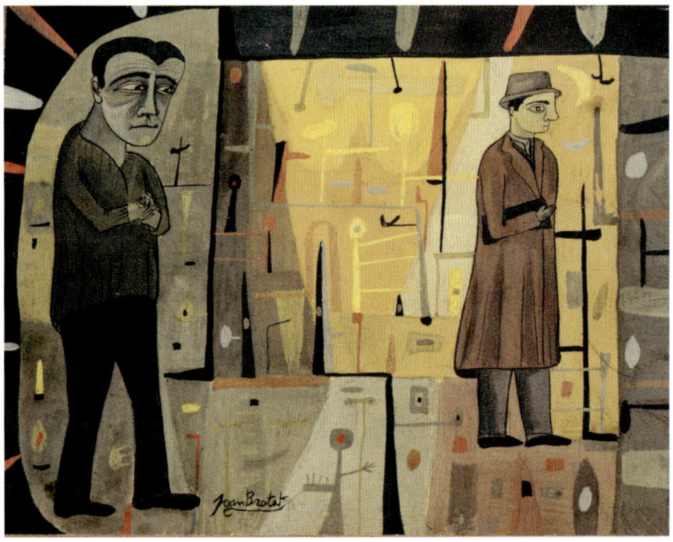

Happiness	Hate
Happiness	Jealousy
Pain	Fear

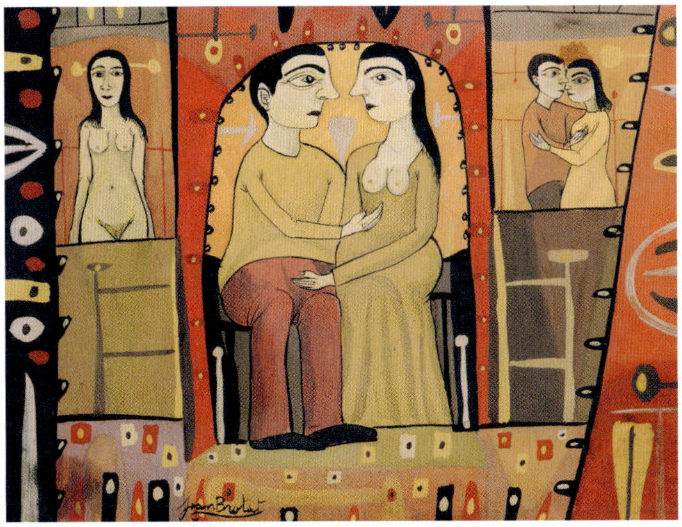

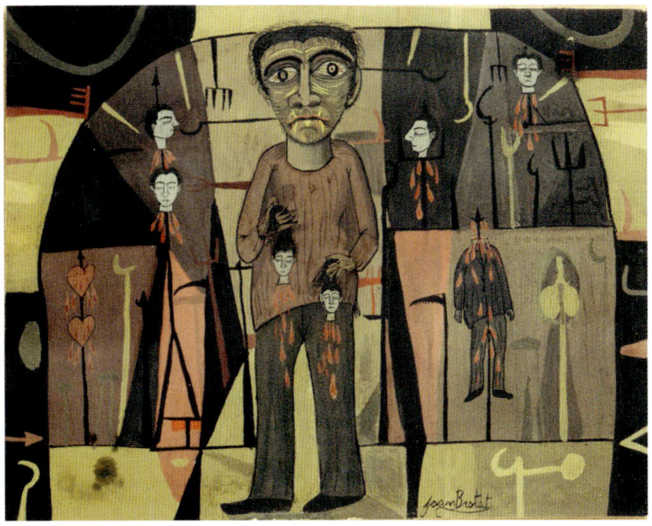

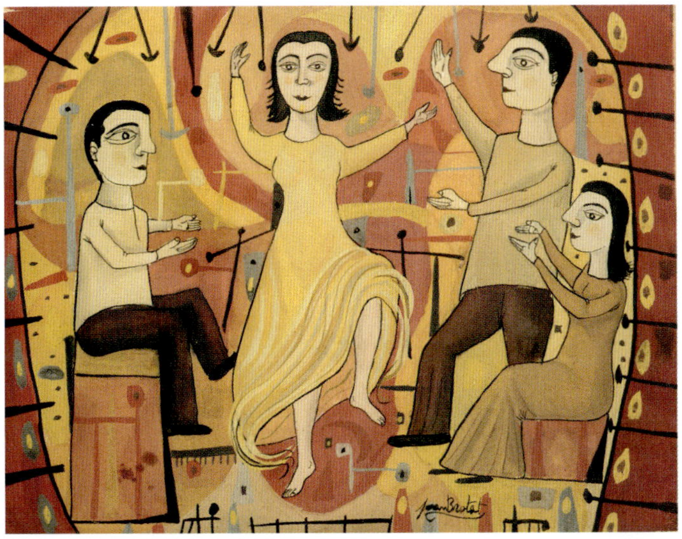

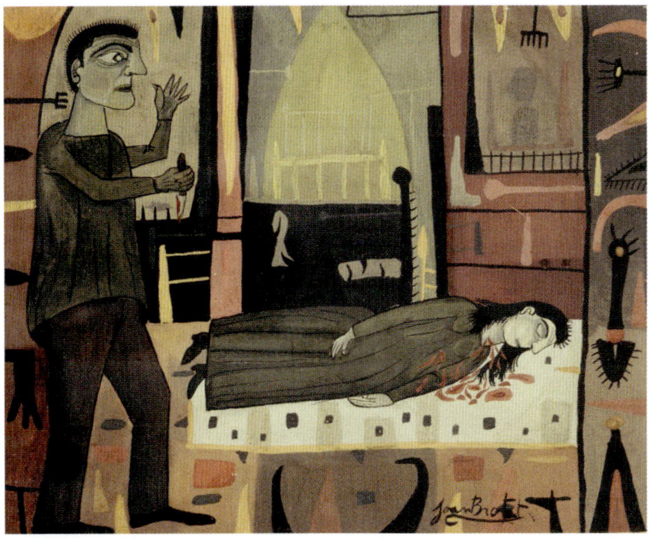

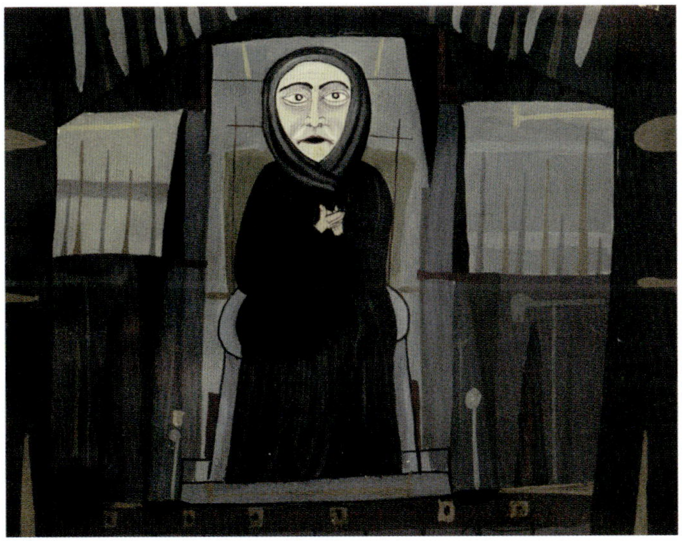

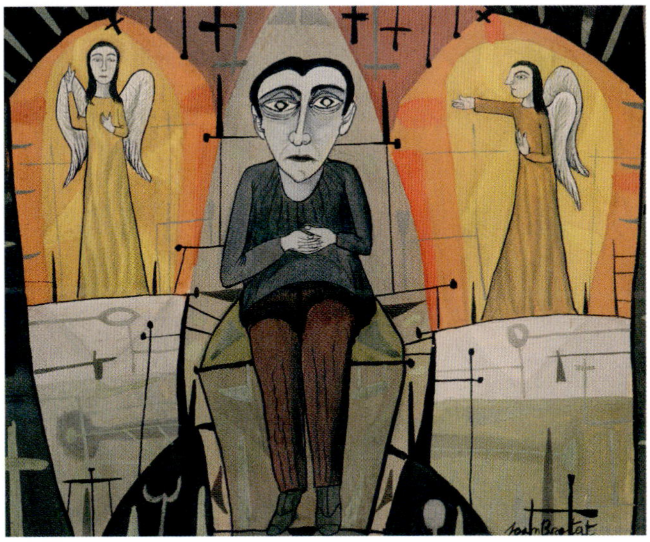

ANTONI GUANSÉ
Tortosa, 1926 – Paris, 2008)
The Station
1953
Oil on canvas
73.5 × 54.5 cm
Museu Nacional d'Art de Catalunya

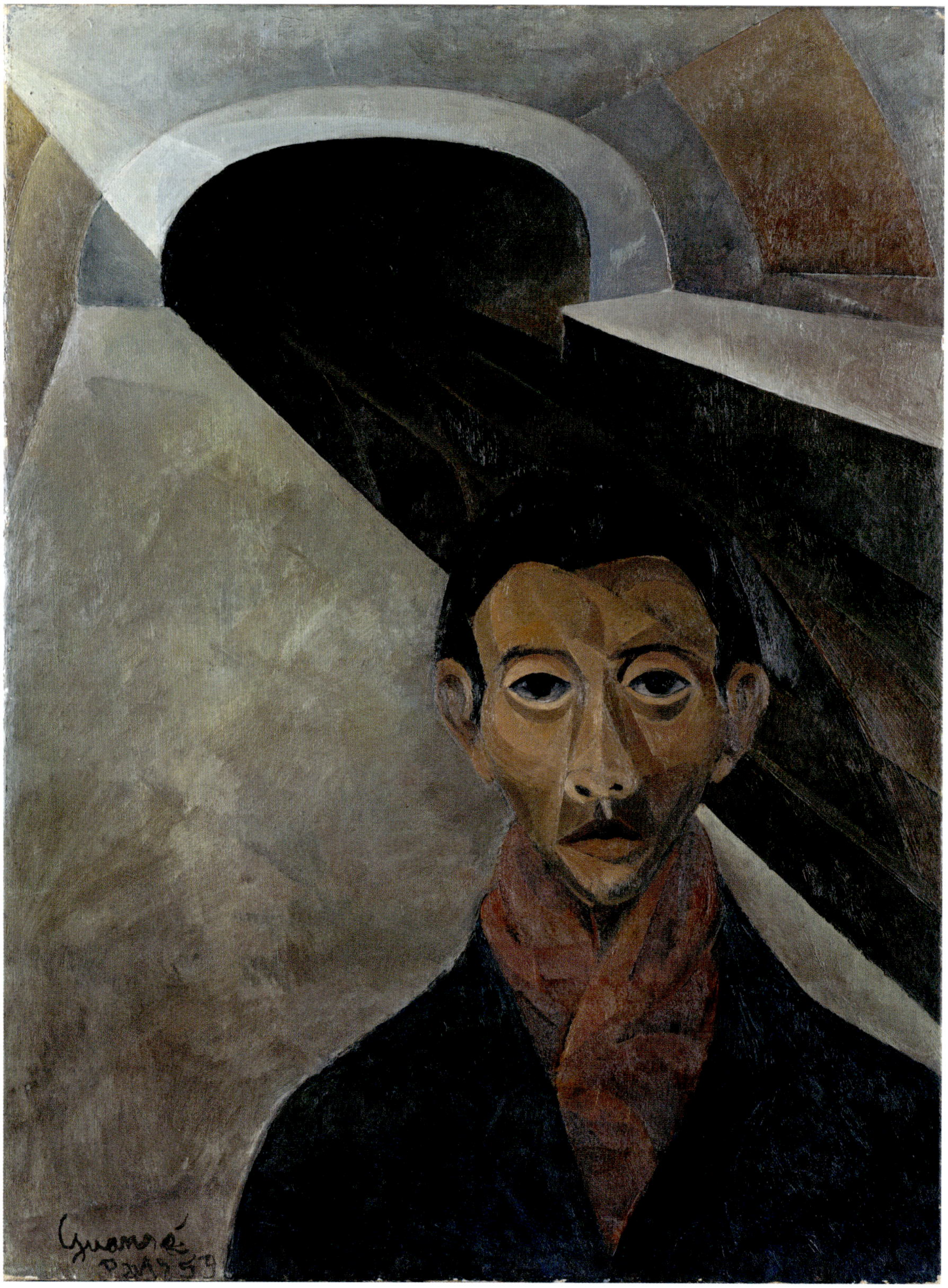

MARIA GIRONA
(Barcelona, 1923-2015)
Portrait of Isabel Garriga
1959
Oil on canvas
73.5 × 60 cm
Deposit of the Generalitat de Catalunya
Col·lecció Nacional d'Art, 2020; acquisition, 2018
Museu Nacional d'Art de Catalunya

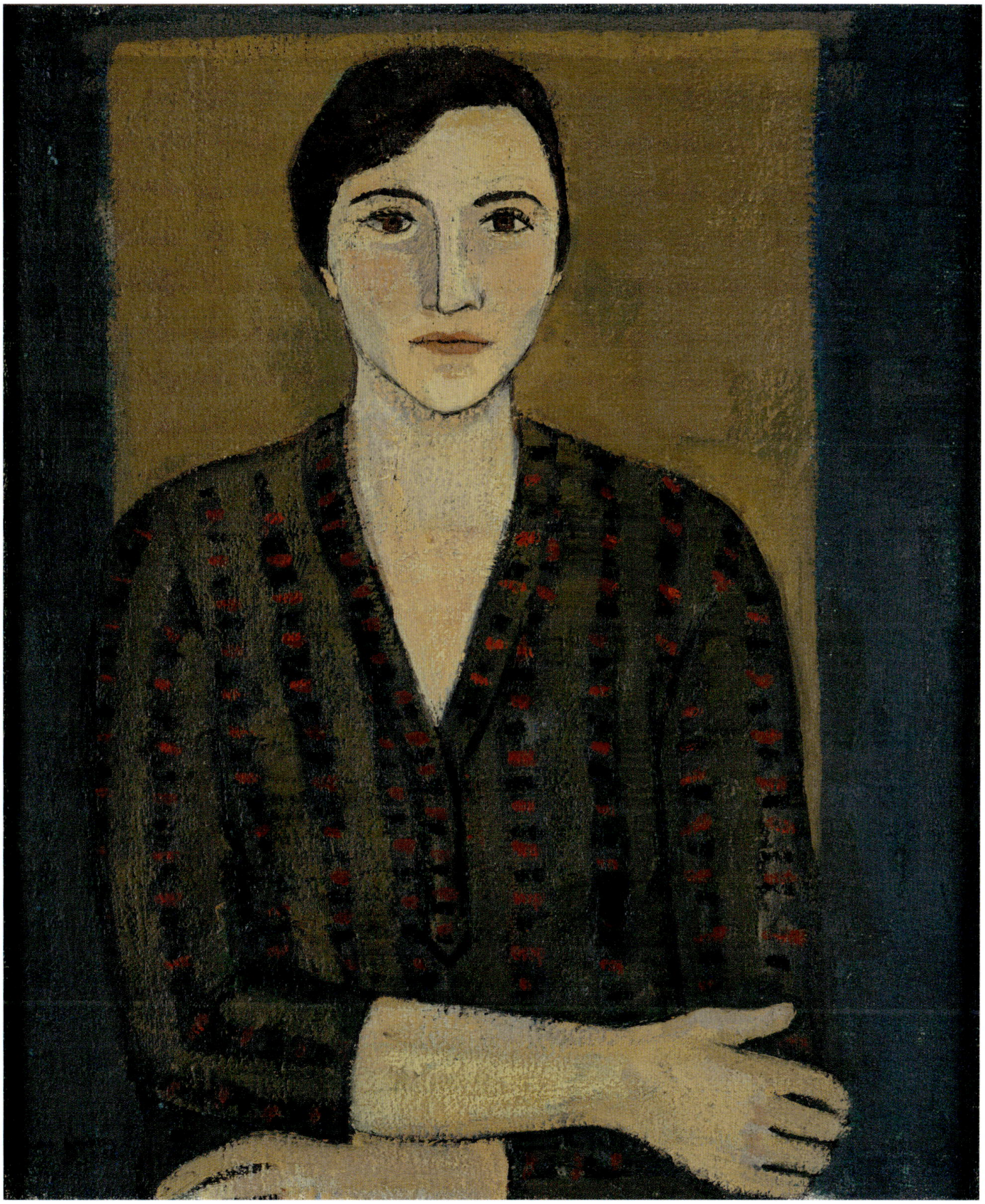

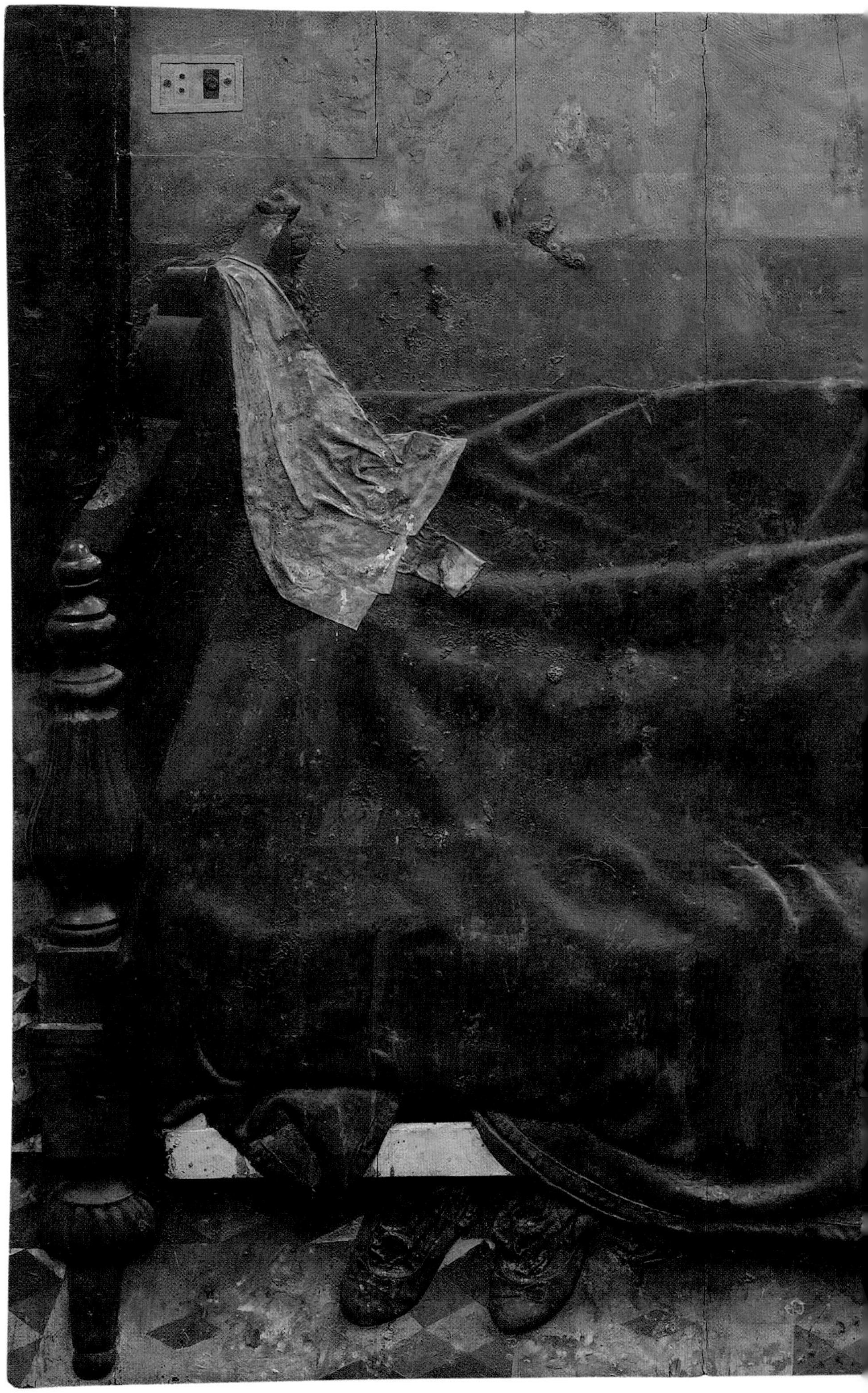

ANTONIO LÓPEZ
(Tomelloso, Ciudad Real, 1936)
Woman Sleeping (The Dream)
1963
Carving, glued, and polychromy
121 × 205 × 12 cm
Museo Nacional Centro de Arte Reina Sofía

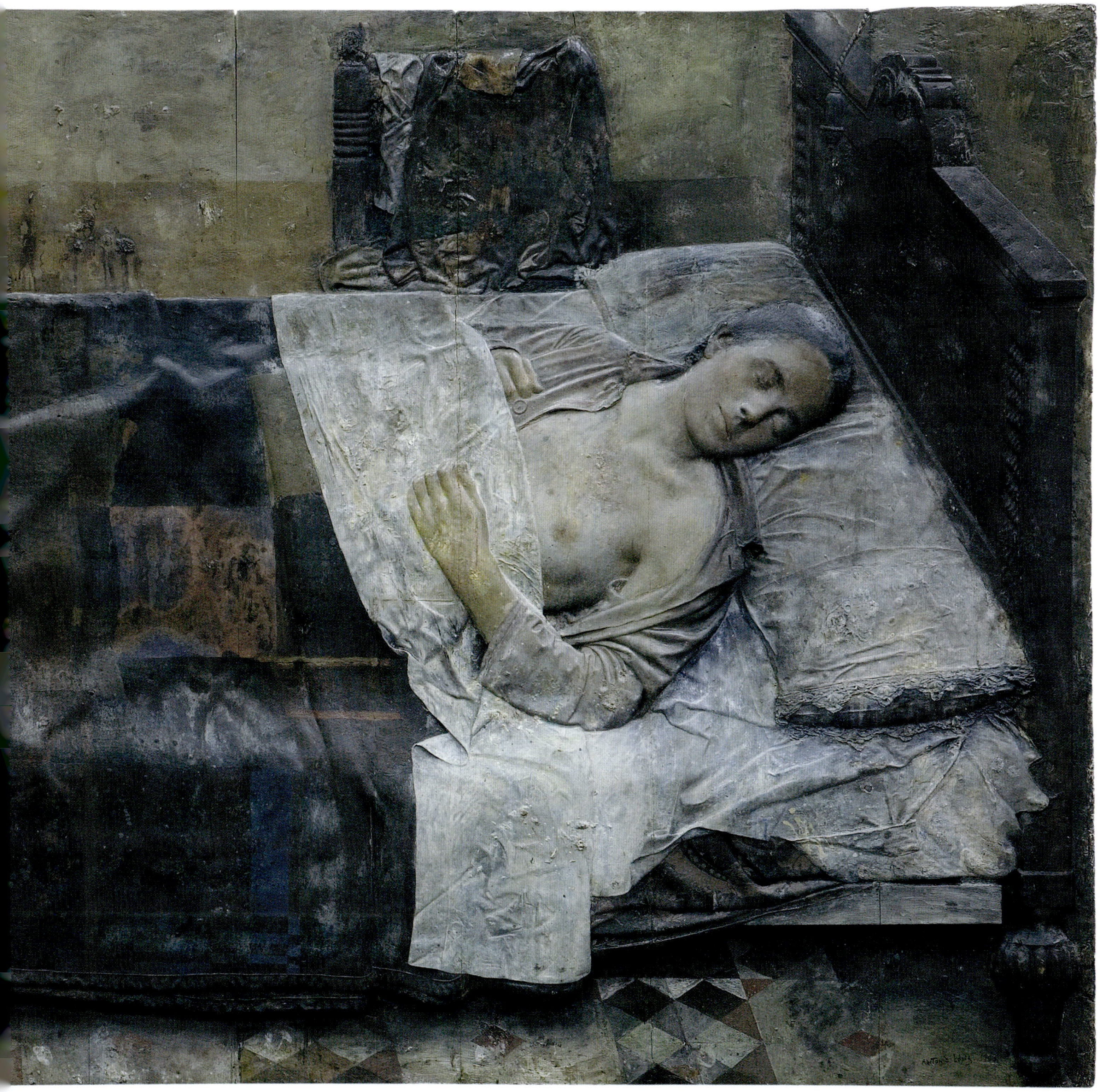

JOAN COLOM
(Barcelona, 1921-2017)
Barrio Chino, Barcelona
1960
Gelatin silver on baryta paper
57,58 × 47,4 cm
Collection of the Agrupació Fotogràfica de Catalunya, 2003
Museu Nacional d'Art de Catalunya

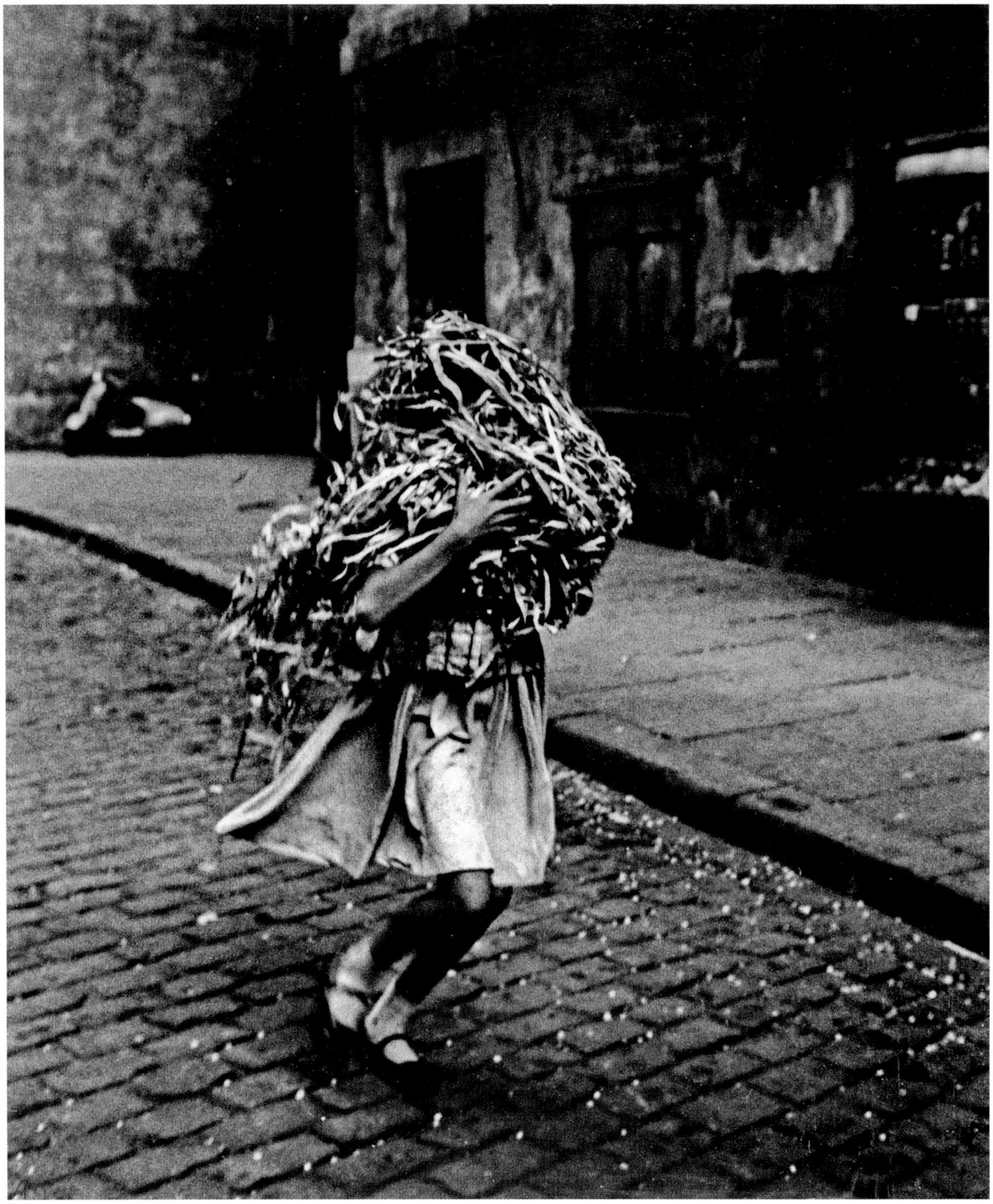

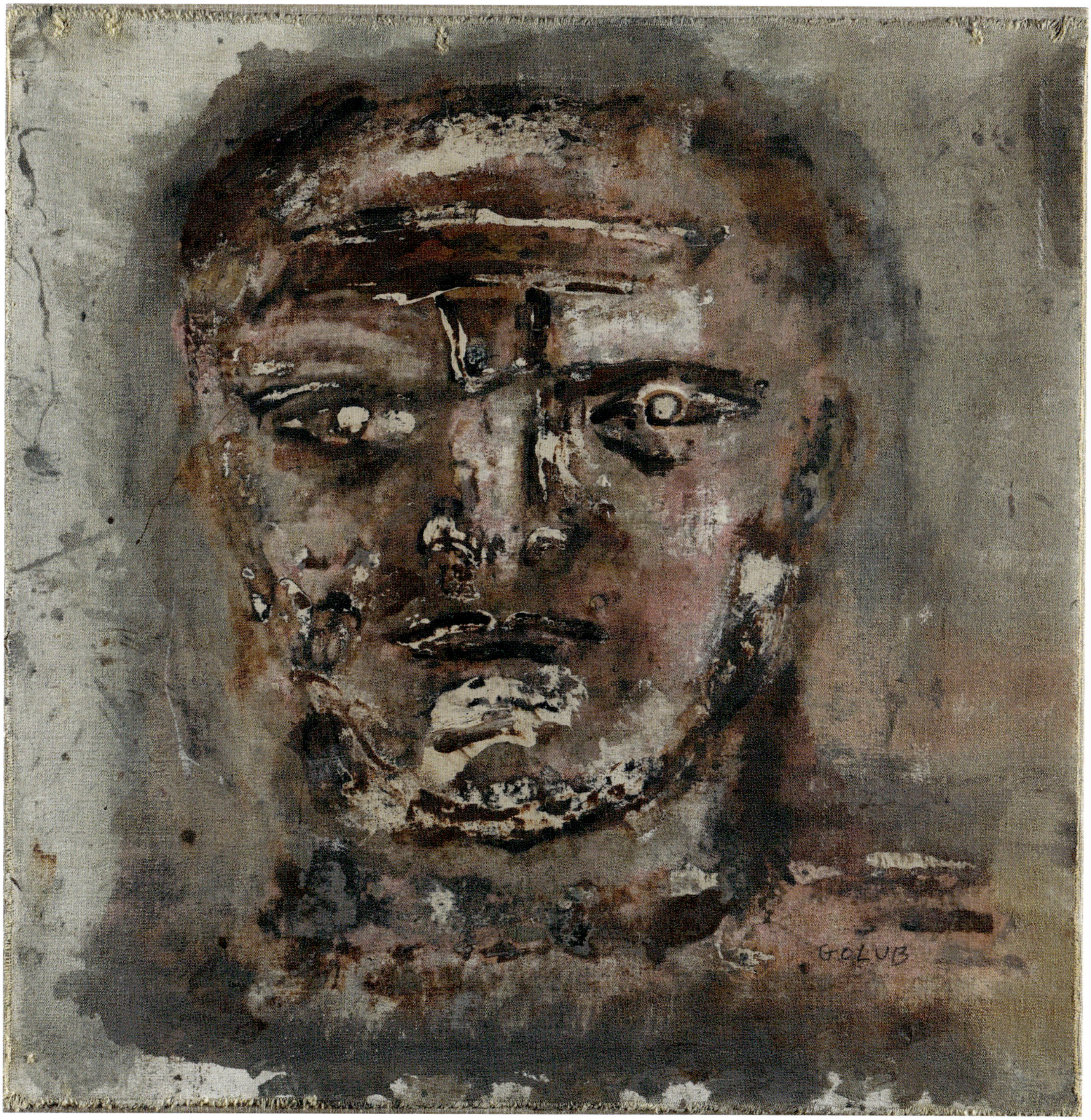

LEON GOLUB
(Chicago, 1922 – New York, 2004)
Untitled
1962
Oil on canvas
57 × 56 cm
Private collection, Palermo

NORMAN NAROTZKY
(New York, 1928)
The Philosopher
1961
Oil on canvas
162 × 162 cm
The artist's collection, Barcelona

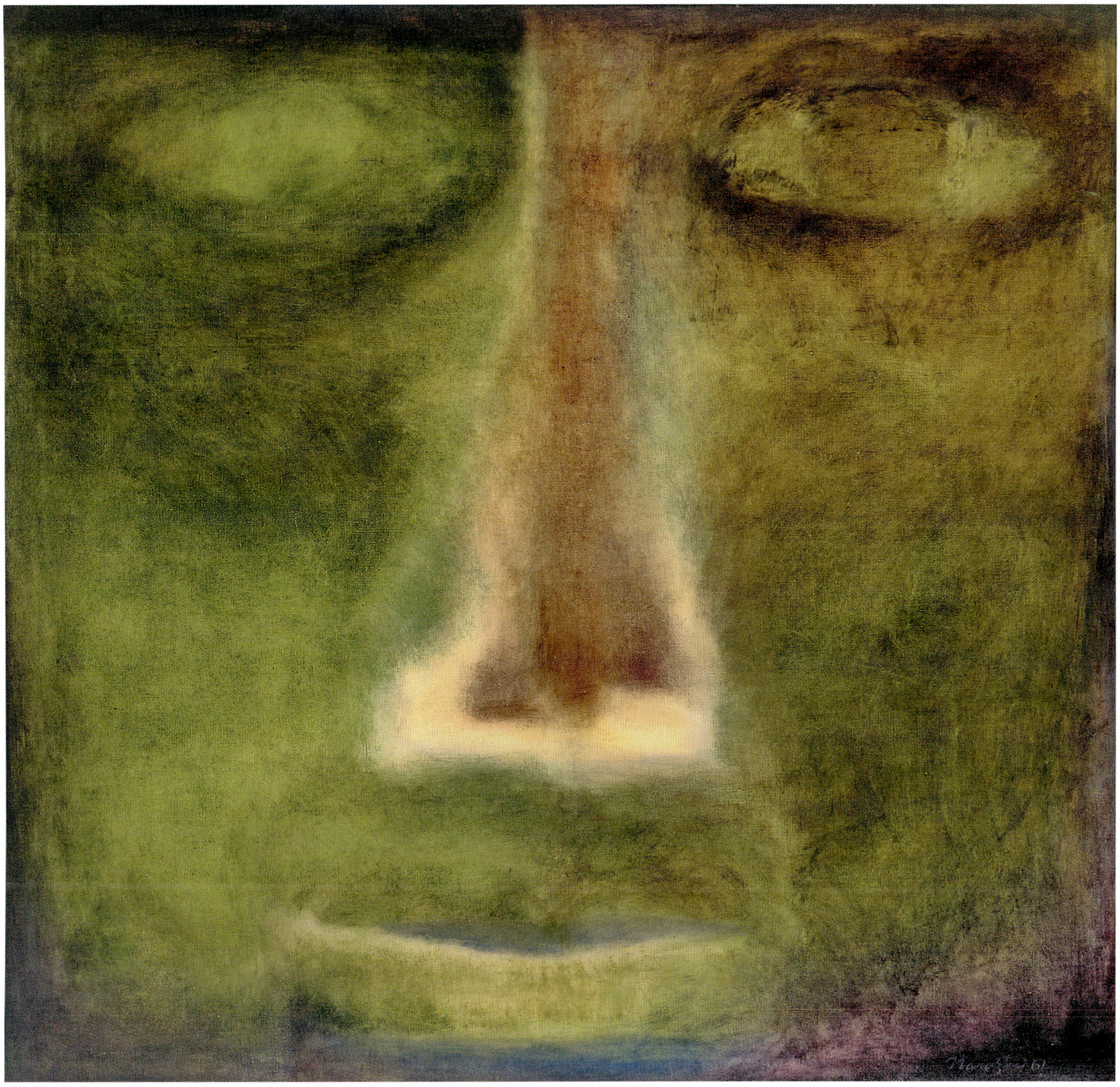

The idea of reviving a humanity oriented towards happiness, harmony and justice was not abandoned, but this could not be achieve through stereotypes of progress. Radical avant-garde artists such as Miró, as well as other, more marginal practitioners, suggested the possibility of a poetic optimism based on vigorous, archaic primitivism. This is the evocation of a new innocence. By reconstructing of an optimism that stems not from politics but from the survival instinct, maternity can appear as a metaphor for vitality.

FROM PRIMITIVE NOSTALGIA TO HOPE

ANTONI TÀPIES
(Barcelona, 1923-2012)
Man
1945
Oil on canvas
54.5 × 45 cm
Private collection, Barcelona

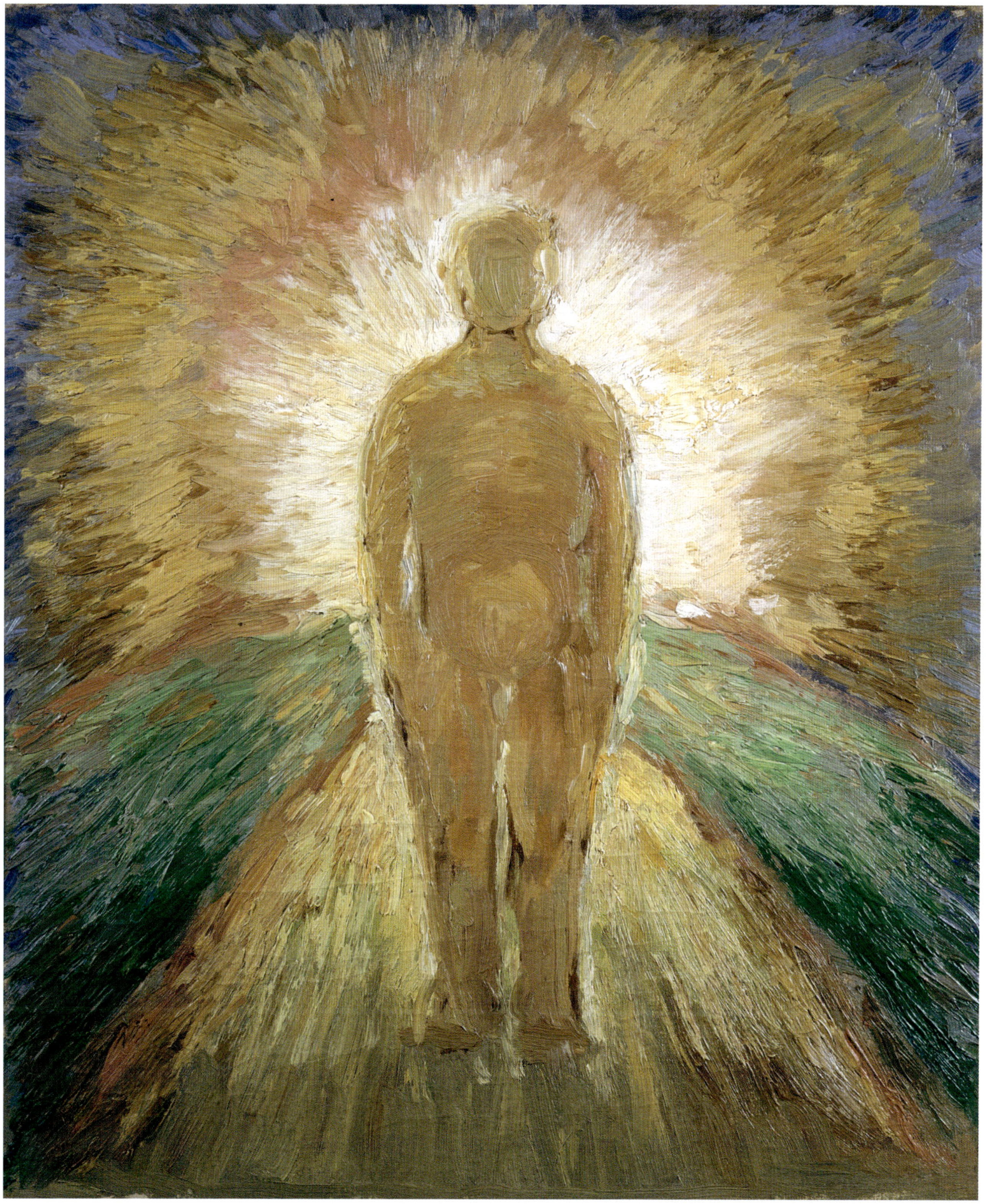

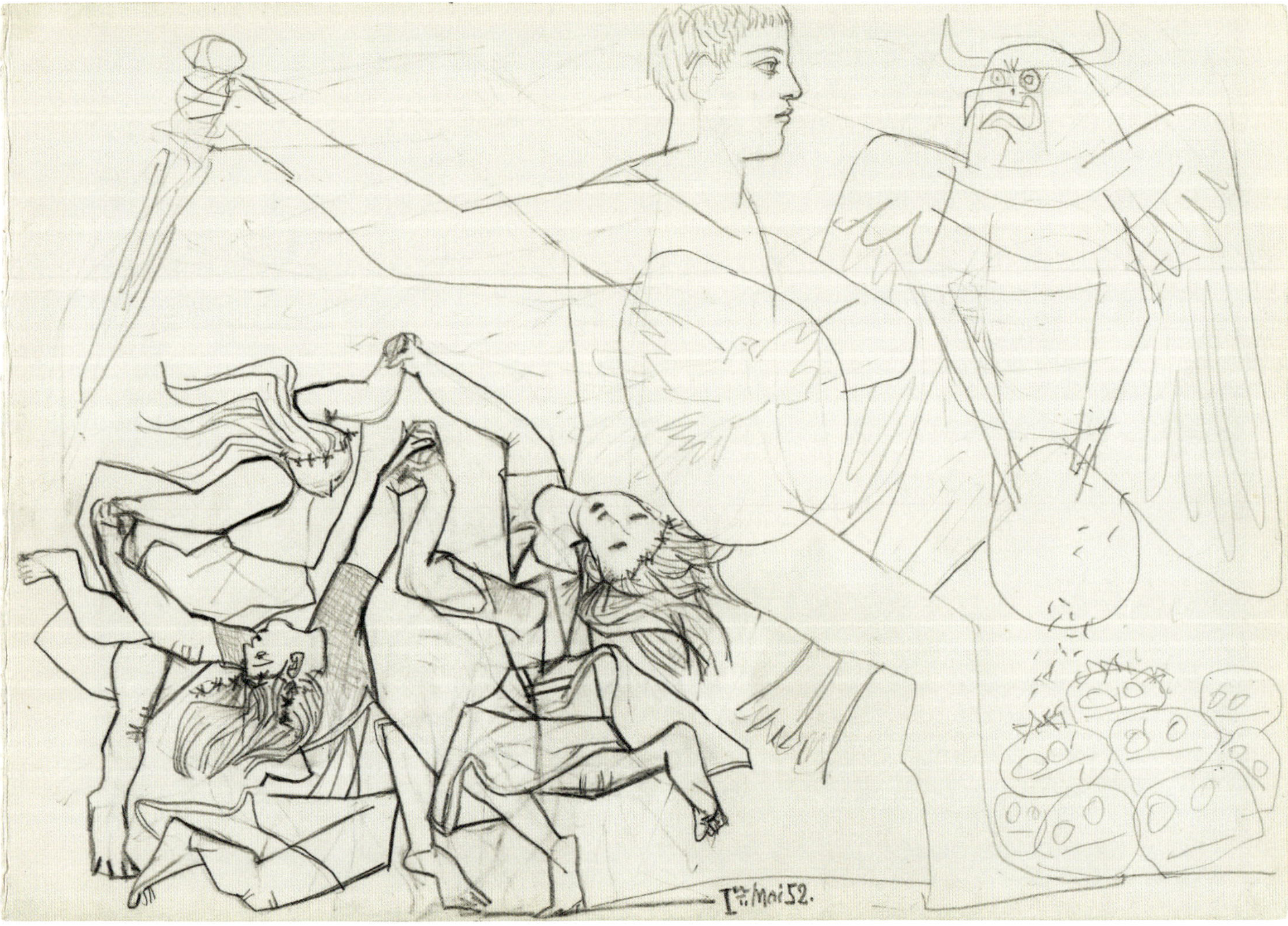

PABLO PICASSO
(Málaga, 1881 – Mougins, France, 1973)
Study for War and Peace, 1 May 1952
1952
Graphite pencil on paper
25.4 × 35.4 cm
Musée national Picasso-Paris Dation Pablo Picasso, 1979
MP1409

LUCIEN HERVÉ
(Hódmezővásárhely, Hungary, 1910 – Paris, 2007)
L'Unité d'habitation à Marseille. Le Corbusier beside a panel from the Modulor
1946-1952
Modern copy, 2023
Getty Research Institute, Los Angeles (2002.R.41)

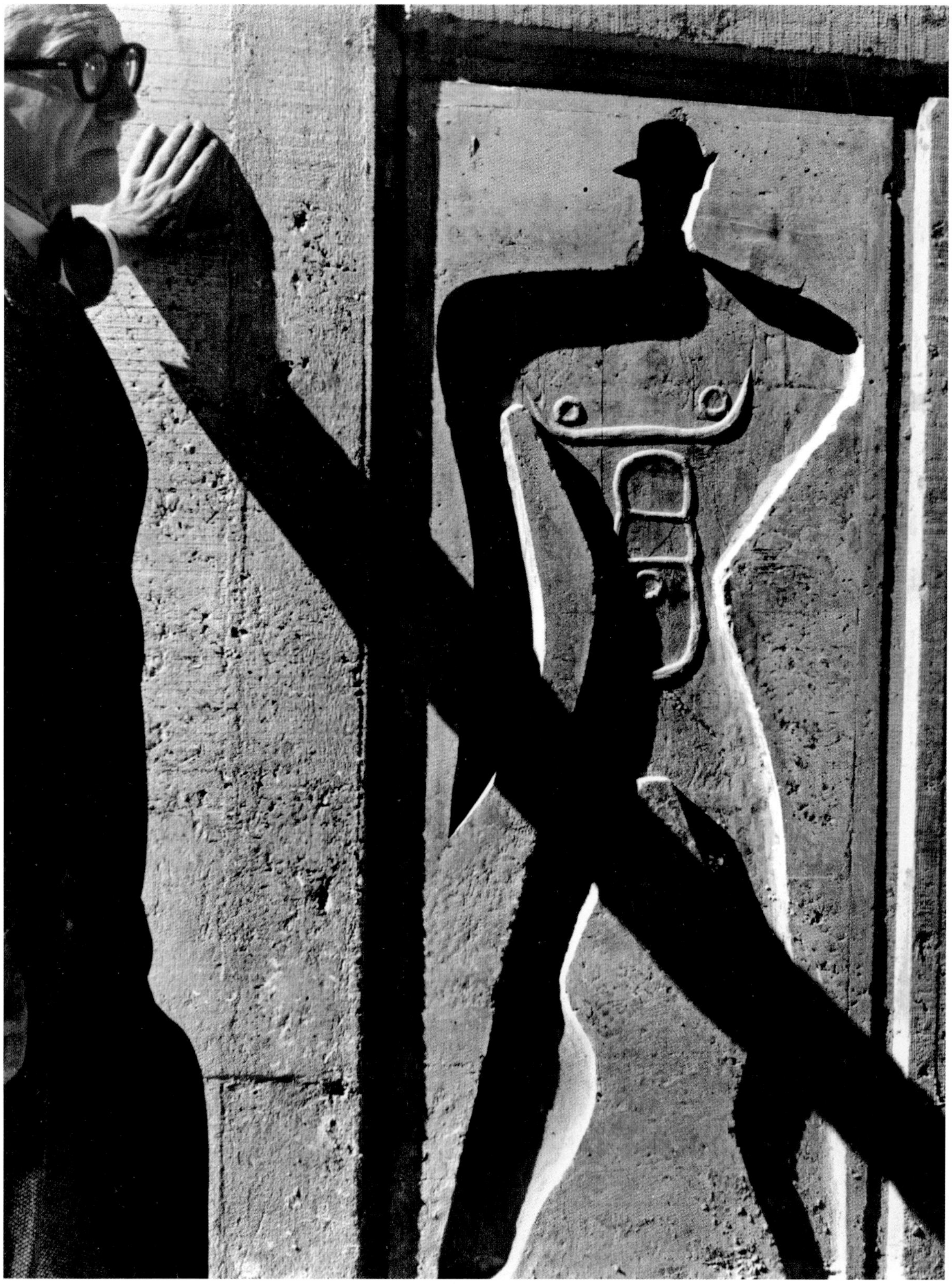

JOAN MIRÓ
Barcelona, 1893 – Palma de Mallorca, 1983)
The Morning Star
1946
Oil on canvas
146 × 114 cm
Fundació Joan Miró, Barcelona
On loan from a private collection

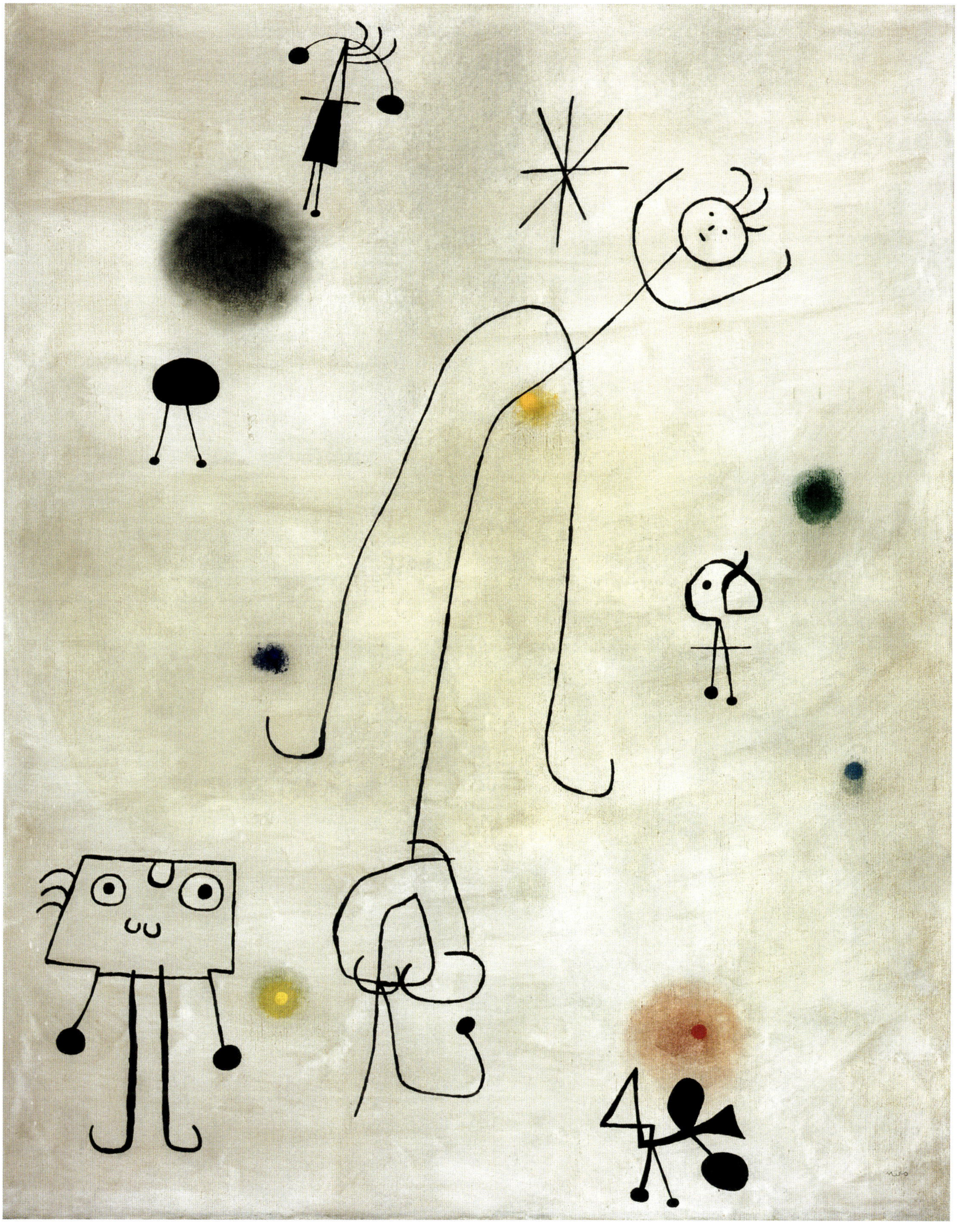

KAREL APPEL
(Amsterdam, 1921 – Zurich, 2006)
Boy with Ball
1950
Oil on canvas
98.5 x 58.5 cm
Galleria Nazionale d'Arte Moderna
e Contemporanea, Rome

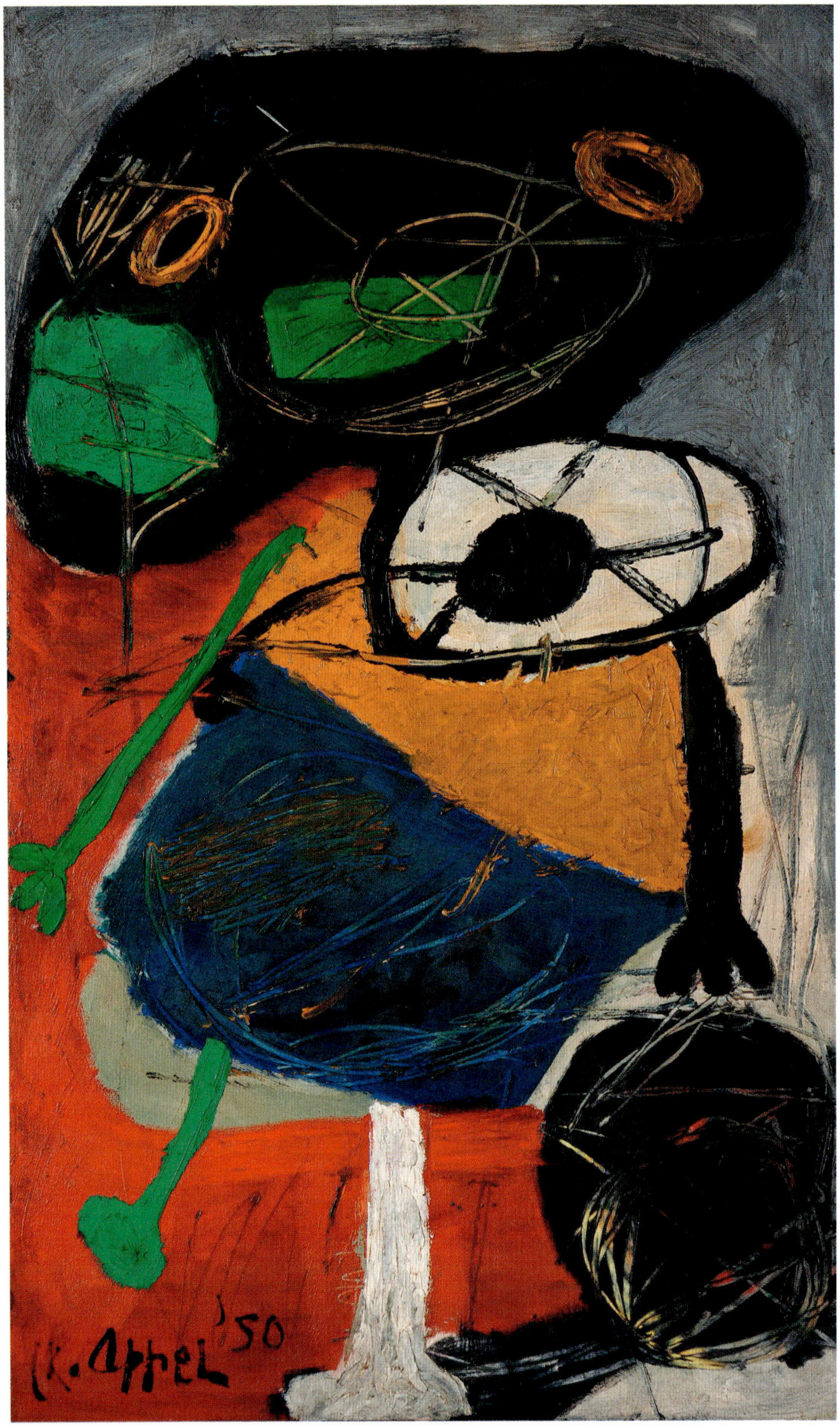

ROGER BISSIÈRE
(Villeréal, France, 1886 – Marminhac, France, 1964)
Pastoral (Composition 130 b)
1946
Oil on canvas
100 × 65 cm
Artist donation, 1959
Centre Pompidou, Paris
Musée national d'art moderne-Centre de création industrielle

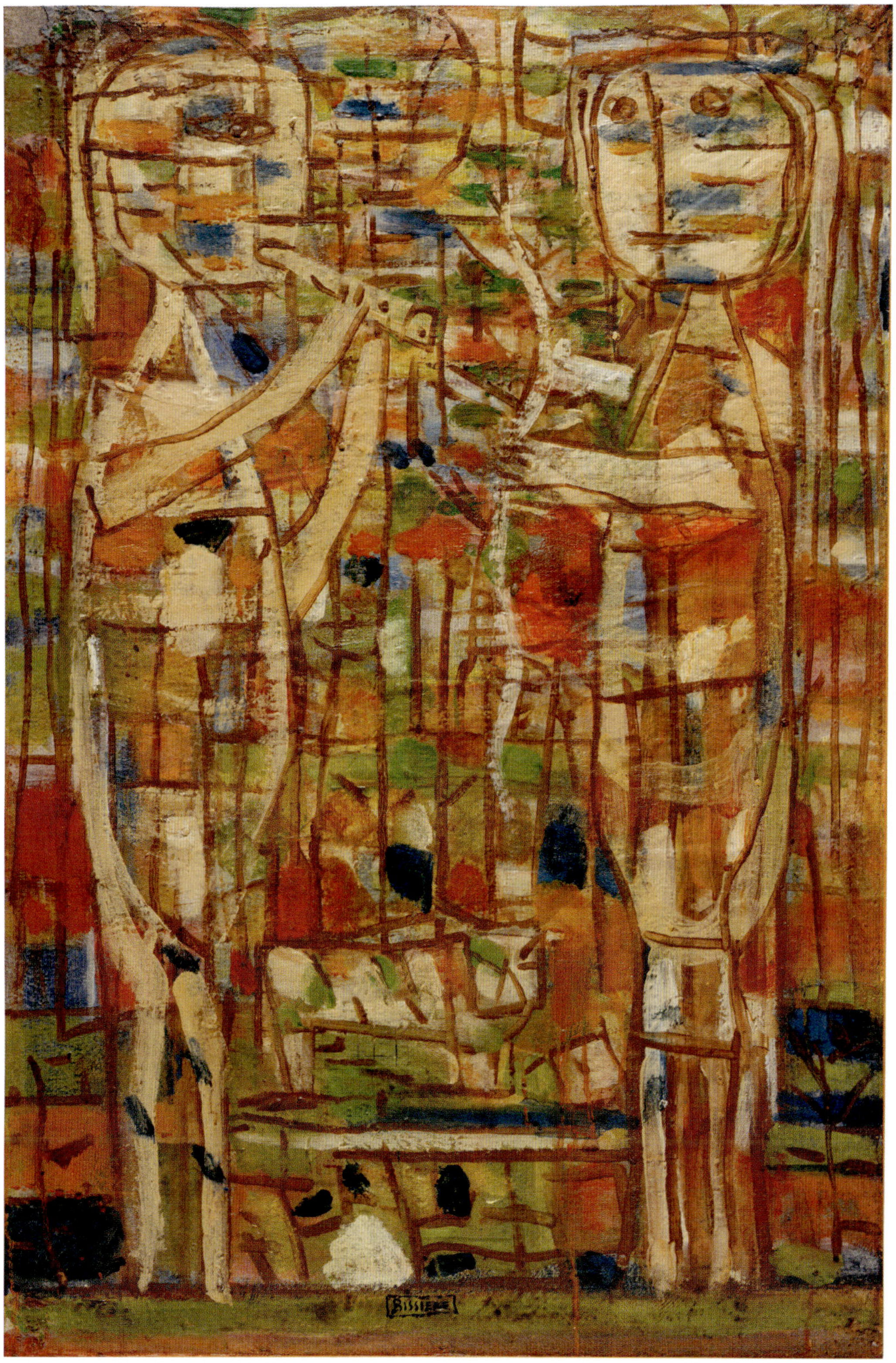

JOSEP MARIA GARCIA-LLORT
(Barcelona, 1921-2003)
The Prayer
1951-1952
Oil on panel
63 × 52 cm
Garcia-Llort Family

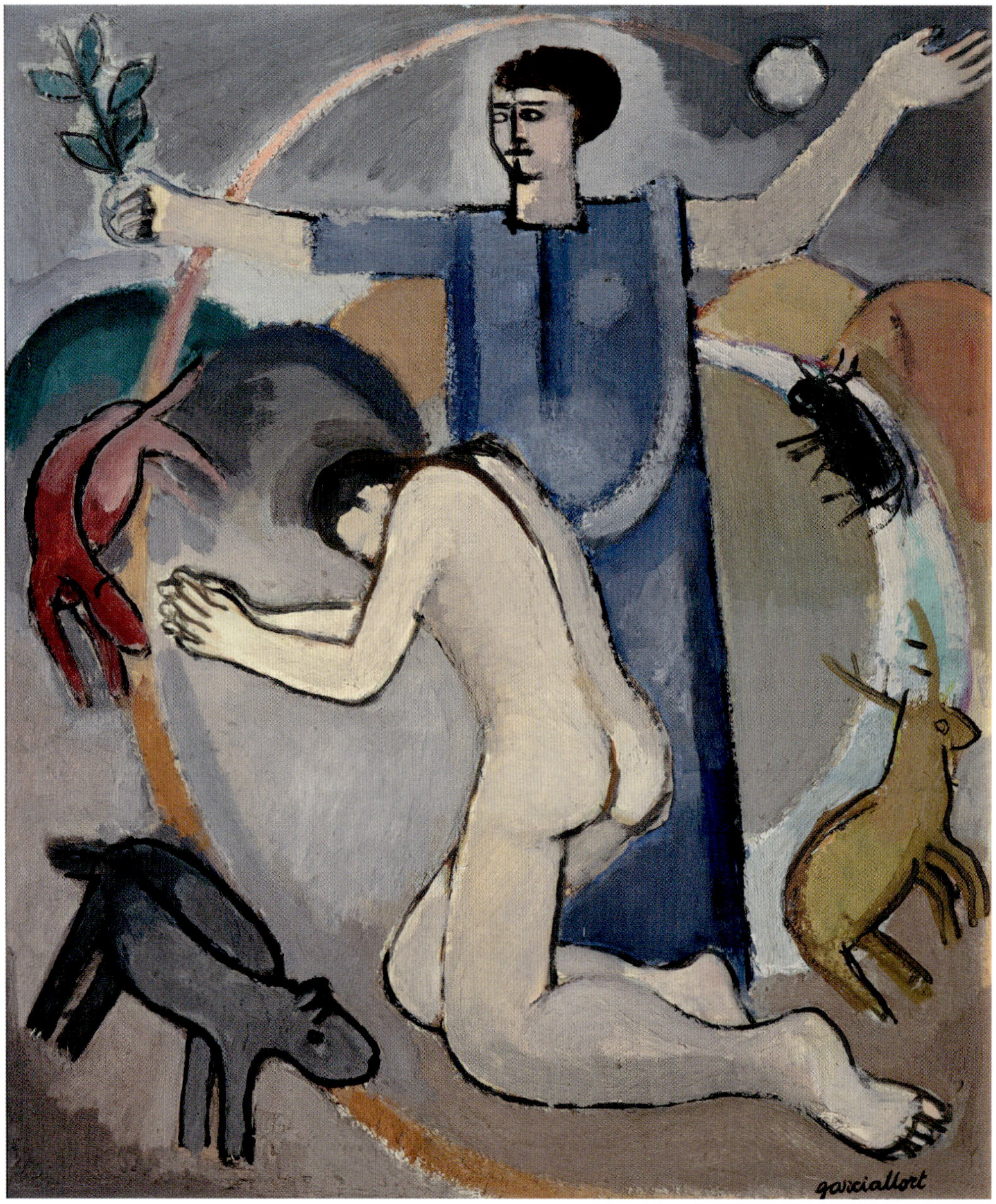

LAURENT JIMÉNEZ-BALAGUER
(Hospitalet de Llobregat, 1928 – Boulogne-Billancourt, France, 2015)
Untitled
c. 1953
Oil on canvas
164 × 142 cm
Donated by Valérie Jiménez, 2023
Museu Nacional d'Art de Catalunya

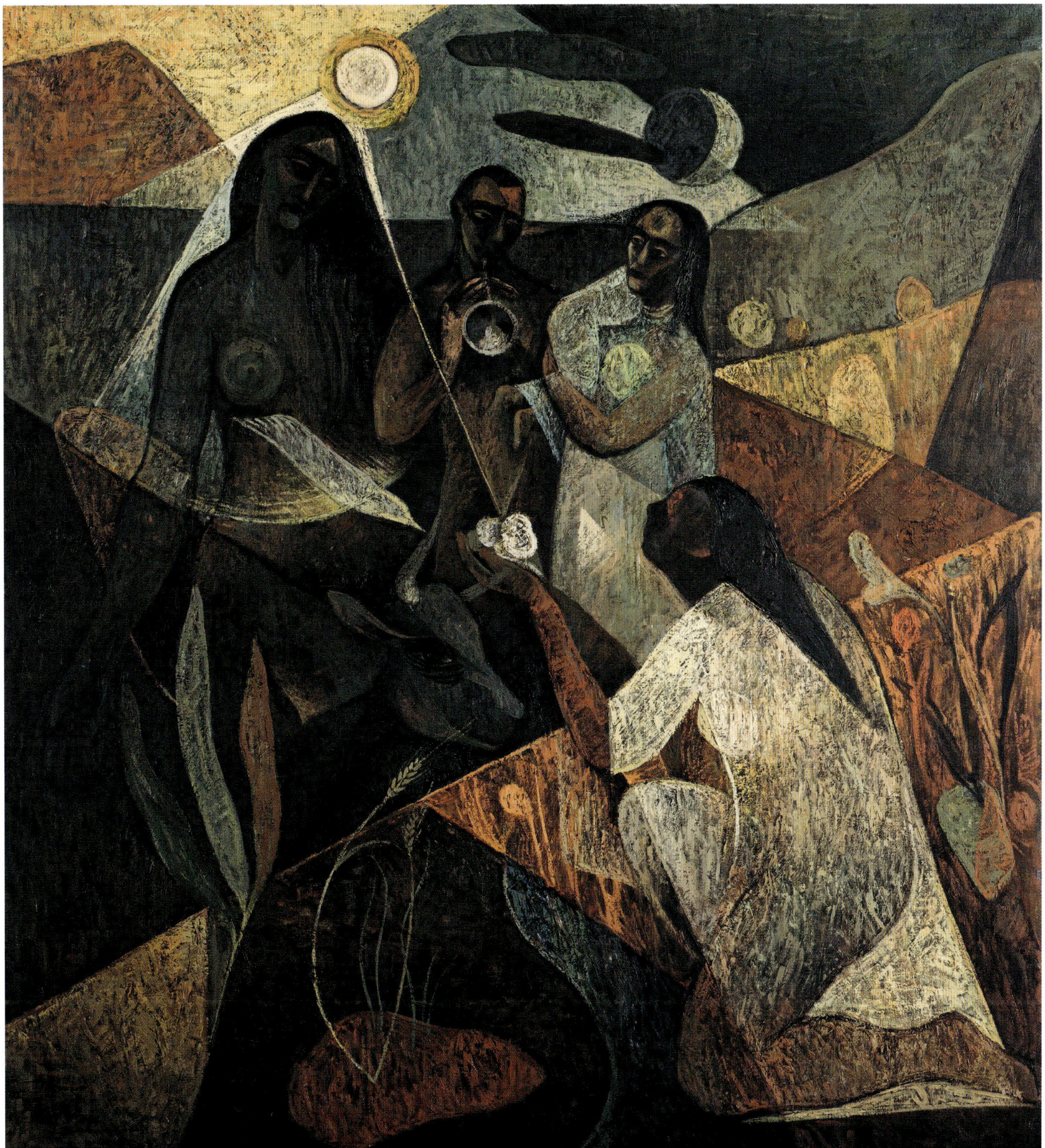

JOAN BROTAT
(Barcelona, 1920-1990)
Lion Hunters
1955
Oil on canvas
60 × 73 cm
Rodríguez-Aguilera Collection

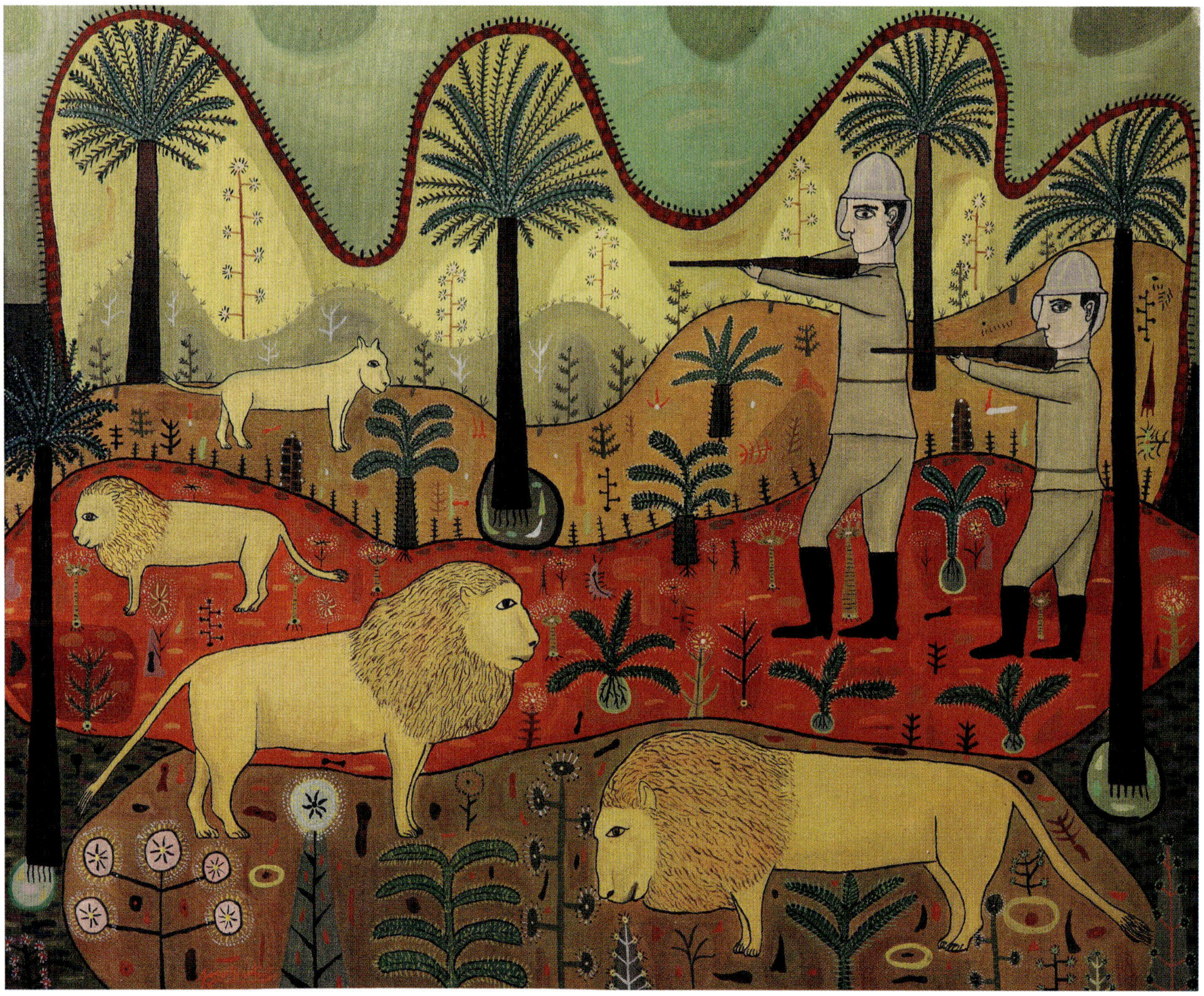

MANUEL GIL
(Valencia, 1925-1957)
Paradise
1955
Mixed technique on canvas
109 × 150 cm
Fundación Bancaja Collection

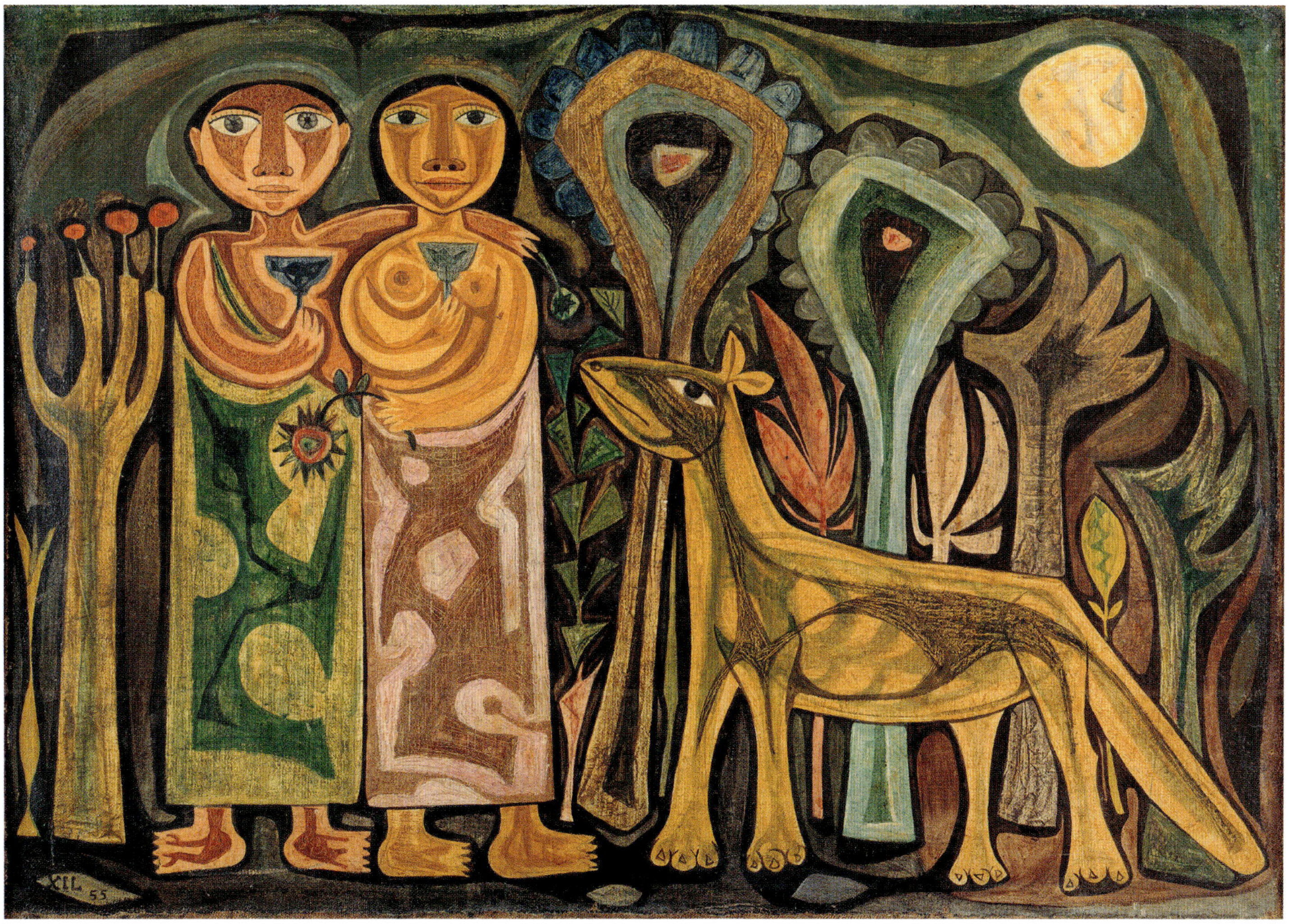

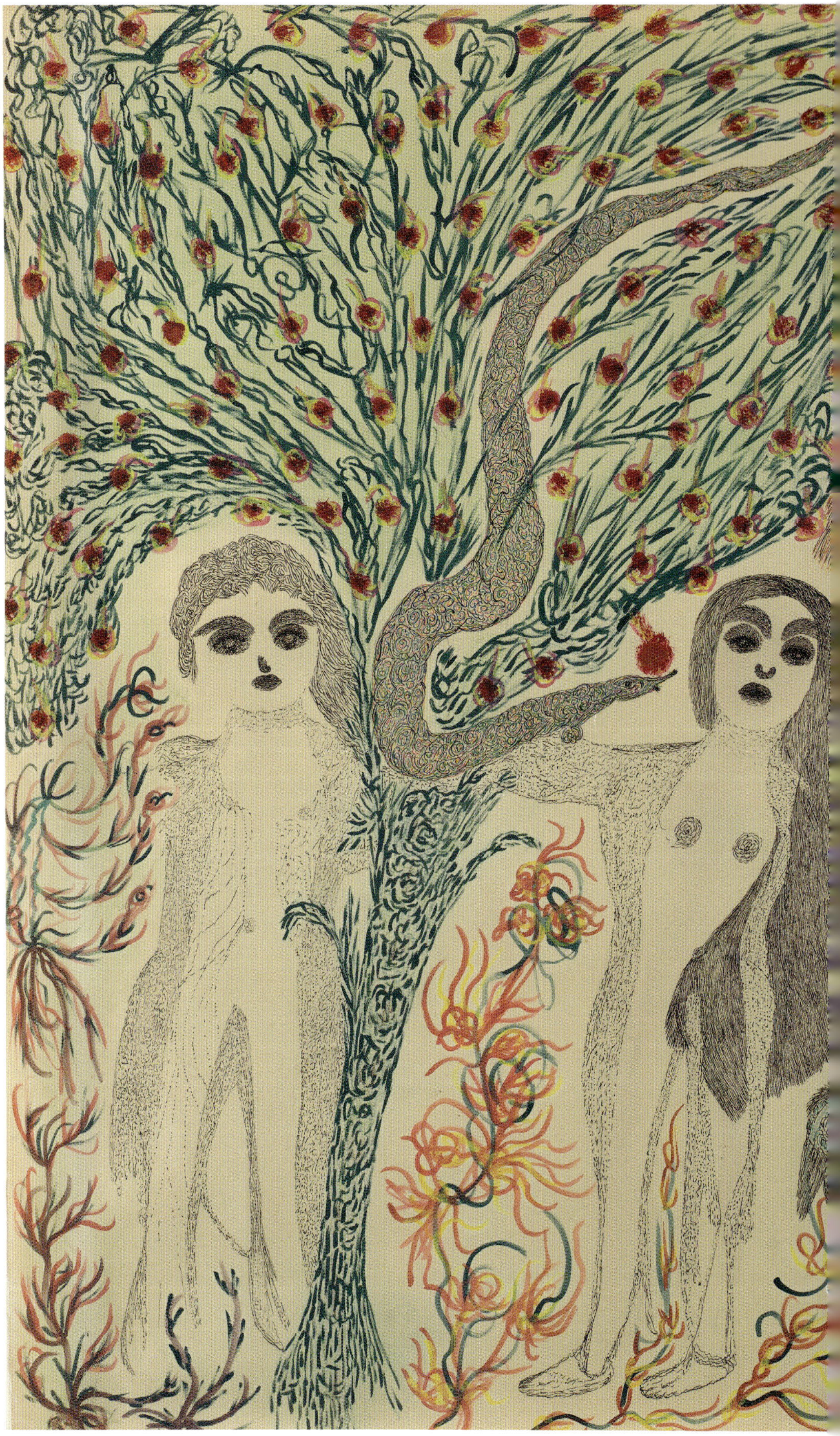

JOSEFA TOLRÀ
Cabrils, 1880-1959)
Adam and Eve
1957
Watercolour, black ink, felt-tip pens
and gouache on card
67.5 × 100.6 cm
Museo Nacional del Prado, Madrid

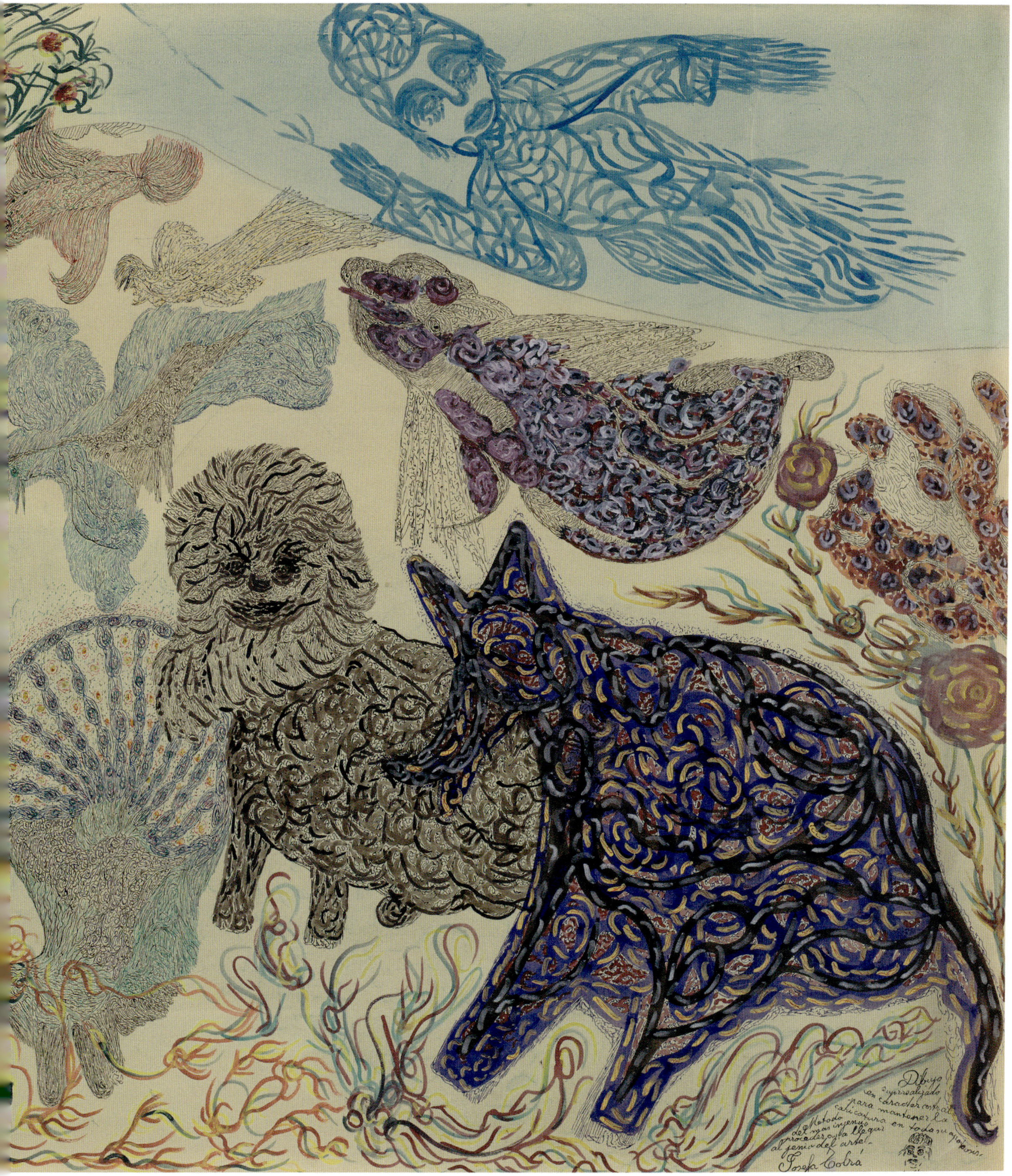
Dibujo
Josefa Tolrá

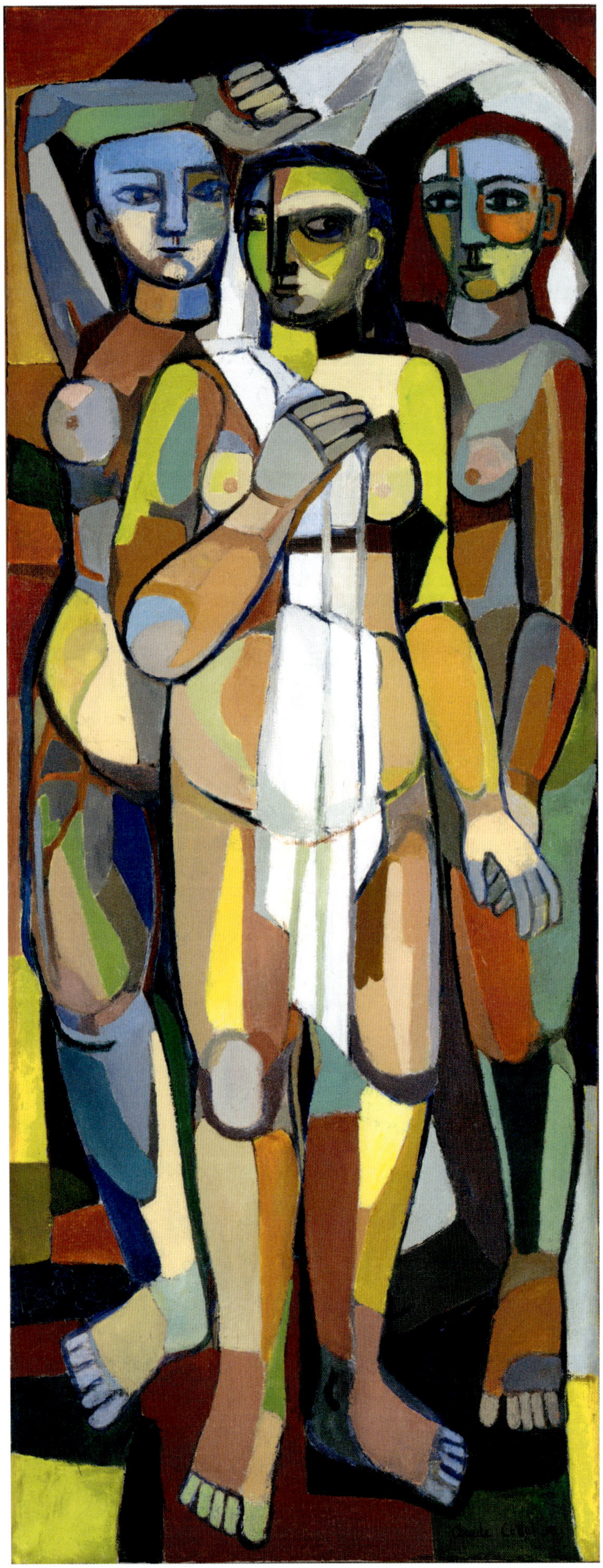

CLAUDE COLLET
(Geneva, 1929 – Barcelona, 2007)
The Three Graces
1958
Oil on canvas
183 × 70 cm
Acquisition financed by the Fundació Amics del Museu Nacional d'Art de Catalunya, 2022
Museu Nacional d'Art de Catalunya

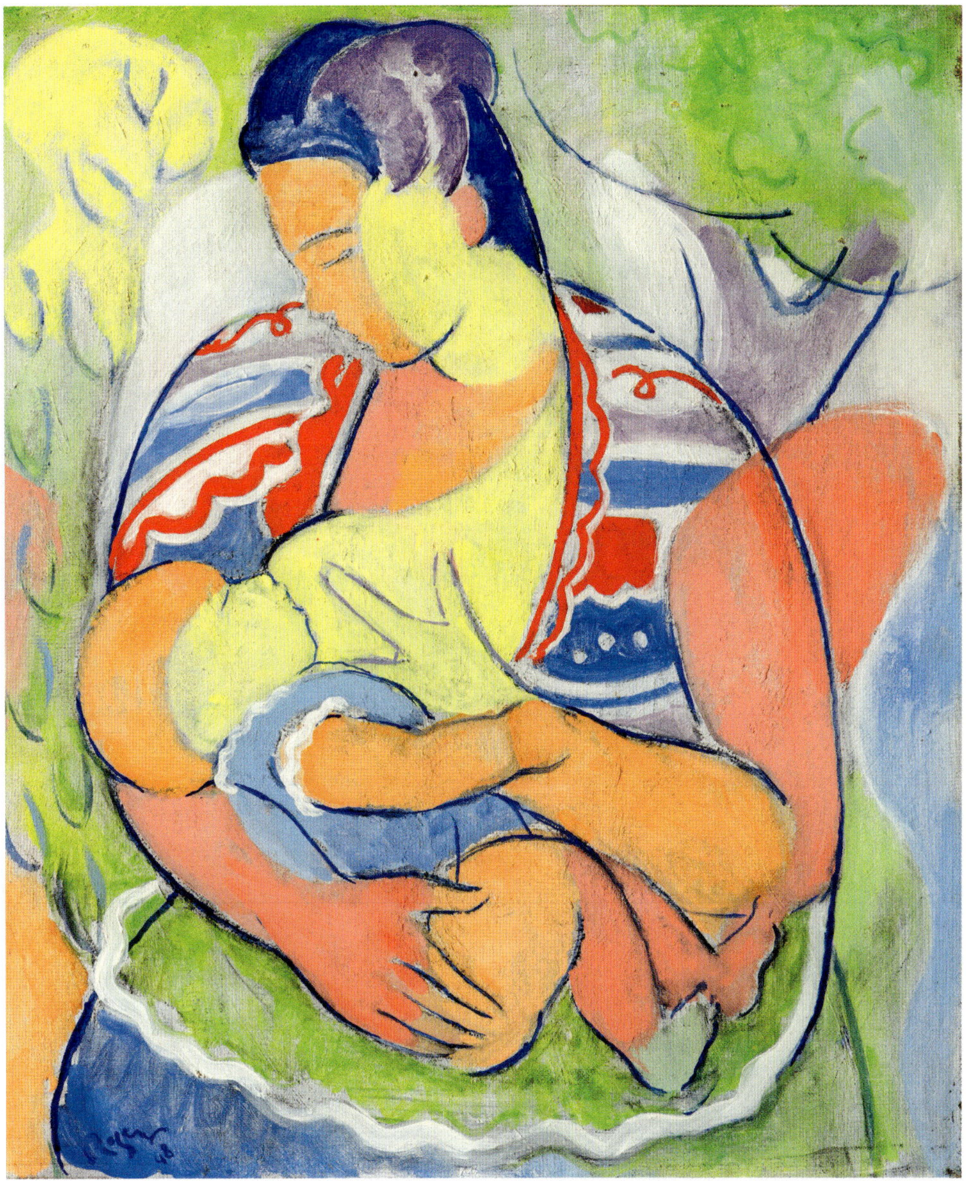

RAMON ROGENT
(Barcelona, 1920 – Plan-d'Orgon, France, 1958)
Maternity
1948
Oil on canvas
63 × 53 × 2 cm
Private collection, Barcelona

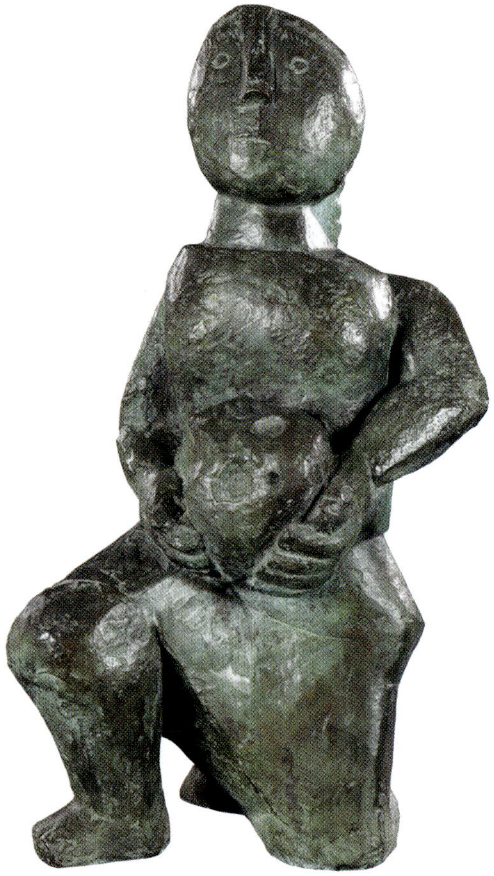

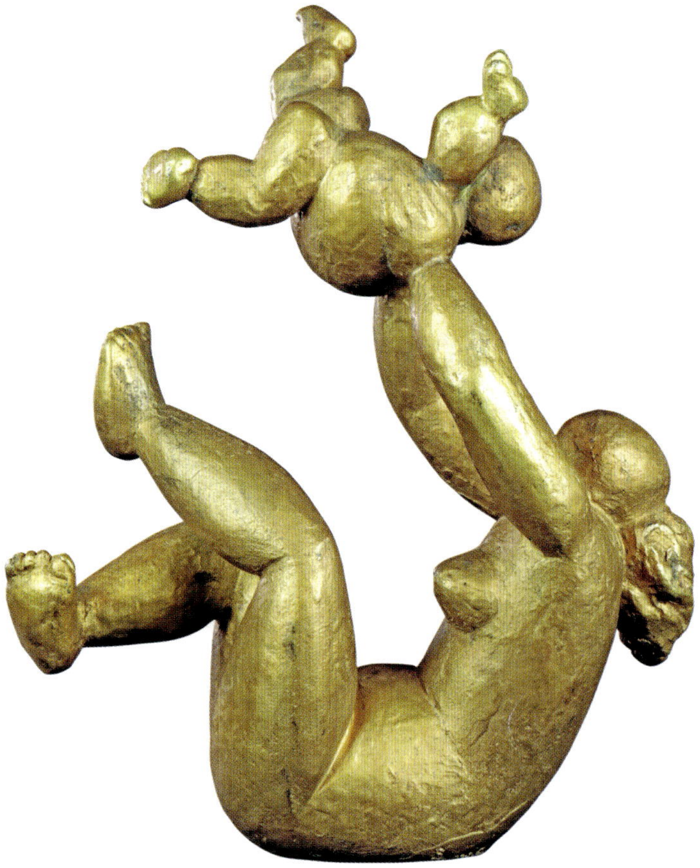

BALTASAR LOBO
(Cerecinos de Campos,
Zamora, 1910 – Paris, 1993)
Woman with Death's Head
1942
Cast in bronze, green patina
33 × 17.6 × 13 cm
Museo de Zamora. Junta de Castilla
y León. Collection of Zamora City Council

BALTASAR LOBO
Cerecinos de Campos,
Zamora, 1910 – Paris, 1993)
Maternity
1946
Bronze
23 × 18.4 × 8 cm
Excmo. Ayuntamiento de Zamora
Fundación Baltasar Lobo

MARCEL MARTÍ
(Alvear, Argentina, 1925 –
Palafrugell, 2010)
Woman with Child
1950
Wood and stone base
62 × 25 cm
Private collection, Barcelona

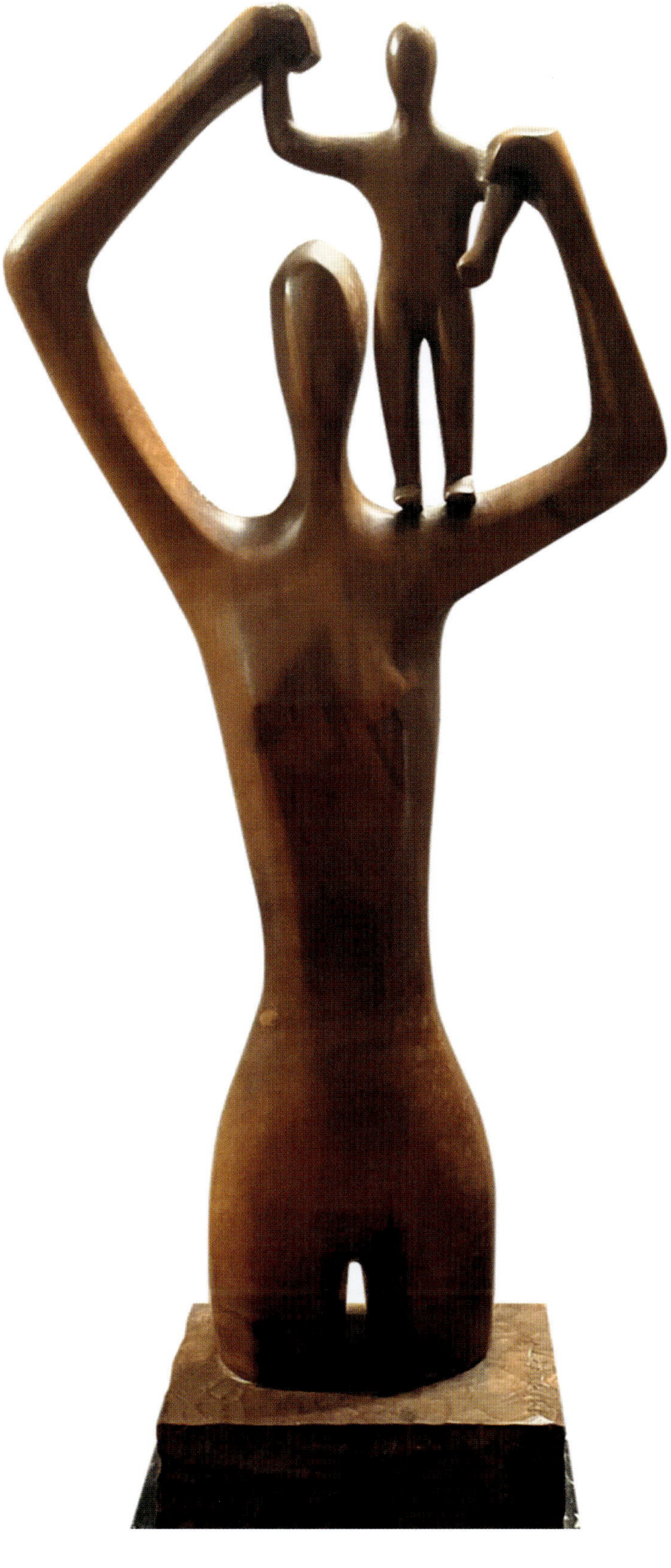

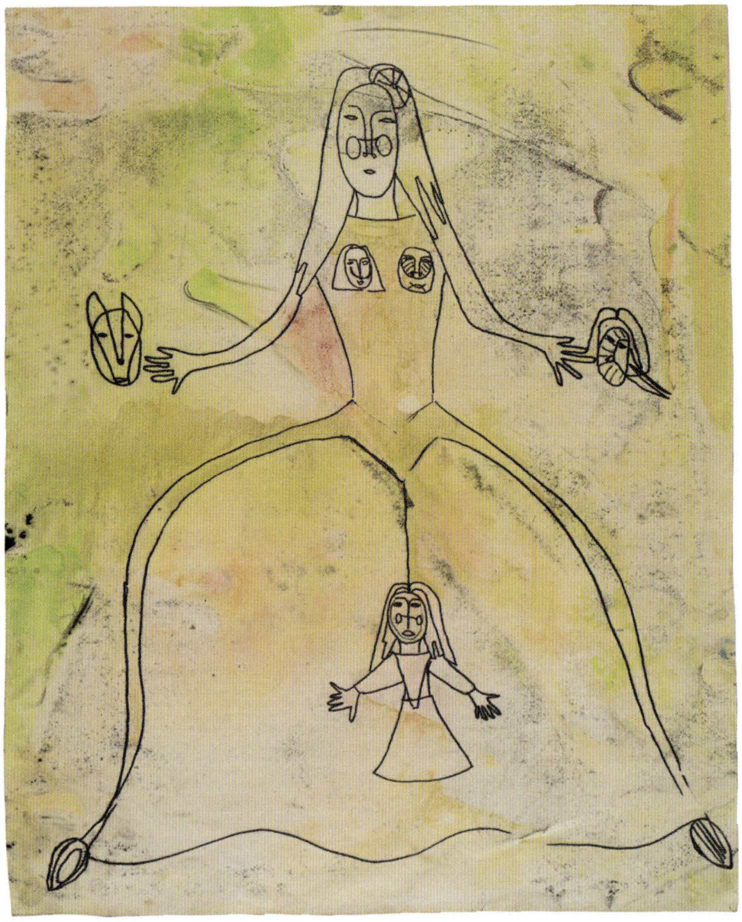

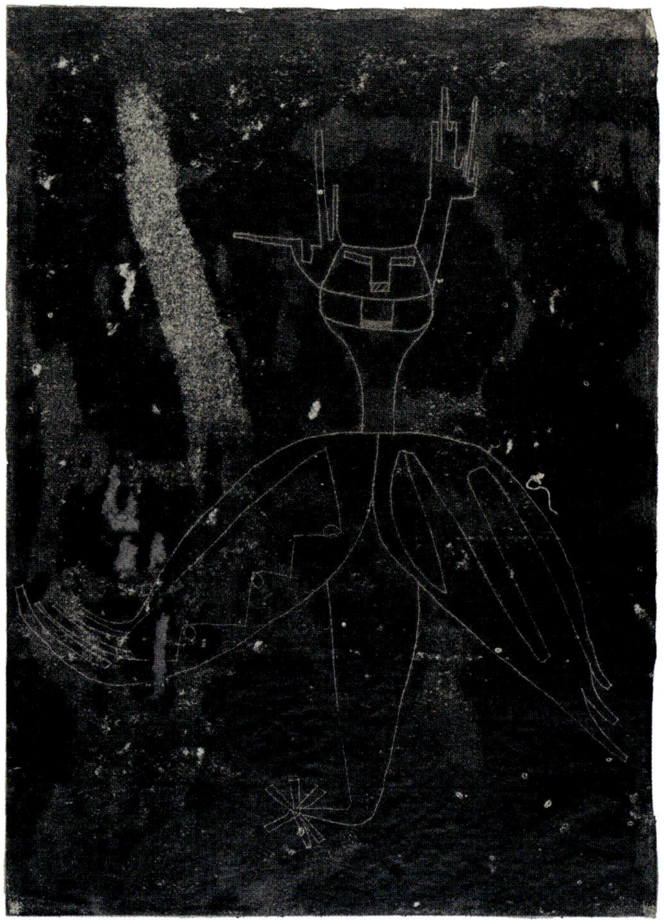

PARVINE CURIE (ARLETTE MARTÍ)
(Nancy, France, 1936)
Meninas no. 4
1959
Mixed technique on paper
44.5 × 35 cm
Donated by the artist, 2023
Museu Nacional d'Art de Catalunya

PARVINE CURIE (ARLETTE MARTÍ)
(Nancy, France, 1936)
Untitled
c. 1959
Monotype on paper
49 × 34.5 cm
Donated by the artist, 2023
Museu Nacional d'Art de Catalunya

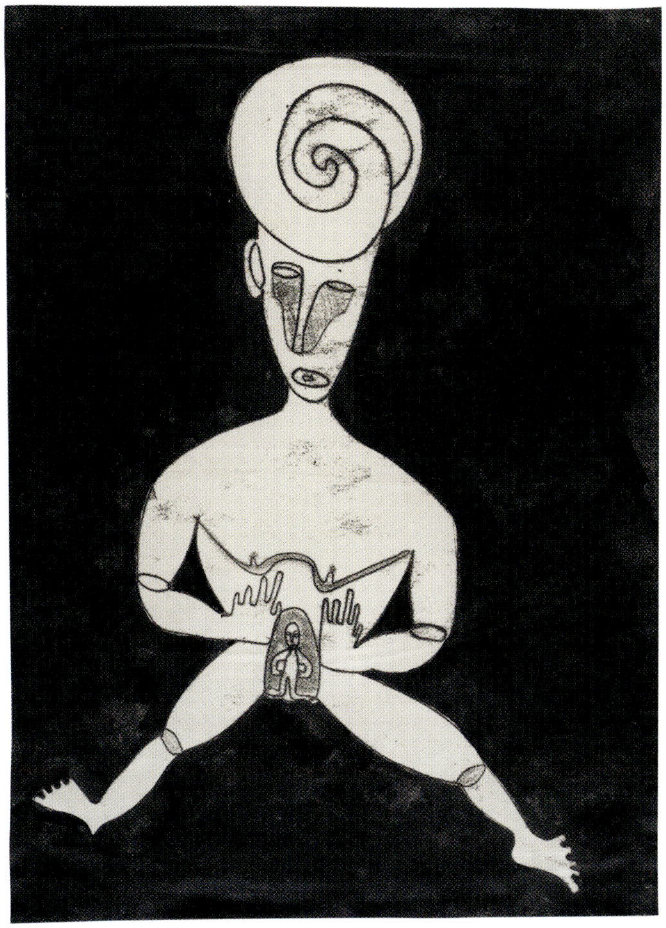

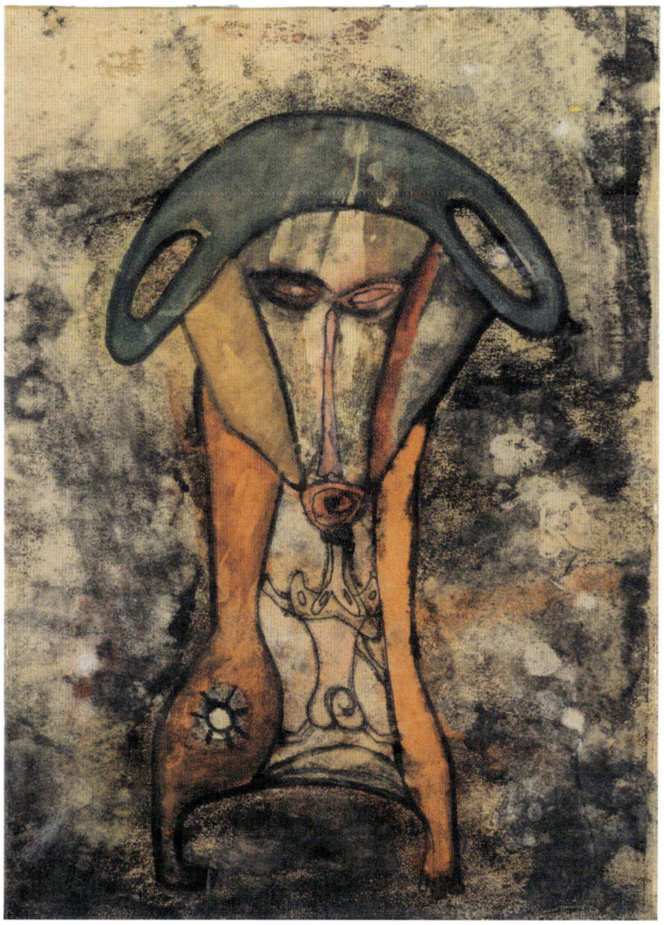

PARVINE CURIE (ARLETTE MARTÍ)
(Nancy, France, 1936)
Birth
1960
Ink on paper
46 × 34.3 cm
Donated by the artist, 2023
Museu Nacional d'Art de Catalunya

PARVINE CURIE (ARLETTE MARTÍ)
(Nancy, France, 1936)
Untitled
c. 1959
Mixed technique on paper mounted on frame
46 × 33 cm
Donated by the artist, 2023
Museu Nacional d'Art de Catalunya

ROSER BRU
(Barcelona, 1923 – Santiago de Chile, 2021)
Maternity
c. 1960
Oil on canvas
120 × 80 cm
Private collection, Barcelona

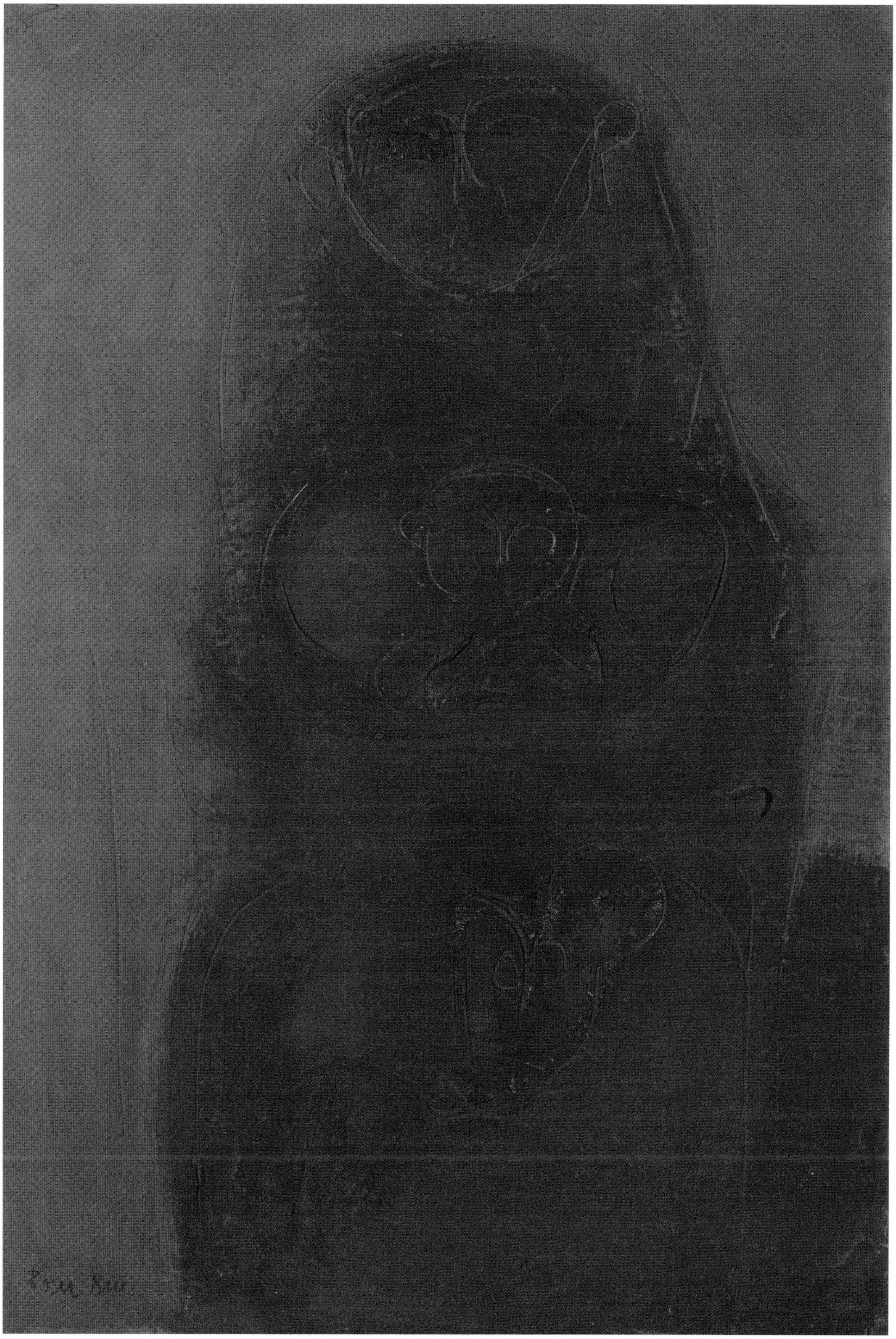

The 1960s saw the disappearance of philosophical existentialist solitude and the consolidation of new, more specific debates that focused on the collective: feminism, civil rights, the possibility of revolution, decolonisation, and resistance to dictatorial regression. In the context of consumerist hedonism and the conflicts that marked the decade, new humanist debates emerged, driven by political and communal concerns.

THE NEW DEBATES

MARI CHORDÀ
(Amposta, 1942)
Human head
1966
Paint on wooden box
60 × 40.5 × 8 cm
Galeria Mayoral, Barcelona

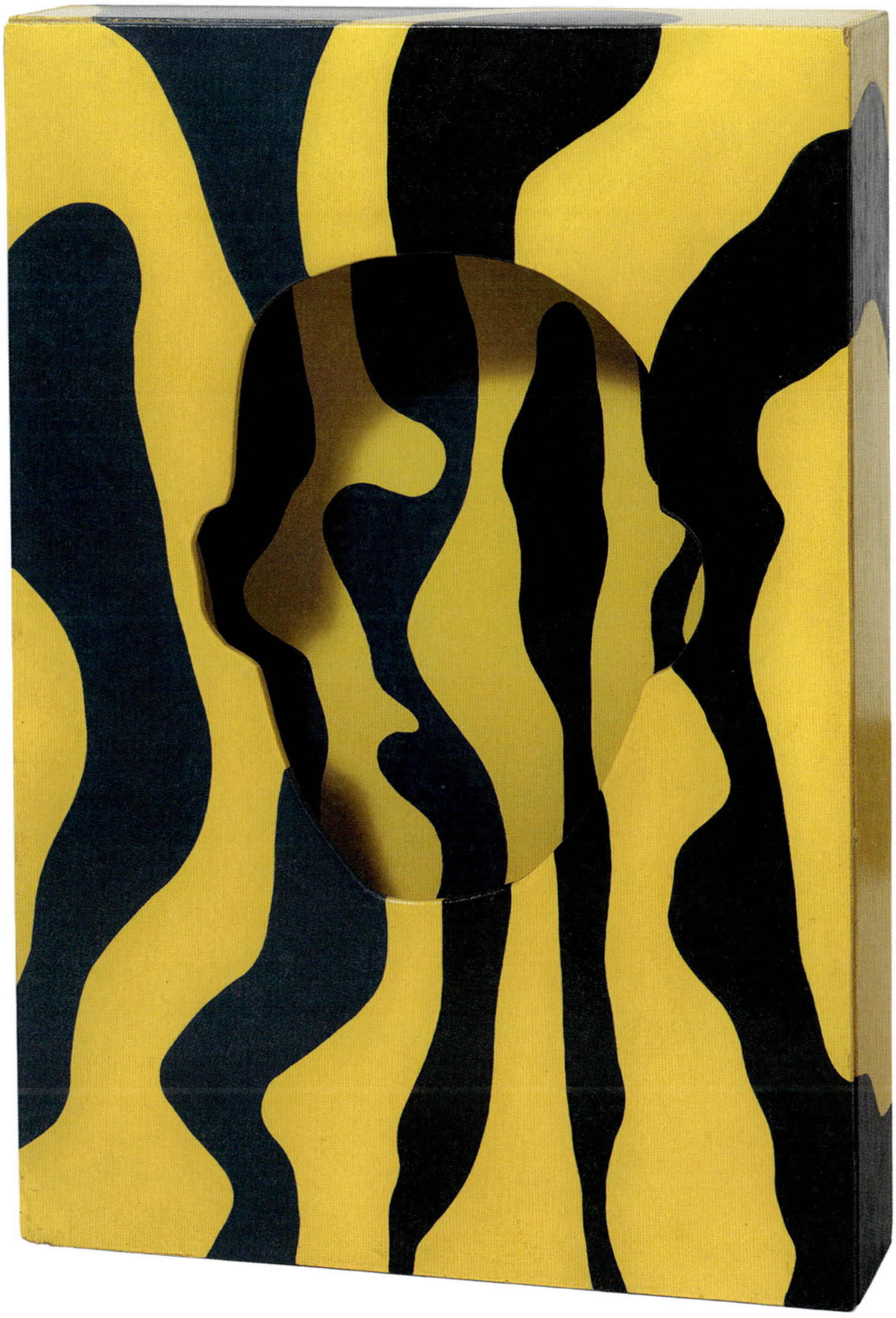

Tirs par Niki de Saint Phalle
Broadcast: 25/04/1961
Production: Office de radiodiffusion-télévision française
Director: Yvan Jouannet
1:18
INA. Institut national de l'audiovisuel

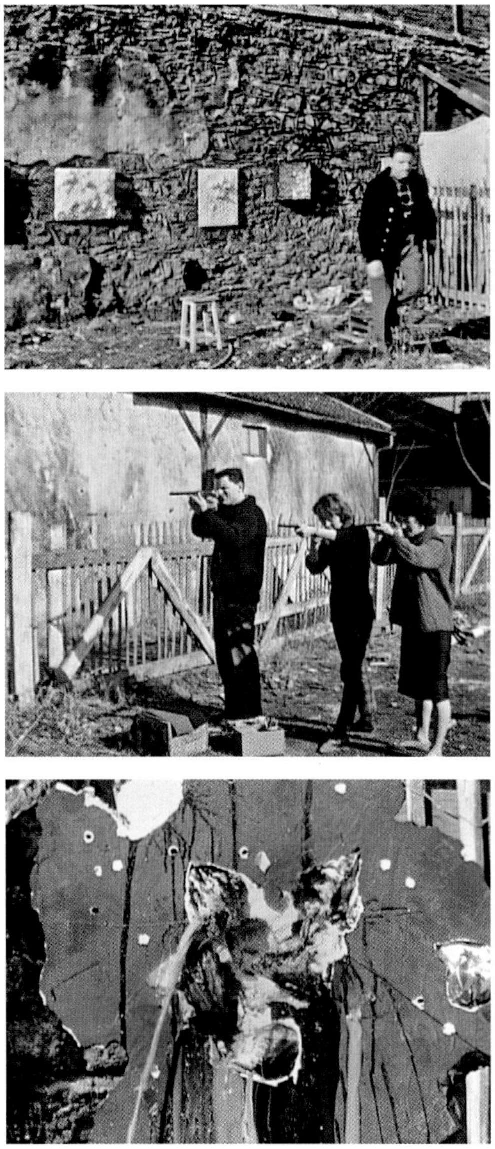

FRIEDRICH RAUCH
(Germany, 1928-1993)
Niki de Saint Phalle
(Neuilly-sur-Seine, France, 1930 – San Diego, United States, 2002)
Niki de Saint Phalle, 'Tir Gambrinus' at the Galerie Becher, Munich
1963
Modern copy, 2023
INTERFOTO / Friedrich Rauch

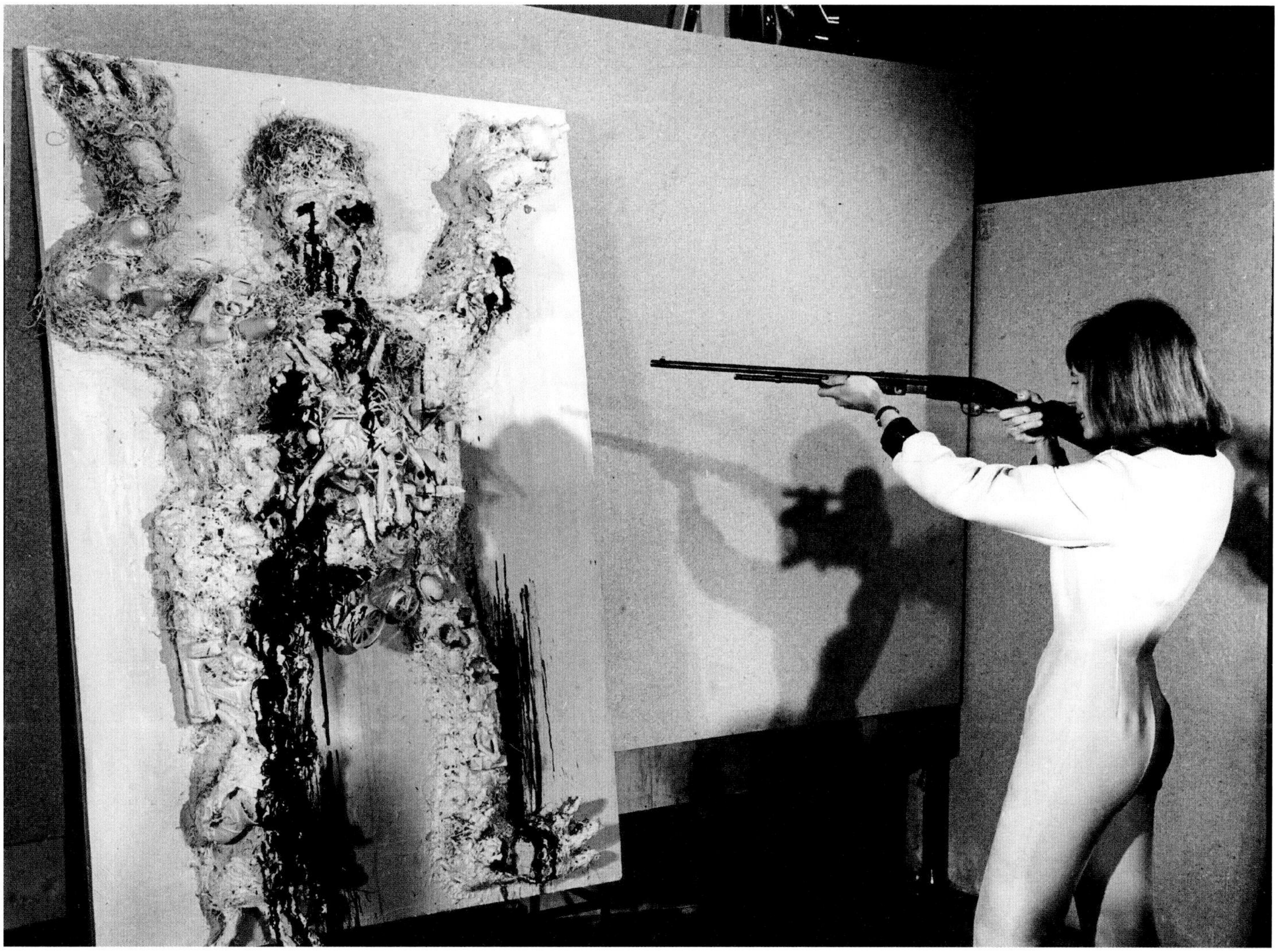

LLUÍS GÜELL
(Banyoles, 1945 – Begur, 2005)
Black Man Wounded by Bullet
1965
Mixed technique
32 × 49 × 197 cm
Donated by Tànit del Mar Güell Damont, 2021
Museu Nacional d'Art de Catalunya

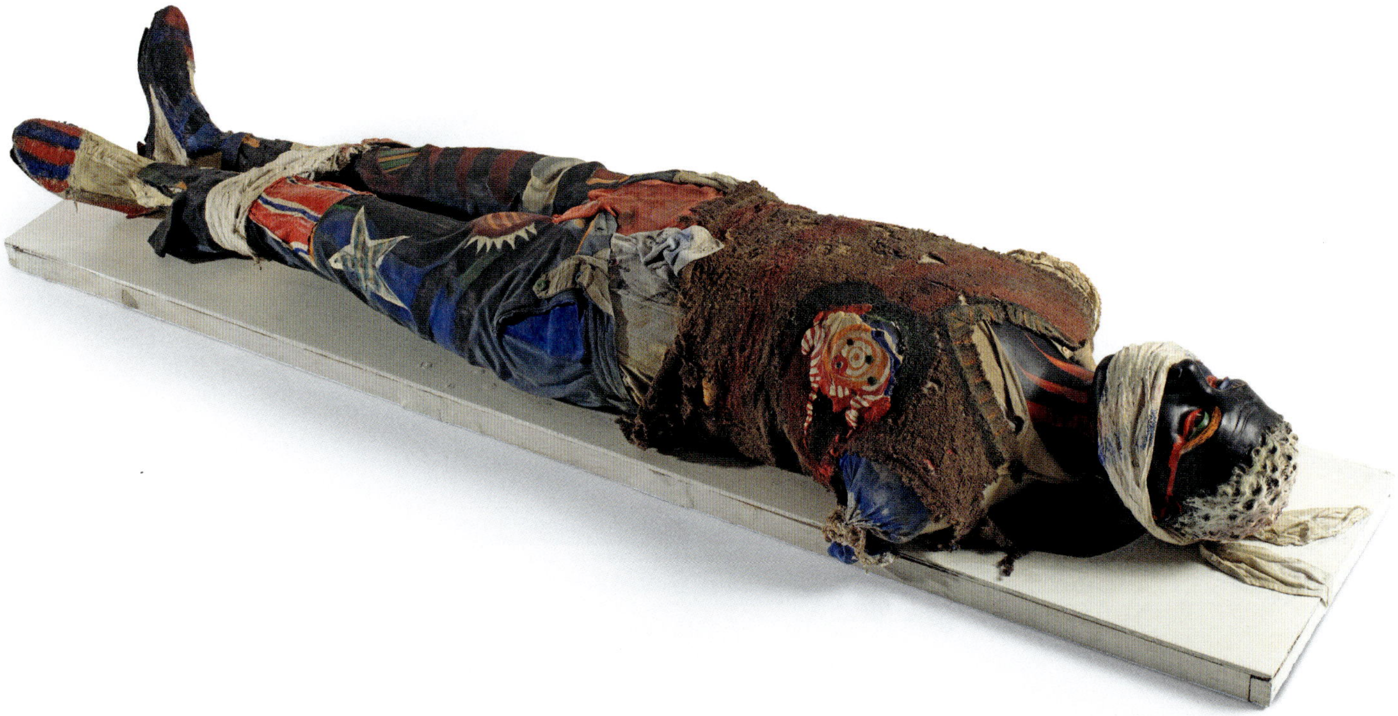

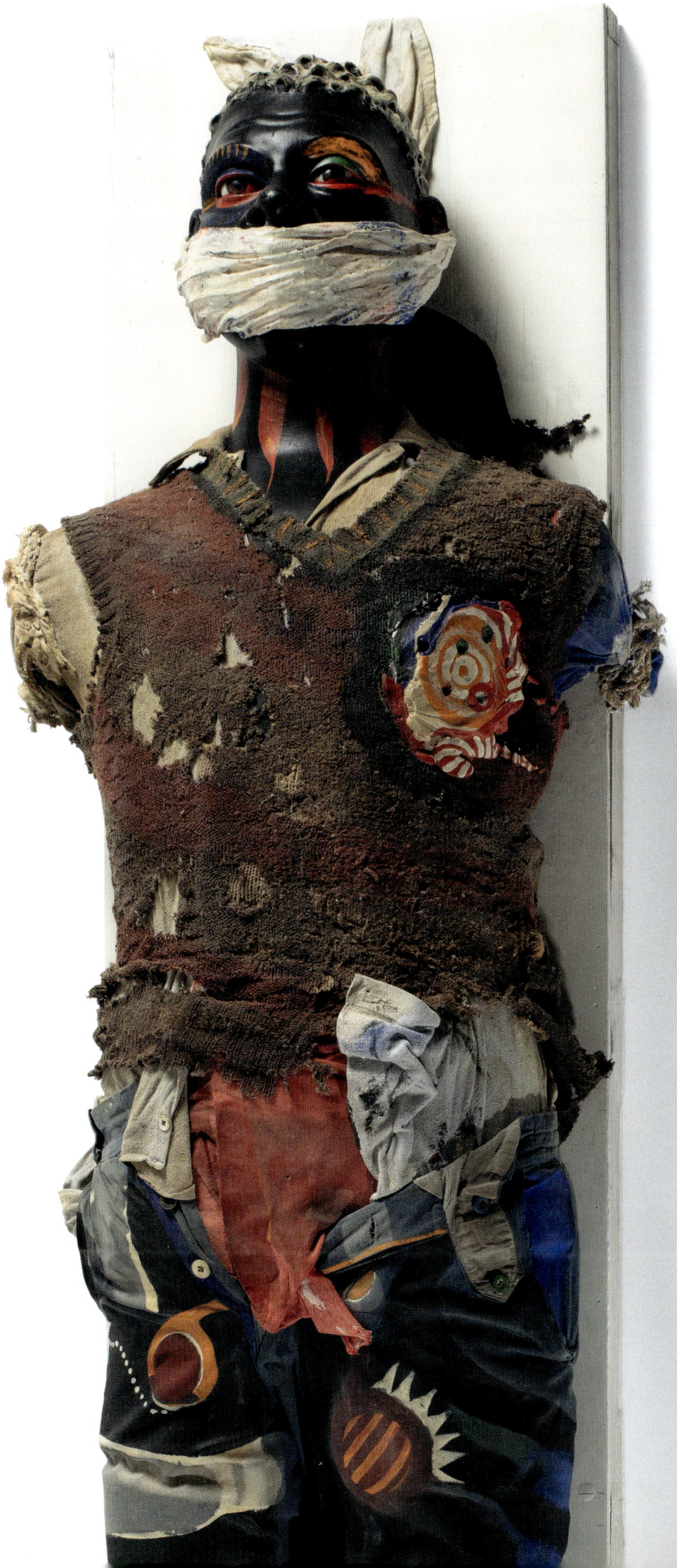

JUAN GENOVÉS
(Valencia, 1930 – Madrid, 2020)
The Door
1966
Oil and acrylic on canvas
140 × 90 cm
Museo Nacional Centro de Arte Reina Sofía

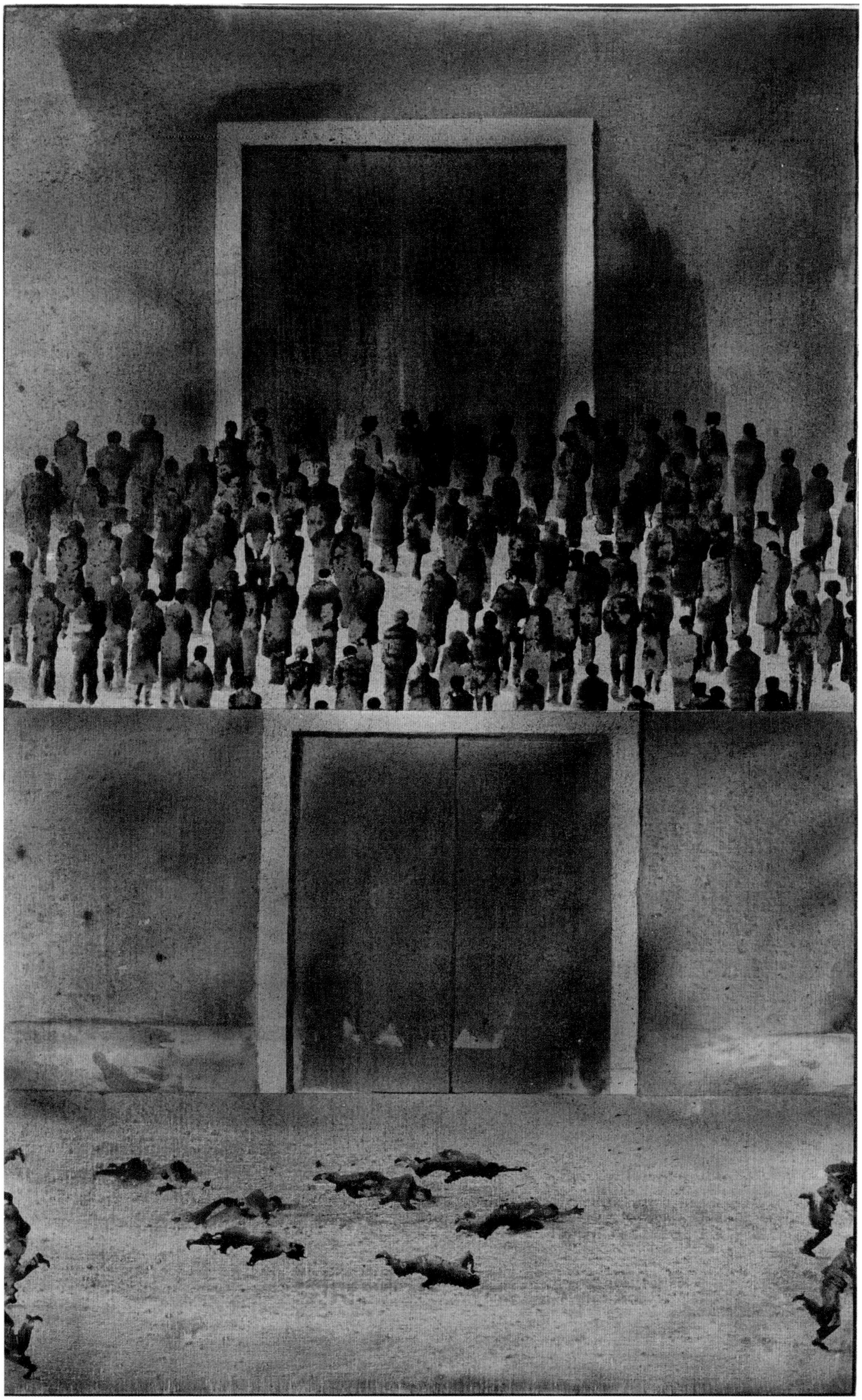

Museu Nacional d'Art de Catalunya

Lenders

Acervo Museu Lasar Segall-Instituto Brasileiro de Museus/
Ministério da Cultura
Agnès Varda Estate. Galerie Nathalie Obadia, Paris/Brussels
Arxiu Històric de la Ciutat de Barcelona (Ajuntament de Barcelona,
Institut de Cultura de Barcelona)
Carmen Thyssen Bornemisza Collection
Centre Pompidou. Musée national d'art moderne-Centre de création
industrielle, Paris
Colección Banco Santander
Colección Fundación Bancaja
Colección Rodríguez-Aguilera
Colección Studiolo Candela A. Soldevila
Col·lecció Bassat
Col·lecció Gastó
Collection Delphine Creuze
Collection of Stéphane Holvoet. Courtesy Louise Bourgeois
Trust and Xavier Hufkens, Brussels
Collection of the Themerson Estate
Collection Van Abbemuseum, Eindhoven
Daniel Blau, Col·lecció particular, Salzburg
Diputació de Tarragona. Museu d'Art Modern
Espai Subirachs
Familia Garcia-Llort
Fondation Giacometti, Paris
Fundació Antoni Tàpies, Barcelona
Fundació Espai Guinovart Agramunt
Fundació Joan Miró, Barcelona
Fundació Mercè Rodoreda. Institut d'Estudis Catalans, Barcelona
Fundación Baltasar Lobo, Excmo. Ayuntamiento de Zamora
Fundación Foto Colectania, Barcelona. Archivo Paco Gómez
Fundación "La Mirada Ingenua"
Galeria Mayoral, Barcelona
Galleria Nazionale d'Arte Moderna e Contemporanea, Roma
Grosvenor Gallery, London
Guggenheim Bilbao Museoa
Institut national de l'audiovisuel (INA), France
Jorge Oteiza. Fundazio Museoa, Alzuza (Navarra)
Kirklees Collection: Huddersfield Art Gallery, United Kingdom
Kunstmuseum Basel, Switzerland
LaM – Lille Métropole Musée d'art moderne, d'art contemporain
et d'art brut, France
Musée national Picasso, Paris
Musei Vaticani, Città del Vaticano
Museo Nacional Centro de Arte Reina Sofía, Madrid
Museo Nacional del Prado. Madrid
Museo de Zamora, Junta de Castilla y León.
Depósito del Ayuntamiento de Zamora
Museu d'Art Contemporani de Barcelona
Museu de Valls
Muzeum Narodowe w Poznaniu, Poznań, Poland
Osborne Samuel Ltd.
Successió Cuixart

Exhibition

Organisation and Production
Museu Nacional d'Art de Catalunya

Direction
Pepe Serra

Administrator
Josep Desquens

Curator
Àlex Mitrani

Documentaction
Mireia Berenguer

Coordination and Registration
Ana Izquierdo

Restoration
Elisa Bonet
Àngels Comella
Pere de Llobet
Elena López
Àlex Masalles
Carme Masdeu
Luz Morata
Núria Pedragosa
Núria Prat
Carles Ribó
Marta Serra

Exhibition Design
A2Espaie, S.L.

Graphic Design
Lali Almonacid

Acknowledgements

Archivo Ottavio Roth
Josep Maria Cabané
José Corredor-Matheos
Madalena Elek Machado
Mercè Ibarz
Philippe Lanfranch
Ana Be Machado
Gal Vallois
Marie-Christine Vila

Publication

Museu Nacional d'Art de Catalunya

Author
Àlex Mitrani

Texts
Paula Barreiro
Boris Cyrulnik
Nausikaä el Mecky
Jordi Ibáñez
Sarah Wilson

Editorial Coordination
Núria Giralt

Documentation
Carmen Mora

Correction and Translation
Susanna Méndez
Jofre Homedes
Adolf Fuertes
Beatriu Krayenbühl
Alan Moore
Mercè Ubach

Graphic Design and Layout
Jaume Roure

Photomechanical Services
XPS Arts finals- Xavi Parejo

Printing
Serper, S.L.

MIX Paper FSC® C110625

Edition: October 2023
Legal deposit: B 17460-2023
ISBN: 978-84-8043-404-1

EXHIBITION CATALOGUES

Amsterdam 1986
A Tour in Words and Watercolour. The Swiss artist Louis Ducros accompanies Dutch tourists in Italy in 1778. / Images et souvenirs de voyage. Le dessinateur suisse Louis Ducros accompagne des touristes hollandais en Italie en 1778, by J.W. Niemeijer, French edition by Pierre Chessex, Rijksmuseum, Amsterdam 1986; Musée Historique, Lausanne 1990

Atlanta 1988
From Liotard to Le Corbusier. 200 Years of Swiss Painting, 1730–1930, with contributions by Ulrich Jost, Brandon Brame Fortune, and edited byWilliam Hauptman, Swiss Institute for Art Research, The High Museum of Art, Atlanta 1988

Bassano 1988
Giovanni Volpato 1735–1803, edited by Giorgio Marini, Museo-Biblioteca-Archivio, Bassano del Grappa 1988; Istituto Nazionale per la Grafica, Gabinetto Disegni e Stampe, Rome 1988

Berne 1810
Verzeichnis der Kunstwerke und andern Gegenstände (...), Schweizerische Kunst-und Industrieausstellung, Berne 1810

Berne 1991
Emblèmes de la Liberté. Image de la République dans l'art du XVIe au XXe siècles, edited by Dario Gambino, Georg Germann and François de Capitani, 21e exposition du Conseil de l'Europe, Kunstmuseum Bern, Historisches Museum Bern, Berne 1991

Florence 1994
Luoghi di delizia: un Grand Tour olandese nelle immagini di Louis Ducros, 1778, by Taco Dibbits and J. W. Niemeijer, Istituto universitario olandese di storia dell'arte, Florence 1994; Museo Diego Aragona Pignatelli Cortes, Naples 1995

La Chaux-de-Fonds 1997
La Grotte dans l'art suisse du XVIIe au XXe siècle, edited by Edmond Charrière, Musée des Beaux-Arts, La Chaux-de-Fonds 1997

Lausanne 1953
Aquarelles de Abraham-Louis-Rodolphe Ducros, 1748–1810, Introduction by Louis Junod, Musée cantonal des Beaux-Arts, Lausanne 1953

Lausanne 1986
A.L.R. Ducros (1748–1810). Paysages d'Italie à l'époque de Goethe, edited by Pierre Chessex, contributions by Luc Boissonnas, André Corboz, Olivier Masson, Westby Percival Prescott and others, Musée cantonal des Beaux-Arts, Lausanne 1986; Museo di Roma, Palazzo Braschi, Rome 1987; Centre culturel suisse, Paris 1993

Lausanne 1989
Chefs-d'oeuvre du Musée cantonal des Beaux-Arts Lausanne. Regard sur 150 tableaux, edited by E. Billeter, with contributions by Pierre Chessex and others. Musée cantonal des Beaux-Arts, Lausanne 1989

Lausanne 1994
La collection du Musée des Beaux-Arts, Lausanne, by Catherine Lepdor, Patrick Schaefer and Jörg Zutter. Musée cantonal des Beaux-Arts, Lausanne 1994

Lausanne 1995
La genèse des formes. Œuvres sur papier de la collection, by Catherine Lepdor, Patrick Schaefer and Jörg Zutter. Musée cantonal des Beaux-Arts, Lausanne 1995

Lausanne 1998 a
Musée cantonal des Beaux-Arts Lausanne, by Jörg Zutter, Catherine Lepdor and Patrick Schaefer. Institut suisse pour l'étude de l'art, Lausanne 1998

Lausanne 1998 b
Abraham-Louis-Rodolphe Ducros. Un peintre suisse en Italie, edited by Jörg Zutter, Musée cantonal des Beaux-Arts, Lausanne 1998. Musée du Québec, Québec 1998–1999; Norwich 1999.

Lausanne 1999
Le sommeil ou quand la raison s'absente, by Jörg Zutter, Catherine Lepdor and Caroline Nicod. Musée cantonal des Beaux-Arts, Lausanne 1999–2000

Lausanne 2001
L'attrait du trait. Dessins anciens et modernes de la collection, by Catherine Lepdor, Dominique Radrizzani and Julie Enckell. Musée cantonal des Beaux-Arts, Lausanne 2001

Zurich 1999
Der Weltuntergang & das Prinzip Hoffnung, by Harald Szeemann, Kunsthaus, Zurich, 1999

Valetta 1989
Louis Ducros in Malta, edited by Dominic Cutajar, contributions by Pierre Chessex and Lorenza di Nuzzo, The New Gallery, Auberge of Provence, Valletta (Malta) 1989

London 1985
Images of the Grand Tour, Louis Ducros 1748–1810, by Pierre Chessex, Francis Haskell and Lindsay Stainton and others. The Iveagh Bequest, Kenwood, London 1985; The Whitworth Art Gallery, Manchester 1985

London 1996
Grand Tour. The Lure of Italy in the Eighteenth Century, edited by Andrew Wilton and Ilaria Bignamini. Tate Gallery, Londres 1996; Palazzo delle Esposizioni, Rome 1997

London 1996
Vases and Volcanoes. Sir William Hamilton and his Collection, edited by Ian Jenkins and Kim Sloan. British Museum, London 1996

Nantes 1985
Les Frères Sablet (1775–1815), by Anne Van de Sandt. Musées départementaux de Loire-Atlantique, Nantes 1985; Musée cantonal des Beaux-Arts, Lausanne 1985; Museo di Roma, Palazzo Braschi, Rome 1985

Naples 1962
Il paesaggio napoletano nella pittura straniera, edited by R. Causa. Palazzo Reale, Naples 1962

Naples 1990
All'ombra del Vesuvio. Napoli nella veduta europea dal Quattrocento all'Ottocento, edited by Giuliano Briganti, and Nicola Spinosa. Castel Sant'Elmo, Naples 1990

Paris 1989
La Révolution française et l'Europe, edited by Jean-René Gaborit. 20e exposition du Conseil de l'Europe, Galeries nationales du Grand Palais, Paris 1989

Rome 1954
Acquarelli di A.-L.-R. Ducros, pittore svizzero, introduction by Luc Boissonnas. Istituto svizzero, Rome 1954

Rome 1987
Ducros 1748–1810. Paesaggi d'Italia all'epoca di Goethe, edited by Pierre Chessex with contributions by Luc Boissonnas, André Corboz and Olivier Masson and others. Museo di Roma, Palazzo Braschi, Rome 1987

Rome 1994
Il paesaggio secondo natura, by Paolo Chiarini, Palazzo delle esposizioni, Rome 1994

Stockholm 1982
På Klassik Mark. Målare i Rom på 1780–talet, Nationalmuseum, Stockholm 1982

50. SAUT DU DOUBS, NEAR BRENETS, NEUCHÂTEL, c.1807–1808

Watercolour and oil on paper laid down on canvas, 86.5 x 136.7 cm
Lausanne, Musée cantonal des Beaux-Arts
Inv. 799

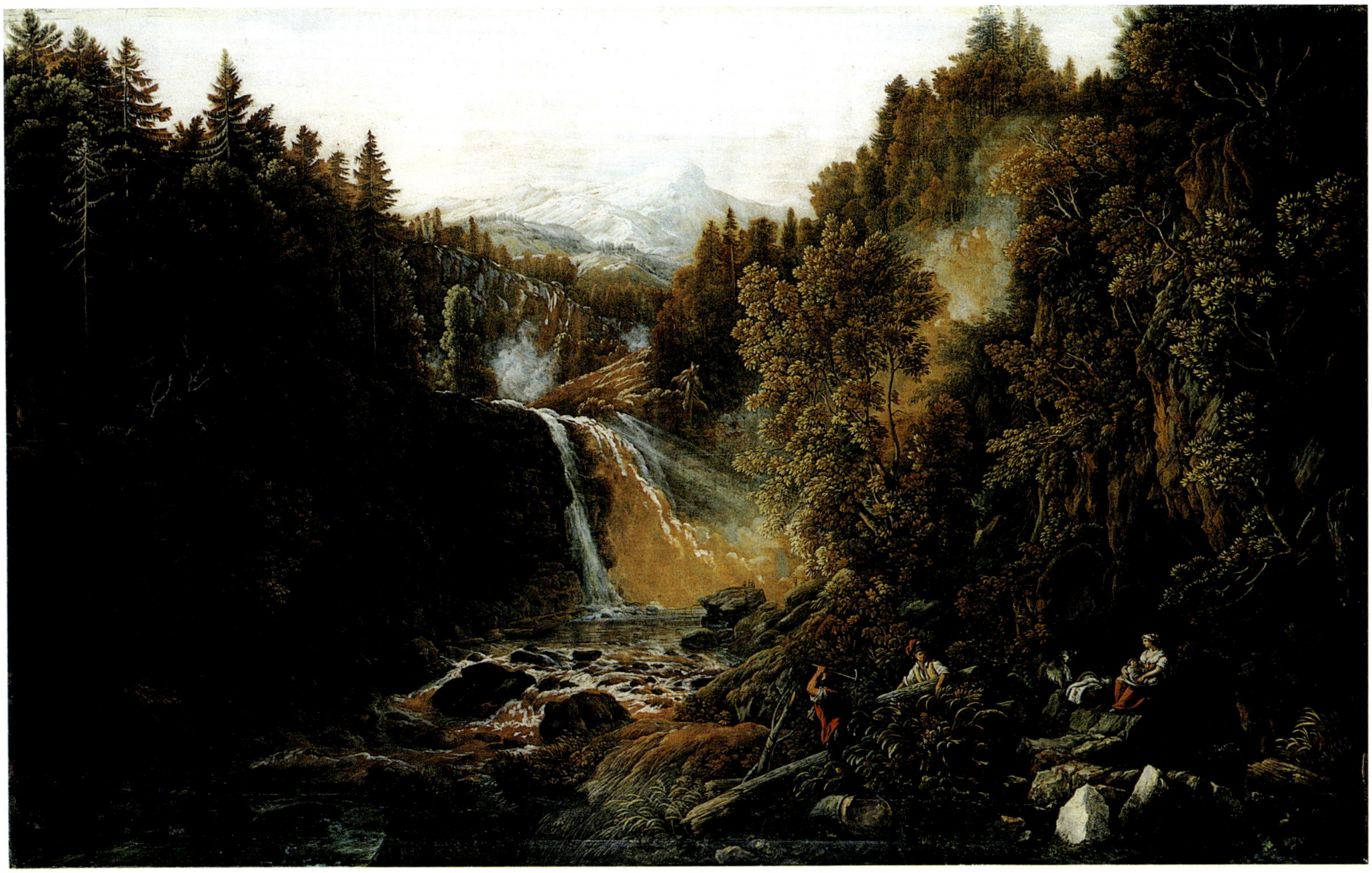

BIBLIOGRAPHY

ARCHIVES

ACV
Archives cantonales vaudoises, Chavannes-Renens (Fonds privés Hennezel, Plumitif du Conseil d'Etat et onglets du département de législation, Papiers Sévery – carnets d'Effinger von Wildegg)

AEB
Archives d'Etat du canton de Berne, Berne (Manual der Akademischen Kuratel)

AV
Archivio del Vicariato, Rome (*Stati d'anime* of the Parish of San Lorenzo and Santa Maria del Popolo)

BCU
Bibliothèque cantonale et universitaire, Lausanne (Fonds Pellis, Fonds Frédéric César de la Harpe)

BPU
Bibliothèque publique et universitaire, Genève (Ms Bonnet, Archives Tronchin, Ms 2399)

BOOKS AND ARTICLES

Agassiz 1927
Daisy Agassiz, 'A.-L. Du Cros, peintre et graveur, 1748–1810', *Revue historique vaudoise*, (1927), pp. 3–14, 33–40, 66–76, 97–104 et 129–138

Agassiz 1928
Daisy Agassiz, 'Un paesaggista svizzero a Roma: Luigi Rodolfo Du Cros', *Roma, Rivista di studi e di vita romana*, VI, (1928), pp. 545–552

Barghouth 1995
Laurence Barghouth, 'Ducros, Bridel et Francillon: trois amateurs d'art autour de 1800', *Revue historique vaudoise*, (1995), pp. 337–368

Bridel 1783
Jean-Louis-Philippe Bridel, 'Quelques petites choses sur les Beaux-Arts', *Etrennes Helvétiennes curieuses et utiles pour l'An de Grâce MDCCLXXXIII*, (Lausanne 1783)

Bridel 1790
Jean-Louis-Philippe Bridel, 'Lettre sur les artistes suisses maintenant à Rome (28 juillet 1789)', *Etrennes Helvétiennes et patriotiques pour l'An de Grâce 1790*, n. VIII, (Lausanne 1790)

Bridel 1803
Jean-Louis-Philippe Bridel, 'Lettre sur quelques artistes suisses (Rome 1er mai 1802)', *Etrennes Helvétiennes et patriotiques pour l'An de Grâce 1803*, (Lausanne 1803)

Brilli 1987
Attilio Brilli, *Il viaggio in Italia: Storia di una grande tradizione culturale dal XVI al XIX secolo*, (Milan 1987)

Chessex 1982
Pierre Chessex, 'Quelques documents sur un aquarelliste et marchand vaudois à Rome à la fin du 18e siècle', *Revue historique vaudoise*, XC, (1982), pp. 35–71

Chessex 1984 (a)
Pierre Chessex, 'A Swiss Painter in Rome: A.L.R. Ducros', *Apollo*, June (1984), pp. 430–437

Chessex 1984 (b)
Pierre Chessex, 'Ducros' Italienische Landschaften', *Daidalos, Berlin Architectural Journal*, n. 12, June (1984), pp. 70–78

Chessex 1986
Pierre Chessex, 'Documents sur la première exposition d'art en Suisse: Genève 1789', *Revue suisse d'art et d'archéologie*, Bd. 443, Heft 4, (1986), pp. 362–367

Chessex 1989
Pierre Chessex, 'Tradition et innovations dans la peinture de paysage à l'époque de la Révolution française. L'exemple de Louis Ducros (1748–1810)', *L'Art et les révolutions*, section 1, *Actes du XXVIIe congrès international d'histoire de l'art*, Strasbourg 1–7 September 1989, (Strasbourg 1992), pp. 143–156

Chessex 1992
Pierre Chessex, 'L'émigration artistique à la fin de l'Ancien Régime: quelques points de repère', *Nos monuments d'art et d'histoire*, n° 4, (1992), pp. 491–501

Cusatelli 1987
Giorgio Cusatelli, 'Alla scoperta dell'Europa', *Europa 1700–1992. Storia di un identità. La disgregazione dell'Ancien Régime*, Enrico Castelnuovo (ed.), (Milan 1987), pp. 236–246

De la Rive 1832
Pierre-Louis De la Rive, *Notice biographique de M. P.-L. De la Rive*, (Geneva 1832)

Eckhardt 1979
Götz Eckhardt (ed.), *Ein Potsdamer Maler in Rom. Briefe des Batoni-Schülers J.-G. Puhlmann aus den Jahren 1774 bis 1787*, (Berlin 1979)

Gerning 1802
Johann Isaac Gerning, *Reise durch Oesterreich und Italien*, 3 volumes, (Frankfurt 1802)

Giacomotti 1995
Christine Giacomotti, *Les Suisses en Italie. Bibliographie analytique de leurs écrits conservés dans les collections manuscrites et imprimées de la Bibliothèque cantonale et universitaire de Lausanne, XVIIe-XIXe siècle*, (Lausanne 1995)

Haskell, Chessex 1985
Francis Haskell, Pierre Chessex, *Roma romantica. Vedute di Roma e dei suoi dintorni di A.L.R. Ducros*, (Milan 1985)

Hermann 1968
Luke Hermann, 'The William Spooner Collection and Bequest', *The Burlington Magazine*, July 1968, p. 401

Hugli 1983
Jean Hugli, 'Histoire et préhistoire d'une école d'art', *Cette école d'art. De l'école cantonale de dessin à l'école cantonale des Beaux-Arts et d'Art appliqué de Lausanne*, Institut d'Etude et de Recherche en Information visuelle, (Lausanne 1983), pp.7–113

Knight 1985
Carlo Knight, 'La quadreria di Sir William Hamilton a Palazzo Sessa', *Napoli Nobilissima*, fasc I–II, (1985), pp. 45–59

Niemeijer, De Booy, Dunning 1994
J.W. Niemeijer, J. Th. De Booy, A. Dunning, *Voyage en Italie, en Sicile et à Malte (1778). Journaux, lettres, dessins*, 2 volumes, (Brussels 1994)

Nordhoff, Reimer 1994
Claudia Nordhoff, Hans Reimer, *Jakob Philipp Hackert. Verzeichnis seiner Werke*. 2 volumes, (Berlin 1994)

Spinosa, Di Mauro 1996
Nicola Spinosa, Leonardo Di Mauro, *Vedute napoletane del Settecento*, (Naples 1996)

Zeri 1976
Federico Zeri, 'La percezione visiva dell'Italia e degli Italiani nella storia della pittura', in *Storia d'Italia*, vol.VI, (Turin 1976), pp. 53–214